James Edward Murdoch

A Plea for Spoken Language

An Essay upon Comparative Elocution, Condensed from Lectures Delivered

throughout the United States

James Edward Murdoch

A Plea for Spoken Language
An Essay upon Comparative Elocution, Condensed from Lectures Delivered throughout the United States

ISBN/EAN: 9783744755801

Printed in Europe, USA, Canada, Australia, Japan

Cover: Foto ©Thomas Meinert / pixelio.de

More available books at **www.hansebooks.com**

FOR

SPOKEN LANGUAGE.

*AN ESSAY UPON COMPARATIVE ELOCUTION,
CONDENSED FROM LECTURES DELIVERED THROUGHOUT THE
UNITED STATES.*

BY

JAMES E. MURDOCH,
Actor, Reader, Instructor of Elocution, and Author of "The Stage."

VAN ANTWERP, BRAGG & CO.

CINCINNATI. NEW YORK.

(ii)

Dedication.

THIS VOLUME,
A LABOR OF LOVE,
I DEDICATE TO MY LOVED ONES,
MY DAUGHTERS

Ida, Rosalie, and Fannie;

WHOSE CONSTANT SYMPATHY AND AFFECTIONATE DEVOTION
HAVE LIGHTENED MY LABORS AND ALLEVIATED MY CARES;
A PRECIOUS LEGACY
LEFT TO ME, LONG AGO, BY

One

TO WHOSE MEMORY THEY BIND ME
MORE CLOSELY AS THE YEARS ROLL ON:
A THREEFOLD GOLDEN CORD.

PREFACE.

IN making my plea for the study of spoken language I have worked in the patient spirit of faithful investigation, aided by long experience and close observation; in short, I have labored to make plain to others what I believe and know of the matter in question.

Should my impressions and convictions meet with the approval of conscientious and impartial thinkers, I shall be content to await the final result of public appreciation. I hope I am not mistaken in believing that I have taken a step in the right direction, and that, ultimately, many will walk where but few now tread, in the light of knowledge derived from a thorough analysis of the constituent elements of the system, before seeking to understand and employ its combined principles for the purposes of education. I feel the importance of the subject I have undertaken to expound;

know its bearings and reach; and am also convinced of the inefficiency of its present treatment, as far, at least, as underlying principles are concerned, in spite of the efforts of many able writers to reduce their theories to practical detail.

I may, therefore, well be appprehensive of the result of my own labors in the direction of a more comprehensive exposition of the elements of the art of spoken language than that which has hitherto occupied the mind of the educator.

I have, however, made a well considered attempt, and I trust that the spirit of a progressive age will not lightly treat my claims to a patient hearing.

The subject matter contained in this volume, and that of the manual which forms the second part of the work, is a condensation of numerous lectures, notes, and observations made during my career as instructor in this art.

For the adaptation of my manuscript to the purposes of the present publication, I have availed myself of the clerical labors of my pupil, Miss Cora E. Gordon, whose valuable services it gives me pleasure to acknowledge.

J. E. M.

CINCINNATI, *June*, 1883.

CONTENTS.

	PAGE
INTRODUCTION	9

PART FIRST.

CHAPTER
I. The Early Writers on Elocution.	19
II. The Inflective System.	28
III. Wright and Sheridan.	29
IV. Sir Joshua Steele.	47
V. Development of Systems.	62
VI. Dr. James Rush.	65
VII. Rush's System of Notation.	79
VIII. Rush's System—Continued.	91
IX. Reception of the Rush System.	98
X. The Author's Early Experience.	105
XI. Reasons for the Neglect of Elocution.	116
XII. Capabilities of the English Language.	125

PART SECOND.

I. Power of Voice and Gesture Compared.	139
II. The Development of Language.	152
III. Significance of Sounds.	169

PART THIRD.

I. Popular Errors Regarding Elocution.	187
II. The Principles of Elocution.	204
III. Necessity of Training the Voice.	211
IV. Art not Opposed to Nature.	224
V. Advantages of Methodical Study.	233

APPENDIX.

CHAPTER	PAGE
I. The Principles of Rhythmus	247
II. Essay on Rhythmus by Dr. Barber	261
III. Selections Scored for Illustration	270
The Hermit.—*Beattie*	272
Apostrophe to Light.—*Milton*	275
St. Paul's Defense before King Agrippa	278
The Ocean.—*Byron*	280
Without God in the World.—*Rev. Robert Hall*	284
IV. Hill's Essay	285
Application I.—Of Joy	288
Application II.—Of Grief	291
Application III.—Of Fear	292
Application IV.—Of Anger	295
Application V.—Of Pity	298
Application VI.—Of Scorn	299
Application VII.—Of Hatred	300
Application VIII.—Of Jealousy	302
Application IX.—Of Wonder	304
Application X.—Of Love	306
An Example of Joy in Love	309
An Example of Grief in Love	309
An Example of Fear in Love	310
An Example of Anger in Love	310
An Example of Pity in Love	311
An Example of Hatred in Love	311
An Example of Jealousy in Love	312
An Example of Wonder in Love	312
An Example of Love Unmixed and Solitary	313
Questions and Answers	314

A PLEA

FOR

SPOKEN LANGUAGE.

INTRODUCTION.

My object in the present publication is to offer to educators, and others interested in the universal spread of knowledge, an account of whatever elocutionary principles or methods I have found useful in my study and practice of the voice in speech. More especially, I desire to awaken such an interest in the subject of the culture of spoken language as will lead to a satisfactory consideration of the causes which have led to the present too prevalent idea on the part of school authorities that elocution, as a special study, is inexpedient; or worse, that it can not be successfully taught in connection with the multifarious studies of the schools.

Elocution, as taught at present, is, in most cases, considered and treated in theory and practice as little more than an imitative art, and as such yields its rightful position of honor and dignity as a branch of study based upon philosophic or scientific principles. Still, I feel from general indications of a reviving interest in this subject that nothing short of rational modes and methods of study will ultimately satisfy the earnest student.

I am convinced, however, that the multiplication of mere rules and precepts can be of no avail until an active and a general interest amongst the thinking public, as well as amongst educators, is aroused in the true philosophy and full scope of the theory of the principles of expressive speech.

Believing this, I have thought it advisable to demonstrate, through an historic and comparative treatment of the subject of elocution, its claims as a scientific study, and its possibilities as a disciplined art; and thence to show how a thorough universal system of instruction may be attained through intelligent and conscientious employment of materials already in our possession.

No art or science ever sprang into existence in a full state of perfection. Each must have its beginnings, rude and simple, and only reach a condition of complete development through gradual, oftentimes slow and discouraging, growth. This is exemplified in the history of the origin and progress of music, which proceeded slowly, from the simplest beginnings, through long periods of time in which it languished, was utterly neglected, and finally rose again to advance in triumph toward the consummation of its powers.

The progress of a science, through its various stages, is always the outcome of some inherent vital principles, recognized but dimly at first, in some generalistic form. As it advances, however,

Introduction.

in the course of development brought about by time and investigation, it gradually becomes divested of assumption and error, and the mind finally grasps those truths which, in the beginning, had been but vaguely apprehended, and more rapid growth toward final perfection is the result.

The history of Elocution in modern times shows that it is no exception to this general law of gradual development, as I hope to show in the present volume, by tracing the progressive ideas which secured its advancement, from their origin with the English writers of the last century to their more complete development in the work of an American author of the present century [Dr. James Rush], which marked a new era in the study of spoken language, and placed it upon a firm scientific footing it had never before attained.

Although Dr. Rush's work, "The Philosophy of the Voice," has been acknowledged by the ablest authorities to be founded in truth and expressed in reason, an opinion of its impracticable character has been asserted by those who have not fully comprehended the principles therein set forth; and being thus unacquainted with the practical features of their application, either elementary or aggregate, they have been disposed to regard it as a merely visionary or learnedly mystified presentation of the nature and functions of audible speech.

Such opinions have also resulted from a lack of investigation into what may be termed the historic facts of the subject.

The possibility of defining and describing the

sounds of the speaking voice, and of creating a notation and nomenclature similar to that which marks the nature and duration of the sounds and symbolizes the movements of the voice in song, was, for a long time, a favorite idea with some of the brightest intellects of the last century; but the results of Dr. Rush's treatment of the subject, as we shall learn from the following pages, is but the exposition of a more perfect development of ideas which had their inception with these early writers, and but a complete evolution of truths that had long been recognized, though obscurely, to underlie the science of speech. He may be said to have simply renewed work upon an old vein of scientific inquiry which had been abandoned by others, and through their indications, and the aid of more efficient methods, succeeded in striking the solid ore of truth.

Although our modern elocutionists, through a period of fifty years, owe much to Dr. Rush's "Philosophy," still, its principles have never been accepted as an entirety either in letter or spirit; hence, there has been as yet almost *no intelligent co-operation*, and therefore *no uniformity of result* towards their general establishment in elocutionary instruction.

A conscientious study of the Philosophy of the Voice, and long professional experience in the application of its principles, have convinced me that it is the true method, and my veneration for the Art of Elocution has filled me with an earnest desire to lead others to a like conviction. It has long been, therefore, with me, a cherished desire to see these principles universally recognized and accepted in their integrity, and then educationally placed upon such a basis as will secure their sound and steady growth in the direction of perfection in the artistic uses of spoken language.

As I have been laboring during a considerable part of my life, both in lecturing and teaching, to establish the truths comprehended in "The Philosophy of the Voice," I now feel justified in becoming their advocate in the present volume, and their practical expositor in the work which follows.

I have no desire to be known as an originator of a theory or system. I only claim to have found the right way. I think it is De Quincey who has said, that he who brings to light, in any way, any thing of value to the general welfare that has been lost, obscured, or neglected, confers as great a favor upon mankind as an original discoverer or inventor. It may be asked, why has not "The Philosophy," in its original form, met the necessity of the public. The question is easily answered by quoting Dr. Rush's own words: "He who renovates a science rarely adds the clearest economy of system to his work."

The voluminous character of the book, therefore, in its elaboration of detail, argument, and explanation, has rendered it unwieldy, from a mental standpoint, as well as from a question of time, with the average student. Moreover, it is not, and does not claim to be, a *series of formulas and methods, and stated rules.* It is rather a comprehensive statement of wide-reaching truths, and a suggestive exposition of means for reducing them to practice.

Such a contribution to the subject of elocution as I propose in the present book and its companion volume, will enable the student, not only to follow the march of ideas in their progress through truth and error up to light, but also to arrive at such a crystallization of all the truths on this subject as must form the basis of any efficient working system that should be the standard of elocutionary excellence, and the root from which to expect sound elocutionary growth. It will be seen, therefore, by such a treatment of the subject of elocution, as represented in the old and new systems, how the elements of truth contained in the former will be illuminated, and thus rendered available and enduring, through a proper understanding and acceptance of the system of Dr. Rush.

I fervently desire to enlarge the area of information on this subject, and thus to lead to a more extended investigation into its claims and merits, not only as a science, but as a fine art.

I feel assured that if a true presentation of this system of elocution can be placed in the hands of those who will recognize its dignity and value from an educational stand-point, the study of spoken language can not fail to be advanced, through their disciplined intelligence and unity of action, to the honorable position it deserves as an important feature in all liberal education.

The book which follows immediately upon the present volume will contain carefully graduated elementary exercises in vocal drill, for the cultivation of the voice in speech; studies in articulation and enunciation, and their syllabic combinations; together with the five modes treated of in "Rush's Philosophy of the Voice," under the heads of Quality, Force, Time, Pitch, and Abruptness, with explanations of the theory and rules for their practical application to expression.

It is hoped that the work may prove of value to the private student, the minister, lawyer, lecturer, or actor; in short, to all whose professional necessities or private tasks require of them a disciplined and artistic treatment of the subject of spoken language.

Part First.

The Past, Present, and Future of the Vocal Art in Speech.

Chapter I.

The Early Writers on Elocution.

Elocution is but an artistic copy of intelligent, significant, and expressive speech, as employed in our communication with each other, either in the energized enforcement of deliberate argument, the sympathetic and endearing expressions of affectionate intercourse, the bursts of passion, or the ordinary statement of facts and circumstances which concern our business or other relations.

In all such communication nature supplies a subtle power, a more wonderful agency than mere words—the intuitive accompaniment of vocal significance. To arrive at some definite knowledge of the exact nature of these speech-sounds and their modifications, or, in other words, at a knowledge of the art-means for reproducing them in the premeditated language of reading and speaking, has been an object of research amongst nearly all of our English writers on the subject of elocution within the period of a century. Where the earliest of these writers found the subject, and the skepticism which prevailed concerning the possibility of describing or recording, with any degree of accuracy, vocal phenomena so fugitive, may be inferred from the following, quoted from one of the works of Thomas Sheridan, the celebrated actor, writer, and lexicographer [1775]:

"As words are marks of ideas; so are tones, of energies and affections of the mind; and, as we can not make known our ideas to others without a sufficient number of words to mark, not only their difference in gross from each other, but also the nice distinctions of degrees in the same idea, together with their various relations, so can not we manifest or communicate to others the several feelings of the mind in conceiving and uttering its ideas, and the various proportions of those feelings, without a suitable number and equally regular and nice distinction of tones. But *here art has entirely deserted us*, and left us to guide ourselves as well as we can. And, indeed, all of her exertions seem to have been confined within the bounds of written language, where she has the faithful eye to guide by sure and fixed marks; nor has she hitherto amongst us dared to make any excursions into the more extensive and nobler provinces of spoken language; the ways through which are to be found only by the information of the uncertain ear, which, if not well instructed and early cultivated, must ever form a false guide.

"Hence, it comes to pass that words, as marks of our ideas, are tolerably well regulated and reduced to order; while tones, the marks of our feelings, are left wholly to chance; the natural consequence of which has been that many discourses, good in themselves, are pronounced without affecting the hearers; and that, in a nation abounding in good writers, a good speaker is a prodigy."

The art of elocution was carried to a high degree of perfection amongst the Greeks, and we have reason to believe that they possessed a scientific analysis of the speaking voice, and a system of vocal culture founded thereon; but, owing to the loss of so many of their works on the subject, particularly of the primary manuals of the grammarians, and to the fact that the living tones of the language had long passed away, the moderns have had no means of judging how far the elements of vocal sound in speech were discovered and taught. The accentual marks—acute (´), grave (`), and circumflex (^ ˇ)—of the Greek language were understood to indicate certain sliding movements of the voice, through acuteness and gravity, or the scale of pitch, upon certain syllables over which they were placed. No exact knowledge, however, is transmitted of the definite character of these slides, or *inflections*, as they were called, nor of their exact uses in speech, farther than could be derived from such general statements as the following, from Quintilian.

"As music, by means of tones, expresses various conditions of the mind, so does the raising, lowering, or other inflection of the voice in oratory tend to move the feelings of the hearers; and we try to excite the indignation of the judges in one modulation of phrase and voice, and their pity in another."

The grammar of the Greeks was taught in connection with the study of music, and many of the vocal characteristics of the latter was said to belong to their spoken language. Among the musical attributes claimed for their speech was that of *melody*, or an agreeable order in the succession of its syllabic sounds through the scale of pitch, and *rhythmus*, or a certain measure in their progress; but as to the detail of their application to speech, and of the differences between the science of speech and that of song, almost every thing, as in the case of the accents, was left to conjecture. Such were the only data possessed by our early English writers concerning a science of spoken language from which they might proceed to a philosophical research into the vocal attributes of the living tongue.

The first of the English writers who seems to have discovered that the modulation or variation as to acuteness or gravity of the voice in speech was something more than simple variations by means of long or short syllables, or swift or slow movement in their succession, was Charles Butler, of Magdalen College, Oxford, an old English grammarian.

But he developed the idea no farther than that a question beginning with a verb is to be read, not only in a higher tone, but with a different "turn" of the voice from the other questions. This same vague direction was again repeated many years after in a grammar by a Scotch writer named Perry.

But no new light was thrown upon the subject of the vocal movements in speech until the publication of a work by John Walker, who may be looked upon as the father of the English system of elocution. He was also a Lexicographer who achieved the high honor of giving the British nation a standard for pronunciation, and at a time, too, when the materials for his work were both scattered and incomplete.*

---

* The two great American works of definition and pronunciation of Webster and Worcester, which are now rivals for popular supremacy as authorities, are largely indebted to John Walker for facilities in the progress of construction, and for instances of governing laws.

Early Writers.

Walker claims to have been the first to discover the upward and downward sliding movements of the voice in modern speech, to which he applied the terms rising and falling inflections, and published his discovery in a book dedicated to Dr. Samuel Johnson, and entitled "The Elements of Elocution, in which the principles of Reading and Speaking are investigated, and such Pauses, Emphases, and Inflections of Voice as are suitable to every variety of sentence are distinctly pointed out and explained."

After the publication of this book, Mr. Walker discovered that there were certain "turns of the voice" that he could not distinctly class with either the rising or falling inflection; they were rather a combination of the two. These he classified as upward and downward circumflexes, and explained his views of them in some later works.

The truth of these observations of Mr. Walker was disputed by many writers, who imagined that variation of voice as to high or low in the same word was, to use the words of Mr. Wright, "retrograde to the idea of common maxim and good taste," and for years the discovery was disregarded.

Two other works on the art of delivery were published about this time by Thomas Sheridan, to whom I. have already alluded, entitled respectively, "Lectures on Elocution" and "The Art of Reading." Sheridan was also the author of a valuable work entitled "British Education;" and of a dictionary, which, though possessing great merit as a vocabulary, was not considered as elaborate as that of Mr. Walker. These writers were both well grounded in the classics, as well as masters of the English language, and were acknowledged as such in a period which is considered the Golden Age of English literature.

Sheridan's works on elocution and delivery, although eloquently and impressively written, make no attempt at a philosophical analysis or description of the intonations of the speaking voice. He was, however, the first writer to call attention to the power of sound in our language, and to the fact that while scholars were skilled in letters, they were ignorant of the vital part of their native tongue existing in its vocal forms.

Mr. Sheridan had many followers, all of whom set themselves against the system of Mr. Walker, and cried down his theory of inflections as absurd and productive of artificial effects. Toward the close of the century, however, the author of a small treatise, called "The Art of Delivering Written Language," and dedicated to David Garrick, produced a philosophical and convincing proof of the inflection of speaking sounds. This established the matter, and Walker's works became the accepted guides to the art of delivery. His theories were adopted by Lindley Murray in his celebrated grammar, and his symbols of inflection (′ ` ^ ᵥ), designated respectively by the terms acute, grave, and circumflex accents, borrowed from the Greek, from the supposed analogy in their application, were made use of in Enfield's "Speaker." The system now received universal approbation, and was taught by all masters of elocution.

Another writer on the art of spoken language, contemporary with Walker, was Sir Joshua Steele, who published in London, in 1775, "Prodosia Rationalis, an essay towards establishing the melody and measure of speech, to be expressed and perpetuated by peculiar symbols;" the object of which was to prove that the English language possessed those vocal attributes of accent (slide) and quantity supposed to belong exclusively to the classic tongue. It is one of the most valuable contributions to the subject of spoken language ever written, fully establishing the theory that the tones of the voice in speech are capable of a definite measurement and visible notation, as in song.

The work was not intended as a manual of elocution, nor could its principles have been applied to instruction in that art without a special study of its somewhat difficult theory and symbols of notation.

In elocution, Walker's works were, as I have said, the accepted and popular text-books for reading and speaking. Steele's theory, therefore, which was long in advance of the age, finally found a resting-place on the undusted shelves of English libraries.

Contemporary with the writers I have referred to, were many able men who maintained and promulgated the theory that reading and public address could not be taught save in a restricted sense, assuming the ground that their graces and forces were gifts of nature. For many years, therefore, the systems of the authors in question, and of their disciples, had to contend with adverse public opinion, notwithstanding the many and bright examples furnished by their pupils of the efficiency of their instruction.

The combined influence, however, of Walker and Sheridan tended to awaken a new interest in reading, which, up to their time, had been taught in a hard, dry, mechanical manner, entirely devoid of expressive meaning. Save a strict injunction to drop the voice at the end of a sentence, no attempt had been made to give variety to its sounds, but the pupil was allowed to drone on like the buzz of a bee-hive.

"Those who taught the first rudiments of reading," says Sheridan, "thought their task finished when their pupils could read fluently, and observe their stops. This employment, requiring no great talents, usually fell to the lot of old women, or men of mean capacities, who could teach no other mode of utterance than what they possessed themselves, and consequently were not likely to communicate any thing of propriety or grace to their scholars."

It was the idea of giving the *variety of nature* to the reading tone that led Walker to adopt his system of inflections, the notion of which he seems to have conceived by observing the contrary movements of the voice in asking and answering questions.

Although this author claimed the theory of inflections to have been his own, it is possible he obtained his idea of the slide as applied to modern speech from Steele's valuable essay, though evidently adapting the application of the principles to his individual views on the subject. We are left largely to conjecture upon this point, since, although contemporary, each of these authors seems to ignore the other.

Amongst the disciples of Walker and those who may be accounted as original writers on the subject of elocution, were Mr. James Wright, of Magdalen College, Oxford, and Mr. B. H. Smart, of London. Both wrote early in the present century.

Smart's works were written with a view of familiarizing foreigners with the pronunciation and other vocal peculiarities of the English language. Much of his analysis is given up to the alphabetic elements of speech, but he also pursues the inflective idea in his teaching of delivery, displaying in many cases, however, a perception of the nature of vocal effects much beyond that of Mr. Walker. Mr. Smart was the author of a dictionary, and ranked very high as an authority in pronunciation.

Besides these writers on the subject of delivery, there were few others that could be named as in any degree original. Many compilations were made, embodying the Inflective or English System, and it became the authority in this country, as well as in England, in all elocutionary teaching up to the publication [1827] of Dr. James Rush's Philosophy of the Voice, of which I shall speak hereafter.

Chapter II.

The Inflective System.

I WILL first direct the reader's attention to a consideration of those movements of the voice called inflections, and their application to the utterance of language, which formed the great feature of Mr. Walker's system of elocution.

Walker starts out with the proposition that all vocal sounds are either musical sounds or speaking sounds, the latter being such as continue a given time on a precise point of the scale, and leap, as it were, from one note to another; while speaking sounds, instead of dwelling on the note they begin with, slide either upward or downward to the neighboring notes, without any perceptible rest on any; so that musical and speaking sounds are essentially different. Considering this, he found the primary division of speaking sounds to exist in this upward and downward slide of the voice; and that whatever other diversity of time, tone, or force was added to speaking, it must necessarily be conveyed by these two slides or inflections, either simple, or in their compound form of the circumflex. They were the axis, he thought, on which the force, variety, and harmony of speaking turns; the great outlines of Delivery.

The Inflective System.

Walker's entire system of treating spoken language was based upon the idea that the grammatical structure of a sentence, or the rhetorical structure of a period, must determine, not only its sense, but also the character of its emphasis and its variety in the employment of the inflections of the voice,—the rising inflection being found to express a certain suspension or incompleteness of sense, and the falling, the reverse—and the various members of a sentence were shown to preserve their correct relations, and their character of either continuation or completion, by a proper application of these different inflections to the various words concluding either of the phrases. "The inflection which ought to follow the semicolon, the colon, and the period," he tells us, "may be either the rising or falling, according as the sense or the harmony require; *adapting the elevation or depression to different degrees, as may be required*, though the different degrees of rising and falling on the inflection which ends the words, are by no means so essential as the kind of inflection." The following sentences are given by Mr. Walker as examples of what has been described: "As we can not discern the shadow moving along the dial'-plate, so the advances we make in knowledge are only perceived by the distance gone over. As we perceive the shadow to have moved, but did not perceive it mo'ving; so our advances in learning, consisting of insensible steps, are only perceivable by the distance gone over. As we perceive the shadow to have moved along the dial, but did not perceive its moving; as it appears that the grass has grown, though nobody ever saw it gr'ow: so the advances we make in knowledge, as they consist of such minute steps, are only perceivable by the distance."

"In these examples," says Walker, "the words 'dial-plate,' 'moving,' and 'grow,' marked with the comma, the semicolon, and the colon, must necessarily end with the rising inflection; and if this inflection be employed, *it is not of any consequence to the sense whether it be raised much or little*. On the contrary, if the falling inflection be adapted to any of these words, though the degree of it may be little more than perceptible, the sense, as will be found on trial, will be greatly altered. The very same points, however, if the sentence were differently constructed, would require the falling inflection."

Upon this same principle of indicating continuation and completion of sense, all forms of sentences and periods are marked to be read.

Emphasis, or the particular distinctions of some words above others, he claimed, also, to be effected by inflection as well as by a certain stress, or force, thus: "Every emphatic word, properly so called, is as much distinguished by the inflection it adopts as by the force with which it is pronounced."

Still, in giving examples, he only defines the expressive character of the two inflections in this regard negatively, as it were, by showing that the inflection must shift from falling to rising, and *vice versa*, according to the position of the word in the sentence, the structure of which is thus made to govern even the form of the inflective emphasis.

As an example of this we have the following, in which "indifferent" is the word to be distinguished: "Exercise and temperance strengthen even an *indi'fferent* constitution;" while, in the following, the inflection of the emphatic word is changed, as a necessity of developing the sense, in the changed form of the sentence: "He that has but an indi'fferent constitution, ought to strengthen it by exercise and temperance."

He shows us, it is true, that the downward inflection accompanies the most positive form of emphasis, and yet the arbitrary variety he enforces overrides this in a regulated succession of rise and fall. The following is an example: "As two inflections in the same member can not be alike; if the second branch of the first member has the rising, the first branch must, of course, have the falling, inflection; and, as the last branch of the second member forms the period, and therefore requires the falling, the first branch of this member must necessarily have the rising, inflection; this is the arrangement of inflection which seems universally adopted by the ear, and it will be found, upon experiment, no other is so various or musical, thus: 'The pleasures of the imagination, taken in their full extent, are not so gro'ss as those of se'nse, nor so refi'ned as those of understa'nding.'"

Besides the variety arising from annexing inflections to sentences of a particular import or structure, there is still another source of variety, he tells us, in those parts of a sentence where the sense is not at all concerned, and where the variety is merely to please the ear, thus: "The immortality of the soul is the basis of morality, and the source of all the plea'sing ho'pes and secr'et jo'ys, that can arise in the hea'rt of a reas'onable crea't-ure." This he terms "harmonic inflection."

It will not be necessary to supply further examples of the application of inflection, but simply to place before the reader the author's enunciation of the principles upon which, in this theory, it is founded.

"So important is a just mixture of these two inflections that, the moment they are neglected, our pronunciation* becomes forceless and monotonous. If the sense of a sentence requires the voice to adopt the rising inflection on any particular word, either in the middle or at the end of a phrase, variety and harmony demand the falling inflection on one of the preceding words; and, on the other hand, if emphasis, harmony, or a completion of sense requires the falling inflection on any word, the word immediately preceding almost always demands the rising inflection; so that these inflections of voice are in an order nearly alternate."

In the preceding summary we have the substance of Walker's theory of the principles governing the application of inflection to the sounds of the speaking voice. Although he was undoubtedly in possession of one of its leading principles, still, his method of applying this principle was so arbitrary and empirical that his system led, in many cases,

---

* Pronunciation in that time referred to the delivery of a discourse, not, as now, to the utterance of single words.

almost of necessity, to a mechanical style of utterance, rather than, as he intended it should, to a copy of natural speech. In fact, much of that chanting or "sing-song" style of delivery, so offensive in the manner of public reading for nearly a century, may be attributed to the inflective system of elocution.

That I may make manifest to my readers the fact that I have not been single or severe in this observation, I here introduce a few lines from a comprehensive treatise on vocal subjects,—published in London, about fifty years after Walker's first publication. The writer says:

"This system, which is evidently founded on the national tones of this country, rather than upon nature, has been, like most other artificial systems, very much abused, and productive of more injury, in many cases, than of benefit. The reason is, that, in order to teach it thoroughly, and impress it upon the pupil, the inflections must be caricatured, and made more distinct and strong than they are in natural, elegant, and easy pronunciation. The falling slide must be carried several notes downward, and the rising slide several notes upward, instead of a single note or half note, as it ought to be. The pupil being in this manner taught the elements of the system in a caricatured artificial manner, has his ear and his taste so corrupted that he carries the same caricature into his finished manner of delivery, and renders himself ridiculous and disgusting, as it is uniformly set down by the hearers to affectation, the very worst fault which a speaker can be guilty of. It would be better to have the unstudied manner of every-day life in public speaking, however ungainly, than this system of caricatured elocution, so much in fashion among professional students.

"One argument which we think unanswerable upon this point is, that not one of our great public speakers, in any one of the professions, adopts this artificial system of inflection, nor appears to have studied it. Indeed, it would appear finical in the last degree in Mr. Canning, Mr. Brougham, or Dr. Chalmers to mar their great efforts of oratory by such petty rules of slides and inflections of the voice.

"*We do not mean to say that they do not employ them; for they are more or less employed by all who speak the English language;* but we are certain they do not caricature them, as every pupil of teachers of elocution we have ever heard infallibly does, because he has not art enough to conceal his art, and makes the inflections so distinct that they are as offensive to the ear, as glaring colors in a painting are to the eye.

"We hesitate not to conclude, therefore, that, though Mr. Walker has made a most ingenious analysis of the inflections of the voice, we can not help thinking that it is calculated, when brought into actual practice by rule, to produce stiffness, affectation, and a monotonous sing-song manner of speaking, the very reverse of what he intended, and what is expected by those who devote themselves to the artificial study of elocution."

In another connection, the same author has the following:

"Besides the varieties of voice known to the science of music, the ear, by attention, may easily recognize many minute cadences and transitions, which have a very great effect upon the sounds, both of speaking and singing. These transitions, so far as regards speaking, Mr. John Walker distinguished by the name of slides; and, by introducing certain characters and diagrams into the system, endeavored to establish, on this principle, a perfect method of oratorical delivery. But, so far as we are able to judge, this has not been the result. This, however, is only the abuse, and not the judicious employment of the system itself. The author's original exposition of this system is a fine example of analytical observation on the subject of the voice."

It must appear, from the preceding, that the fault does not lie so much at the door of the inflective system, as it does in the uncertain manner in which the inflections themselves were explained and notated by their author. That which caused all the after error was that his analysis of this rising and falling movement of the voice was not sufficiently close to enable him to define the exact, or even approximate, degrees of rise and fall, as well as the relative position of each sound on the scale of pitch.

In the science of music, certain lines and spaces, called the staff, are used to indicate to the eye the divisions of the scale of pitch, as to high or low, with certain marks, denoting the position of particular sounds in any composition, called notes. This is called musical notation, and enables the singer to reproduce the sounds as they stand thus marked, with perfect exactness, by the voice.

The object of employing symbols for the eye in speech was for the same purpose—that the voice following such indications might reproduce certain effects.

But no approach to the determinate character of musical notation existed in the speech notation of Mr. Walker; for, while those inflections, symbolized by the acute, grave, and circumflex accents, indicate general movements of the voice, they give no certain idea of the extent of its upward or downward course, nor of its starting point upon the scale.

Again, his inflective symbols were, in most cases, employed only to mark the words bearing emphasis, or to designate those vocal movements which mark the different members of a sentence, either by a continuation or a completion of its sense, thus furnishing no guide for the eye in the case of the words of the intervening language.

In addition to the accents already described, Mr. Walker, in order to give an idea of his theory of inflection, makes use of a series of inclined planes to indicate "something," as he tells us, "of the wave-like rising and falling of the voice, which constitutes the variety and harmony of speech," thus:

But this means of indicating the movements of the voice, as far as applying it to the purposes of practical instruction is concerned, was even more vague than the marks of inflection.

While the student of this system was enabled to gain, through the treatment of what may be called the sentential points of elocution (or the relation of the voice to the sense of the language as dependent upon its grammatical or rhetorical structure), — some positive instructions concerning the merely intelligent reproduction of the language he read, he found all uncertain and undefined in the directions by which he was to attain to the ability to give fitting vocal expression to the language of *emotion and passion.*

It is true Mr. Walker showed that the use of the circumflex conveyed a certain significance of irony, sarcasm, etc., and that certain portions of discourse were affected, according to the nature of the sentiments involved, to either a high, low, or middle position on the scale; but, as the circumflex was without measure as to kind or degree in the emotions it was used to describe, and as his description of modulation involved no analysis of the mode of transition from one part of the compass to the other, they were both but indefinite indications to the student of vocal effects.

In his treatment of the voice under other modifications, such as time, force, etc., he is even more loose and undefined than in the matter of inflection and modulation. Indeed, he expresses his entire obscurity regarding the matter of the *passionative expression* of speech, as follows: "The tones of the passions are qualities of sound occasioned by certain vibrations of the organs of speech, independent on high, low, loud, soft, quick, slow, etc."

The vital principles of the voice, it has been said, consists in those tones which express the emotions of the mind; and the language of ideas, however correctly delivered, without the addition of this language of the passions, will prove cold and uninteresting. As there are other things, therefore, which pass in the mind beside ideas, and as we are not wholly made up of intellect, but, on the contrary, the passions and the fancy compose a great part of our complicated frame, and as the operations of these are attended with an infinite variety of emotions in the mind, both in kind and degree, it is evident that unless there be some means of analyzing and reproducing the vocal signs of the latter, we have not compassed all the ends of art in reading.

A complete system of analytic elocution, then, must not only prepare the reader to deal with the understanding, but also to add the means of appealing to the feelings and the imagination through a thorough and disciplined knowledge of the laws underlying those vital vocal forces which are the soul of all that naturalness of effect so much to be desired in reading or in any form of premeditated utterance.

In pointing out the imperfections of Mr. Walker's system of elocution (which, from its general acceptance, may be regarded as a generic term for the English system), I do not wish it to be understood that I undervalue his long and serviceable labors to introduce a more correct knowledge regarding the uses of the English language in artistic speech; or, that I ignore the usefulness of his excellent writings upon rhetoric and philology. To this eminent master of elocution, and to Steele, we owe the first attempt to definitely describe and record the variations of the voice in speech. But, valuable as are his distinctions and illustrations of sentential enunciation, his complete work falls short of what may be justly termed an accurate and philosophical treatment of the subject of spoken language.

Chapter III.

Wright and Sheridan.

I HAVE mentioned Mr. James Wright as a disciple of Walker's, and an able writer on the inflective system. He is considerably in advance of the former in his treatment of inflection, as well as in some other points. To quote his own words:

"Very little consideration will convince the student that phraseology is composed of certain members or clauses which modify, and of others which are modified; and, by attending to oral discourse, he will easily discover that there is a characteristic feature of the voice in the pronunciation of a proposition which indicates either continuation or completion. As, therefore, the least signification of one or more clauses may be restrained or altered by the power and influence of others more significant; so, in the delivery of them, that the *progress* and completion of a whole passage may be gradually conveyed to the ear, the attention must be kept alive by suitable degrees of suspension of the voice. If, from this, we take a more enlarged view of oral sounds, we shall find that in the arrangements of diffuse periods there may be members signifying completeness as to meaning which have certain degrees of intonation, and which, to indicate their just relations to a whole, terminate with proportionate qualities of voice. Thus, in the most rude and uncultivated appearance of the subject before us, we are sensible of something like leading principle and rule; but the *indefinite idea of sound and its relation to articulate voice, seems to* have involved the thoughts of those hitherto interested in the inquiry in considerable obscurity. For this reason, perhaps, the method for conveying information to students in elocution has not been sufficiently pertinent.

"Frequently the spirit of a proposition depends more upon the peculiar turn of voice than upon that stress which assists in placing varieties in contradistinction one to another."

He therefore proceeds to treat the subject with more accuracy as regards the measurement of the individual inflections and their relative position on the scale under certain modifications of sense, although the general principle of their uses in sentences remains the same, as seen from the remarks just quoted. In his notation he makes use of the musical staff, with certain symbols, to mark the direction and extent of the slide or inflection, as thus:

A scale of the principle inflections in compact sentences.

Is it A′ or ‵B?

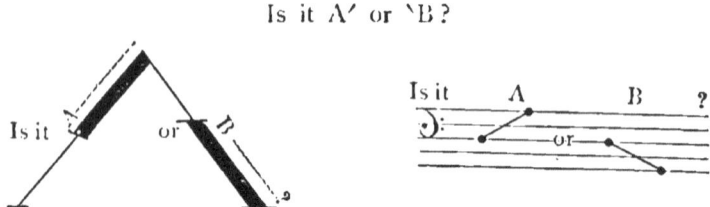

The voice, in pronouncing "A," ascends from the middle of the scale to the top; in pronouncing "B," it descends from the middle to the bottom; these inflections, therefore, are called the extreme rising and falling inflections.

Another scale gives us the principal inflections in loose sentences of two members, as follows:

Is it A′ or ‵B; B′ or ‵C?

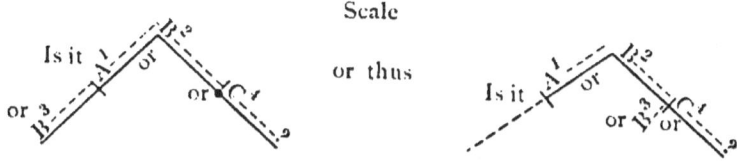

Scale

or thus

Musical Scale

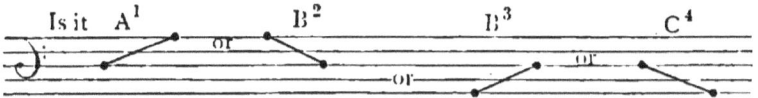

"The musical scale represents the true modulation [variation] of speaking sounds; it also points out an interesting phenomenon for the contemplation of *musicians*. There is no other way of forming the complete cadence of speech, than in sliding the voice downward into another key, as in the above example.

"*A* and *C* are the two extreme inflections, as before explained. The voice, in pronouncing the former *B*, descends from the top of the scale to the middle, and in pronouncing the latter *B*, it ascends from the bottom to the middle; the two *B*'s are therefore called middle inflection.

"The middle falling inflection signifies that a portion of meaning is formed, but that something more is to be added.

"The middle rising inflection prepares the ear for the cadence or entire conclusion.

"The extreme falling inflection implies that the sentence is complete.

"The following sentence is an example, to be read following the principle explained in the above notation :

"Nothing can atone for the want of mo‵desty, without which, beauty is ungra′ceful and wit detes‵table."

In speaking of the relations between inflection and agreeable sound, he observes that "the deliv-cry of a period may be an expressive echo to the meaning. The whole, from the beginning to the middle, and from the middle to the end, should advance with an easy elevation and depression of voice." This variety of inflective progression he designates as "the *tunes* of the voice," and it corresponds in idea to the "harmonic inflection" of Walker.

He also observed that the distance traversed by the inflection is governed by the excited feelings, claiming the musical fifth for the measure of the inflection of ordinary unexcited speech; still, he offers no close analysis of this mental and vocal relationship. As regards the other vocal attributes (besides inflection) of speech, he is practically but little in advance of Walker. His sentential treatment of elocution is, however, equally fine.

Wright was the first writer on elocution to introduce a description of the vocal organs in connection with the theory for the improvement of the speaking voice; the latter, however, was, in his case, but little in advance of what had been given before by Sheridan and Walker, and which had come down from the Latin writers; viz., a distinct pronunciation of the elements, the proper manner of pitching the voice in public address, and a few other general instructions.

I have already said that Thomas Sheridan attempted no scientific analysis of the "tones of the voice," although he was an acknowledged master in their use. He recognizes constantly the variety in speech sounds. He often makes use of the expression "change of note" and "note of the voice" to express this variety, and a general change in the pitch, but makes no attempt to describe in what the change consists. He also constantly speaks of the existence of *certain tones at pauses*, by which the sense as to the relationships of the various parts is indicated, but does not attempt to analyze the elements of this significance. Sheridan's latitude of treatment of the subject in this regard, may, no doubt, be referred to his aversion to the mannerism which arose from the *inflective system*.

In allusion to this he says:

"We are aware that there are few persons, who, in private company, do not deliver their sentiments with propriety and force in their manner, whenever they speak in earnest. This fact gives us a fixed standard for propriety and force in public speaking; which is, only to make use of the same manner in the one as in the other. And this men would certainly do if left to themselves, if early pains were not taken to substitute an *artificial method* in the room of that which is natural. Of ninety-nine persons in a hundred who had just delivered their thoughts extemporaneously upon any subject with propriety of delivery, hardly one could be found who could repeat the same words from the written or printed page without a total change for the worse in tones, emphasis, and cadence. The reason for this is that we are taught from our earliest youth to read in a different way, with different tones and cadences, from those which we use in speaking. Our education substitutes *a few artificial distinctions* for the *endless variety* of inflections, tones, emphases, and cadences furnished us by nature."

Again, he speaks of the "artificial tones annexed to stops by the masters;" which, he adds,

"May justly be called the *reading* tones, in opposition to those of the speaking kind. Of those tones in general, there are but two used,—one which marks that the sense is not completed, another which shows that the sentence is closed. How little fitted they are to answer this end, one may judge by considering that the tones preceding pauses and rest in discourse are exceedingly numerous and various, according to the sense of the words, the emotions of the mind, or the exertions of the fancy. As the one (of what he calls the artificial tones) consists in a uniform elevation of the voice, and the other in a uniform depression of the voice, we need be no longer at a loss to account for that disagreeable monotony which so generally prevails in reading.

" In this case we may apply to reading what Montesquieu has observed of the laws : 'There are two sorts of corruption—one when men do not observe the laws, the other, when they are *corrupted by the laws ; an incurable evil, because it is in the very remedy itself.*' "

The only observation of law he recommends to the reader is a practiced imitation of the natural tones, as they represent the various phases of thought, emotion, and passion in ordinary utterance, a careful copy of "the vivifying, energetic language stamped by God himself upon our natures."

Sheridan entered into a closer analysis of the *alphabetic elements* of the language, with regard to their *vocal value*, singly and in combination, than any other writer of his time, and maintained that the basis of all eloquent delivery consisted in a thorough mastery, in the beginning, of the separate pronunciation of these elements. And, although he did not do much beyond this to positively instruct in the use of the spoken forms,— that is, by his writings,— except as regards accent and pronunciation, which were in an unsettled condition at that time, he certainly did much to arouse an interest and give an impetus to the art of eloquence. His books, apart from their philological and rhetorical treatment of language, may be regarded more as a masterly plea for the study and practice of spoken language as an art, than a statement of practical methods. That is, he recognized and enforced the just *ends* of the art, but offered no scientific means through which these ends might be accomplished. He urges the claims of the spoken language almost to the disparagement of the written; but this was but the re-action of an eloquent man against the indifference of the age to eloquence. The reader will find many of his valuable ideas concerning the *power of sound* in speech embodied in Part Second.

Sheridan's profession as an actor led him to realize the full vocal value of the spoken language, and to feel the necessity of a revival in its study as an art. The same may be said, indeed, of Walker—who was also an actor—though each employed a different method to achieve the same end.*

Sheridan may be said to have favored "word painting" and a progress of sounds, or melody, made up from following the movements of unpremeditated speech, varied and impulsive; while the tendency of Walker's teaching was to create a style of artificial utterance, possessing the graces of oratorical expression founded on the idea of classic forms and measured cadences. As regards the style of their own individual delivery, Sheridan was dramatic, pictur-

---

* The stage in Johnson's time was regarded as the standard of pronunciation.

esque, and impulsive; Walker, more declamatory, studied, and cold.

Foote, in his "Anecdotes," in speaking of Mr. Walker's reading, has the following:

"In the recital of the sublime passages of Milton and our best poets, he has long been justly celebrated; and the editor of these volumes once heard him read the Lord's Prayer in a tone of such fervor and piety as excited a wish that the powers of this impressive science might be more cultivated by the professors of our holy religion. Sheridan was undoubtedly a great and a popular actor; and had he possessed the tact and business qualifications of Garrick, the control of a theater, and, above all, the happy knack of entertaining and managing critics and men of letters in general, he would have divided the throne with the modern Roscius.

"Garrick was more afraid of Sheridan than of any other actor of his day, and employed all his theatrical and personal influence to check his career. Sheridan depended more for his effects upon the power of language in its expressive forms, while Garrick relied more upon pantomime, or physical expression."

Chapter IV.

Sir Joshua Steele.

SIR JOSHUA STEELE'S essay on "The Measure and Melody of Speech," was not published as an elocutionary treatise, or, strictly speaking, as a work on delivery; but its composition was undertaken, he tells us, to prove the contrary of the assertion in Lord Monboddo's "Origin and Progress of Language," that "the English has neither the melody of modulation nor the rythmus of quantity," claimed as attributes of the learned languages. The first few chapters of the essay were communicated to the author in question, who frankly acknowledged the truth of many of its propositions. The remainder of the work was developed through an amicable controversy carried on between these two gentlemen by means of letters, Lord Monboddo proposing his doubts and queries on the subject under consideration, and Sir Joshua answering them in their order.

To give the reader an idea of the spirit and leading features of the work is all that is necessary for the development of my subject.

The fundamental truth upon which Steele based his investigations into the laws governing the sound of the speaking voice, was that the organs and faculties destined for the utterance of speech are, and have been, generally of the same structure and power in all the human species at all times, and that as all spoken language must, therefore, have the same great organic laws in common, our modern tongue could not be so far removed in the vocal character from those of classic times as to warrant the statement of many of the writers on this subject. Under this persuasion, he adds:

"I was of opinion that, by employing my thoughts in and upon my native language, I should sooner be able to discover, to analyze, and to describe separately what appeared to me to be the *essential properties* or *accidents in enunciation*, than if I had determined, in the first instance, to take nothing but what I could derive from the writings of the ancients; or, in defiance of my senses, reject any discovery of my own unless I could make it bend to the vague and discordant rules of commentators. I therefore resolved to depend neither on hypothesis nor on ancient authorities for any facts which I could obtain by actual experiment."

Proceeding upon this rational plan of investigation, he sought to demonstrate the fact that speech and song were but different branches of the same art, having many governing laws in common, but with certain essential and demonstrable differences; and, that as the latter had been reduced to the rules of art by an analysis of its especial attributes, so the former was amenable to similar treatment.

The art of music, he states, whether applied to speaking, singing, or dancing, is divided into two great branches—*sound* and *measure*, more familiarly called *tune* and *time*. For the latter, he employs, as more significant, the terms *melody* and *rhythmus*.

First, then, as to melody. In experimenting on the sounds of the speaking voice with the trained ear of the musician, he discovered that the slide, or *accent* of the Greeks, not only existed in our language, but was the necessary accompaniment of *every syllable* of spoken language. Walker, as we have seen, attributed this slide or inflection to the *entire word*. These *accentual slides* of the voice, as Steele called them, either acute (rising) or grave (falling) or circumflex (rising and falling, or the reverse), he perceived to run through a large extent between acute and grave, and, in their varied order of succession, through this compass of pitch, to constitute a melody of speech, on the same principle that the variety in the successive pitch of the musical notes produces the melody of music.

To understand this more perfectly, the reader must have some knowledge of the modern or diatonic scale of music. This may be defined as a series of sounds moving from grave to acute, or from acute to grave, by a succession of skips or intervals, *each sound or note dwelling, for a perceptible length of time, on exactly the same degree or point of the scale.*

The succession of sounds called the scale (from *scala*, a ladder), from the progressive steps by which they proceed from the lowest to the highest, are seven in number, each sustaining a fixed relation to the first, and separated from its proximate sound by a regulated interval that is large or small in accordance with its position in the scale. The eighth tone from the concordance of its vibrations with those of the first, assumes to the ear the character of the first, and has, therefore, been termed its repetition upon a higher pitch.

The intervals between the first and the second, and the second and the third, the fourth and the fifth, the fifth and the sixth, and the sixth and the seventh sounds of the scale are large, and have been termed full tones. The distances between the third and fourth, and the seventh and eighth, are small, and have been called half-tones or semi-tones.

The scale is graphically represented by symbols placed upon a series of lines and spaces, called the staff, resembling a ladder. Each space and each line represents a certain degree of pitch, from the lowest upward, and the symbols represent higher or lower tones, as they occupy higher or lower positions upon the lines and spaces.

The distance between two degrees of pitch of different elevations is called an *interval*, that is, an intermediate space or distance, and each interval has a name which depends upon the number of degrees of the scale which it embraces. The first degree of pitch of a given series of intervals is called the prime or first, the distance to the next adjoining degree is called the interval of a second.

From the first to the third degree is an interval of a third, from the first to the fourth an interval of a fourth, and so on to the eighth or octave.

Melody in music is an agreeable and regulated variation of its notes through these varied intervals—"Whereas," says Steele, "the melody of speech moves rapidly up and down (by slides), wherein no *graduated distinctions* of tones and semitones can be measured by the ear."

As to the distance traversed on the scale by the syllabic slides, he states that they pass variously through the extent of a fifth, more or less, or as great an extent, at least, as that allowed to the Greek accents.

He conceived the exact measure of these slides could only be made by quarter tones or enharmonic intervals, a division of the scale but little known to the moderns (the semi-tone being the least interval of the chromatic or diatonic scale). In making use, however, of this division of the scale for the purpose of measuring the slides, he says, "It will be sufficiently accurate to call every degree of tone a quarter tone that does nor correspond to any tone or semi-tone of the chromatic-diatonic scale." He does not, however, insist upon so accurate a measurement of the slides for the purposes of ordinary notation, his object being more essentially to show their relative proportions, and the manner of their succession in the natural utterances of language.

In devising a scheme for expressing on paper the notation of the accentual slides, etc., Steele chose one which might come as near as possible to the modern notation of music, in order that it might be intelligible to those whose idea of sounds and measure of time were already formed on that plan.

Taking the lines and spaces of the musical staff, then, and, for example, the words oh, ho, he marks the upward accentual slide on oh, thus:*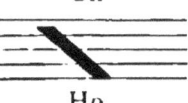

Oh

and a falling slide on ho, thus:

Ho

The circumflex, which he designated severally the *acuto-grave* and the *gravo-acute*, were represented by the following symbols, placed on the musical staff similarly to the accentual slides:

His theory of rythmus was that all utterance follows the great law of pulsation and remission resulting from organic exertion and recovery from exertion, as exhibited in the beating (or systole-contraction, and diastole-expansion) of the heart. Thus: "Our breathing, the beating of our pulse, and our movement in walking, make the division of time by pointed and regular cadences."

---

* Mr. Steele tells us that, in forming his accentual symbols, he had no intention of imitating the form of the Greek accents, and yet, in pursuing his scheme, he hit upon exactly the Greek form. "Why," he says, "did the Greeks mark their accents by exactly such sloping lines, if they did not mean them as we do, for the expression of a slide upward /, or a slide downward \ ?"

The Greeks, however, called their most acute sounds low, and their most grave sounds high. But Mr. Steele explains this circumstance in this way; viz., that it arose from the fact that all grave sounds (slides) must begin comparatively high, in order to end grave, by sliding downwards, and that the acute sounds must begin comparatively grave in order to ascend.

In the original Steele manuscript the slides were sometimes curved instead of being directly upward or downward. This indicated that the sound hung longer on the first part of the slide than on the last.

As it does not affect the melody, we have not deemed it necessary to use it in the example on pages 56 and 57.

The pulsative movement of the voice on a syllable (which corresponds to what, in the present acceptation, we call *accent*) he called *arsis*,* or *heavy poize*, and the remiss he called *thesis*,† or *light poize* (unaccented).

These Greek terms he claims to indicate similar accidents in that language to those he here used them to describe. He showed that by the natural alternations of the heavy syllable, which he marked thus △, and the light or lightest, marked thus . ·. and thus ·· , all speech was divided into regular cadences or measures of time, similar to those of music,— every syllable of our language being affected either to heavy or light, though some are of a common nature, and may be used with either.

As in music, the notes have a relative time or duration in sound, so he observed the syllables of speech to be similarly affected; this quantity or duration of sounds, distinguished by *longer* or *shorter*, being subservient to the cadences of rythmus as fractional parts to integers—the alternations of heavy and light, keeping all the cadences of an equal length by their regular pulsations. Accepting this

---

* *Arsis :* Webster says, its ordinary use is the result of an early misapprehension; originally and properly it denotes the lifting of the hand in beating time, and hence the unaccented part of the rhythm. That elevation of voice now called *metrical accentuation,* or the rythmic accent. It is uncertain whether the *arsis* consisted in a higher musical tone, greater volume, or longer duration of sound, or in all combined.

† *Thesis :* the depression of the voice in pronouncing the syllables of a word. The part of the foot upon which such a depression falls.

The unaccented or unpercussed part of the measure, which the Greeks expressed by the downward beat.

principle as common to both speech and music, he adopted the bar (| |), as employed in the former to mark cadence from cadence to the eye, together with certain symbols, to indicate the different quantities or proportions of time in the syllables, and their corresponding rests or pauses.

The quantity or time of syllables he marked thus, the opposite symbols indicating severally, *longest, long, short, shortest*, while the marks for the *rests*, severally corresponding, are represented thus:

To the symbols or notes of speech, already described, representing the slides and circumflexes, the marks of quantity were attached, so that the extent of the slide or circumflex, and, the time of its duration, were marked by the one symbol, as follows:

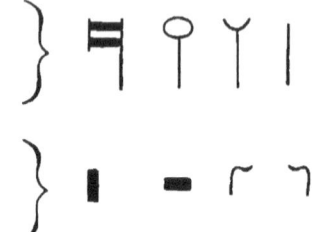

For the several notes thus formed, and for their rests, he adopted the terms of common music, as:

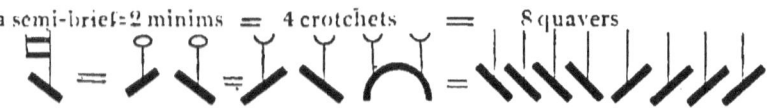

He also employed the method used in common music of lengthening a note by the addition of a point, thus:

[musical notation examples]

Other affections of the speaking voice were indicated by the musical terms, *forte*, loud; *adagio*, slow; *piano*, soft; *allegro*, quick or fast; *largo*, a middle degree between fast and slow; *staccato*, sounds with a short pointed expression, and *sostenuto*, tones equally sustained.

The *forte* and *piano* of the voice he further symbolized as follows:

Increasing in loudness:

Decreasing in loudness:

Loudness uniformly continued:

The following notated passage from Hamlet will illustrate the application of these symbols to the representation of the several attributes of the voice comprehended under melody and rhythmus; as, *accentual slides*, *arsis*, and *thesis* or *cadence*; quantity, or long and short; and *force*, or loud and soft. The Hamlet text stands exactly as Steele gave it; in it, he ignored lines and capitals.

Any one at all familiar with music will be able, with what explanation has been given, to at least approximately follow the movements of the voice here indicated:

A Plea for Spoken Language.

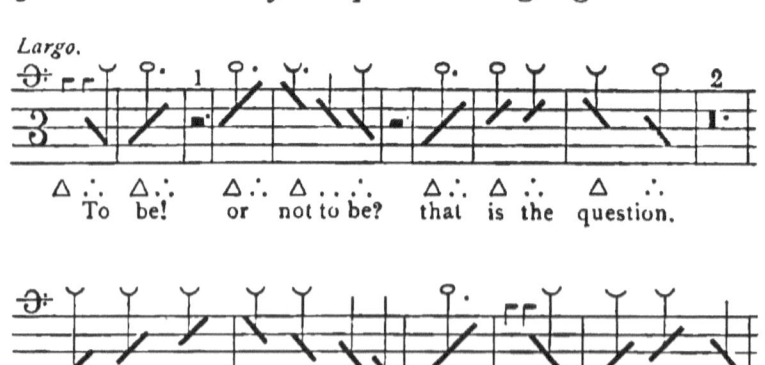

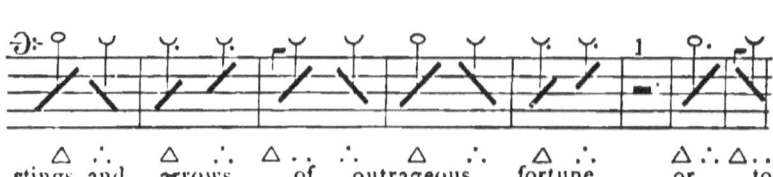

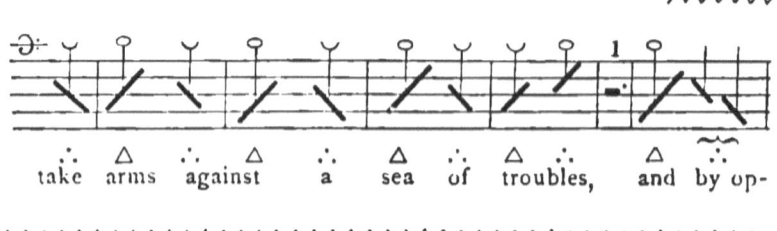

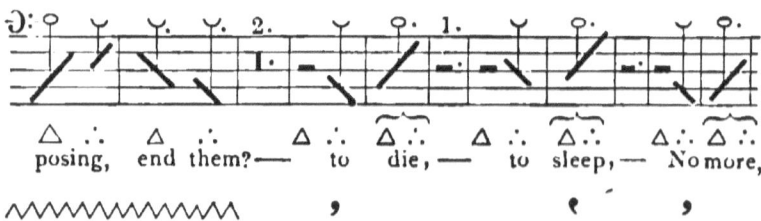

Sir Joshua Steele.

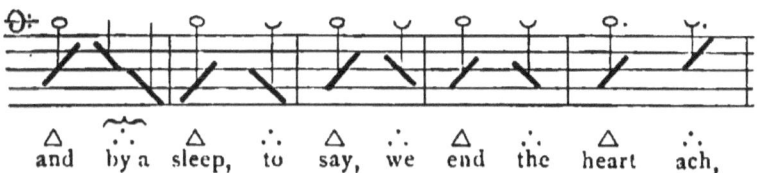

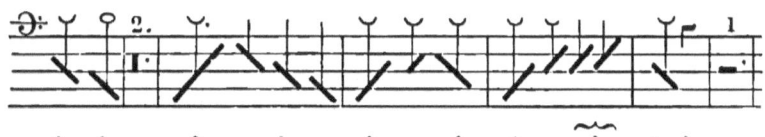

This speech (of which I here give but a part), the author tells us is not noted as a specimen of the correct delivery of the passage, but in the style of the ordinary actor of his time, and simply to illustrate how the sounds of the speaking voice may be recorded.*

---

* When this system was explained to Mr. Garrick, among many judicious remarks and queries, he asked this question:

"Supposing a speech was noted, according to these rules, in the manner he spoke it, whether any other person, by the help of these notes, could pronounce his words in the same tone and manner exactly as he did?"

To which he was answered thus:

"Suppose a first-rate musician had written down a piece of music, which he had played exquisitely well on an exceeding fine toned

This is but a bald outline of the essential properties or accidents of enunciation as discovered and set forth by the author, but it is enough to show what a vast step was here taken toward the formulation of a science of spoken language.

The principles of pulsation and remission, as the result of a universal organic law, have been since practically developed and taught as a primary element in elocutionary training by a few able writers and teachers; but the great principle of melody in speech was long allowed to remain a dead letter in the study of delivery.*

That the theory of melody, though conceded by learned men to be correct, did not meet with a more substantial acknowledgement was owing, no doubt, to its supposed impracticability. We have this opinion expressed in the following commentary on the work, from a learned contemporary of the author:

"I am far from thinking Mr. Steele's notation of the melody of speech was not his own discovery, though it is as old as Pythagoras, and mentioned by almost all the Greek writers on music now remaining, and particularly described by

violin; another performer, with an ordinary fiddle, might undoubtedly play every note the same as the great master, though, perhaps, with less ease and elegance of expression; but, notwithstanding his correctness in the tune and manner, nothing could prevent the audience from perceiving that the natural tone of his instrument was execrable; so, though these rules may enable a master to teach a just application of accent, emphasis, and all the other proper expressions of the voice in speaking, which will go a great way in the improvement of elocution, yet they can not give a sweet voice where nature has denied it."—*Steele.*

* See Pt. 4, Rhythmus.

some. But Mr. Steele has certainly the merit of having reduced it to a practical system. It seems, however, to require so much practice to obtain a facility in executing the slides, and especially the circumflexes with the velocity and neatness necessary to imitate common speech that I despair of its ever coming into use."

Lord Montboddo thus expresses his convictions and those of all the musical men to whom he had shown the treatise concerning the subject of spoken language as treated by Steele:

"It is reducing to an art what was thought incapable of all rule or measure; and it shows that there is a melody and rhythmus in our language, which *I doubt not may be improved by observing and noting what is most excellent of the kind in the best speakers.*"

The principle object of Steele's essay being to prove the existence of certain phenomena, and the possibility of observing and recording these phenomena by means of a system of notative symbols, he does not enter into that close philosophical analysis of the correspondences between the vocal effects he describes and their ultimate producing causes in the mental condition of thought, emotion, or passion in the speaker, which is needed to make a complete exposition of the subject of spoken language for the purposes of elocutionary study.

He recognizes some general facts, however, in the philosophy of these mental and vocal correspondences, as the reader will see from the following extracts: "Wherein," says Lord Montboddo, "does the difference consist betwixt the tone of passion and the musical tones of acute and grave?" Steele's answer is:

"The tones of passion are distinguished by a greater extent of the voice, both into the acute and grave, and by making the antithesis or diversity between the two more remarkable. Also by increasing the *forte* and making contrasts occasionally between the *forte* and *piano*, and by giving an extraordinary energy and emphasis, and blending the *forte* now and then with the heavy poize, or *arsis;* and lastly, by sudden and desultory changes of the measure, and of its modes—that is, from fast to slow, and *vice versa*—and from common to triple time, and *vice versa*. . . . .

"In the various tumults of passion, the voice runs very high into the acute, and very low into the grave. . . . .

"I suppose there are as many circumflexes as there are different tempers and features in men. The dialectic tone of the court, and other polite circles, rises but little above a whisper, and may be compared to that species of painting, called the *chiaro-oscuro*, which is denied the vivacity of expression by variety of colors. There the circumflex, though it can not be left out of the language, is used within very narrow limits, frequently not rising or falling five quarters of a tone, and, for the most part, hurried over with great velocity in the time of a quaver or shorter note. But, in the court language there is no argument; for, in the senate, and where that is used, *the extent of the slides is enlarged* to the extreme, so the circumflex is never so apparent as in the provincial tone.

"In plain, unimpassioned sentences the addition of *piano* or *forte*, to any sensible degree, would convert plain discourse into bombast."

Steele's treatment of the slides at pauses is similar to Walker's inflection at periods and half pauses, though he does not enter into the subject at all explicitly:

"The accent (slide) must always be liable to be changed according to the position of words, whether in question or in answer, in a suspended or in a final sense.

"In our language generally the last syllable of any imperfect sentence (while the attention is to be kept up for the sense of the whole yet in suspense) ends in the acute (rising), and all complete periods end in the grave (or falling), accentual slide."

Chapter V.

Development of Systems.

OF the many problems placed before man for solution, none could be more difficult than that of defining and describing the various movements and other attributes of the speaking voice.

Although the labors of Walker and his disciples failed to accomplish a perfected result in this direction, their works, together with those of Sheridan and Steele, marked an era in the study of the vocal art in speech, and paved the way for the more perfected discoveries of a later day or age.

Both Walker and Sheridan, in spite of their elaborate works devoted to the subject of elocution, and of the long and earnest labor they performed in elucidating their theories and imparting their principles, both as lecturers and teachers, confess to having fallen short of that at which they aimed; for, as they have both averred, they were more successful in making good readers, through the *mere imitative method*, than by teaching the rules of the systems which bear their respective names. Walker thus sums up the result of his labors:

"I have worn out a long life in laborious exertions, and though I have succeeded beyord expectation in forming

Development of Systems.

readers and speakers, in the most respectable circles of the three kingdoms, yet I have had the mortification to find few of my pupils who listen to any thing but my pronunciation. I have been generally obliged to follow the old method—if such it may be called—'Read as I read without any reason for it.'"

In the preface to one of Walker's books, which was intended by him to be exhaustive of the subject of elocution, he says, with a commendable sense of his own diligence, "It is presumed that it is the most perfect of its kind in the language." Nor was this boast without foundation at the time it was uttered. His mind was evidently reaching forward toward a complete exposition of the true science of elocution, as a vine puts forth its feelers in every direction in search of something by which it may climb into the sunlight. But it was reserved to a later time to attain to that to which he aspired, or to complete the work he had but begun. Although, at the close of his career, he realized that he had comparatively failed to identify or describe the subtler attributes of significant and expressive speech, he lost no faith in its ultimate accomplishment, but looked forward to the solution of the problem by some mind more analytic than his own. In speaking of some illustrious exceptions amongst his pupils, to the rule of mere imitation, he says:

"Such satisfactory evidences of the value of systematic elocutionary training, leads me to hope that some more successful practitioner may supply a much needed want by the discovery and use of a more thorough and efficacious system than I have been able to invent."

And again, he says, in speaking of his theory:

"Thus we have endeavored to delineate those outlines which nothing but good sense and taste will fill up; and if, instead of leaving so much to taste as is generally done, we were to push as far as possible our inquiries into those principles of taste and beauty in delivery, which are immutable and eternal; if, I say, we were to mark carefully the seemingly infinite variety of voice and gesture in speaking and reading, *and compare this variety with the various senses and passions of which they are expressive; from the simplicity of nature in her other operations, we have reason to hope that they might be so classed and arranged as to be of much easier attainment*, and productive of much certainty and improvement in the very difficult acquisition of a just and agreeable delivery."

Indeed, he looked to the active genius of the French, "so remarkably attentive to their own language," to lay the foundation of a new and comprehensive analysis of the vocal elements of language, by the aid of which the laws governing its effects in speech might be definitely and philosophically explained. Mr. Walker's hopeful anticipations have been realized, and it is a fact of which we may well feel proud, that it was the genius of America that finally placed elocution upon a firm basis of scientific truth.

Chapter VI.

Dr. James Rush.

Dr. James Rush, of Philadelphia, while pursuing his medical studies abroad, became much interested in the subject of the voice in its relations to artistic speech. In his researches into the subject in connection with his professional studies, he consulted the various works of the authors we have already enumerated; but, becoming fully aware of the imperfect state of the history of the vocal functions in speech, as set forth in the writings in question, he set to work to investigate the subject of elocution as a matter of physiological inquiry. To this work he brought the philosophic training and accurate habits of the man of science, and the just ear of the skilled musician, to which was added a cultivated acquaintance with the fine arts, derived from an extensive European observation and study. He possessed, moreover, the character of an independent thinker, and that large and generous spirit which labors on in the cause of truth undiscouraged by lack of public appreciation, and is bold and fearless in the enunciation of its convictions. What more favorable combination of capabilities could have been desired for the successful analysis of the vocal constituents of language, and their relations to the artistic uses of speech?

When Dr. Rush first turned his attention to the phenomena of the voice (1820), ingenious theories as to the structure and action of the vocal organs were numerous amongst physiologists of the highest rank, but conflicting in their statements and unavailable for the purposes of practical utility to the teacher or student of vocal expression. Thus, whatever facts of physiological research might have been made serviceable for the discipline and development of the voice in speech, were buried in a mass of prejudice and arbitrary assumption, until it seemed doubtful whether any exertion of human skill could extract a single practical ray of truth from the disputed question. Dr. Rush, in pursuing the subject of vocal mechanism, by adhering closely to the laws of analytic investigation, succeeded in clearing away much obstructing matter, but became finally satisfied that no exact truth with regard to the vital principles of speech could be discovered in such researches, on account of the impossibility of observing, with accuracy, all the actions of the living organs during the production of speech sounds.*
He therefore turned his attention to a close observation and analysis of *vocal sound itself*, having con-

---

* Of whatever service the discovery of the laryngoscope has been to pathological science, or to that of vocal music, it has failed to throw any further light on the subject of the production of what may be called the note of speech, owing to the fact that the peculiar action of the organs in the spoken utterance of vowels or syllabic sounds displaces the instrument, and thus prevents any accurate observation of their exact producing causes.

ceived the idea of making his combined knowledge of music and physiology serve him in this labor. Although availing himself of the suggestive ideas of the systems which had preceded him, especially of that of Steele, he passed beyond their uncertain foot-prints, and sought the revelations of truth where most surely to be found—from nature herself.

While his brother physiologists were carefully inspecting the cartilages and muscles of the larynx, that they might invent learned theories concerning the causative mechanism of the various vocal effects, Dr. Rush was applying the keen scalpel of analytical dissection to these very effects, studying and noting their form and degree, together with their exact relations to the various states of mind which are their primary producing causes.

The first valuable facts he obtained he applied to his recollections of the beautiful elocution of Mrs. Siddons, which he regarded as a perfect model of elegant and natural speech; and, continuing his researches into the elementary nature and functions of vocality, he succeeded in measuring the movements of the voice by means of a fixed scale, and in making other valuable discoveries with regard to the nature of the various vocal phenomena exhibited in the variety of natural speech. These phenomena he recorded by means of intelligible symbols, and an accurate nomenclature, and classified them in strict accordance with the natural laws governing their relation to thought and passion, in his work entitled "The Philosophy of the Human Voice." (The first edition was published in 1827;

the second, in 1833; and finally the sixth, in 1867).

A brief analysis of Dr. Rush's mode of investigation, and a synopsis of the chief features of his discoveries, may enable the reader to form at least a general idea of the value of the latter, in their relation to the elocution of the past and of the future.

The slide and its application to certain syllables was known to the ancients; but it is impossible to say, at present, how far the knowledge of this principle extended.

Walker and others used the word slide, or inflection, in a vague and undefined manner.

Steele was more accurate than Walker in his treatment of the slide, showing how it might be carried on the syllables of speech, through the compass of the musical scale. He entered, however, into no discriminative analysis of the vocal properties of this slide and their peculiar functions in the expression of thought and passion; and, valuable as were his contributions on the subject, he fell short of a perfect development of the vocal functions "by assuming identities," says Rush, "which do not exist, between certain points in music and speech." He adds that Steele possessed "power sufficient, when not restrained or perverted, to have developed the whole philosophy of speech."

Dr. Rush, in his investigations into the subject of this vocal slide, by careful observation and experiment, discovered that a vowel sound, in its capacity for prolongation in accordance with the natural law of the vocal mechanism, was susceptible of this continuous movement, rising or falling, from its inception at one point of the scale to its termination at another, through the interval of a second of the simple and familiar diatonic scale. He next traced this stream of sound through other wider intervals of the scale, as the third, fifth, and octave. To this progressive movement of sound, exhibited on each separate impulse of the voice, elemental or syllabic, he gave the name of the *vocal concrete* — sound concreted or grown together — either as expressed on the upward or downward continuous progression of sound; or, on those more extended sweeps of the voice, composed of a blending of the upward and downward movements, or the reverse, which he called a *wave* instead of a circumflex, as more appropriate to its vocal form. The fact that as the concrete carried the voice either upward or downward on each separate syllabic utterance, necessarily involved a repetition of the concrete movement on the next, and hence a fresh starting point, which, being more or less remote, with regard to the preceding concrete on the scale of speech, caused a point, or interval of silence, between the syllabic impulses, thus suggesting, from its separating character, the opposite term, *discrete* movement. The varied succession of these two movements of concrete and discrete pitch, he found to constitute the melody in speech, and to be a constant and measurable accompaniment of all spoken language.

The act of performing the movements of pitch through any interval, concrete or discrete, of the scale in speech, as in song, he called *intonation*. He was the first writer to make use of this term as applied to the sounds of speech, although it had been in use amongst writers on music for at least a century, to denote the precise recognition of intervals.

The concrete intonation was supposed with the Greeks to belong exclusively to speech, and the discrete to music, but Dr. Rush showed that they *both* belonged to speech, and carried with them, both severally and in their successions in melody, a certain significance and power of expression.

Melody, as here described, is not that regular recurrence of sounds constituting the offensive peculiarity commonly called "reading in a tune," but that agreeable variety in their order of succession which constitutes one of the graces of language, adds to its power of expression, and relieves it of tedious monotony or of sameness in effect. This was the principle of the speaking voice Steele so clearly demonstrated to exist, though not pursuing it into its expressive functions, and which the other writers sought to describe under the terms of "tunes of the voice," "harmonic inflection," etc.

Thus Dr. Rush's close study of the natural utterance resulted in the long deferred consummation of a definite and tangible measurement of the extent of the speech intonations, and in a satisfactory and practicable treatment of the melody of speech.

But one of the crowning features of his discov-cries, and one which he may be said to have worked out without even a suggestion from his predecessors, was that this concreted stream of the elementary or syllabic sounds of language was the vocal current on which were borne those peculiar stressful effects of force or of significance which vitalize all utterance, and constitute, in great measure, the *emphasis* of language.

These different forms and varieties of the concrete, he found to spring from one generic root, in the formation of the vowels,—a mere point of sound, produced by an occlusion in the larynx, and the subsequent ejectment of air from the lungs, overcoming the momentary resistance by the means of certain muscular agencies.

He observed that the vocal effect heard in *the natural cough* formed this "root of vocality" in all the vowel sounds, and he made it apparent by the execution of a voluntary cough, imitated from the natural act.

This abrupt effect, he found to mark, in a greater or less degree, the inception of every vowel sound, and hence to be the root of every syllable in speech. He next observed that this vocal impulse was susceptible of a graceful and delicate conclusion, well exemplified in the natural sigh — a gradually diminishing process or vanish of sound, into which the radical attenuates in what he called *the equable concrete of speech*, existing in the ordinary utterance of unimpassioned language.

He then observed in the peculiar extended or drawn out sound of *the yawn*, the type of that swell or expansion of the voice-material on the vocal or syllabic concrete utterance, often heard as a natural and beautiful expressive effect. This he called the *median stress;* while that distinctly marked jerking movement or accumulation of force at the end of the *sneeze* or *hiccough*, served as an illustration of a third natural expressive form of force applied to the syllabic concrete, which he called *vanishing* or *final stress*.

This analysis of the force applied to the vocal concrete, gave a definiteness to the study of the former attribute of the voice, never before attained; for here were recognizable *forms* of force described, where previously there had been nothing observed but the general variations of strong and weak, or *forte* and *piano*. These modifications of degree represented the intensity, or muscular exertion, applied in the formation of the several forms or stresses named.

In connection with this elementary analysis, Dr. Rush also made a masterly exposition of that attribute of the voice known in music as *timbre*, and which he designated as *quality*, or *kind*, descriptive of its peculiar sound, independent of height or depth.

In this connection, he made apparent, through his study of the mechanism of the elements, *the means for improving the natural voice* to its fullest capacity for agreeable sound by a correct practice in their formation.

All previous writers had described the vowels as sounds *flowing through opened organs*, not recognizing the vital part of their mechanism as existing in the closing or occlusion of the inner mouth. A correct practice in elementary training on this root of vocality or radical of the vowel sounds, Rush showed to form the basis of nearly all voice development.

The idea of *a special vocal culture*, or elementary training for speech, originated with this author, and forms one of the great features of his system of vocal principles.

It had been, it is true, an acknowledged idea that the speaking voice could be improved by practice in reading aloud, and Sheridan, Wright, and Smart recommended an elementary training on separate elements for the sake of improving distinctness of articulation, but it was disconnected with any definite idea of improvement of the quality of the voice.

The discovery of the syllabic function of the radical and vanish also enabled Dr. Rush to throw a great light on the subject of *quantity*, which Steele was the first to prove was a positive value in our language. His elucidation of the subject of concrete intonation, particularly in that form called the wave, demonstrates the fact that certain syllables are capable of *indefinite extension*, for the purposes of beauty and expression, without falling into the level note of song or the drawl of speech.

But the great fundamental principle of Dr. Rush's philosophy of spoken language, and one overlooked in any thing like scientific detail, as we have already noted, in former systems, was that *every state* of the mind had its corresponding vocal signs in some of the varied forms of pitch, force, time, and quality. These vocal signs he observed and recorded, not only as we have briefly described, with reference to their individual form and character, *but classified them on the principles of this natural relation to the mental phenomena of which they are the audible indication.* In other words, he found that the concrete interval of the second on each syllabic utterance, proceeding in their succession by discrete intervals of a second, was the proper or natural means for expressing unimpassioned thought or the plain statement of facts; while a syllabic progression through the more extended concretes, with accompaniments of extended discrete movements, or jumps of the voice, and the additional modifications of stress, quality, time, etc., he found to be adapted to the varied expression of feeling and passion. It is a remarkable fact that, among those who have employed and borrowed from Rush's principles of speech, the greater number have overlooked this essential difference between the vocal forms of human thought and human passion.

A description of the various elements of the voice in speech which we have noted in this brief summary, in all their variety of *form, application, and combination* in the progression of syllabic utterance in speaking or reading, goes to make up the sum of Dr. Rush's contribution to the art of spoken language, and to prove that there is a science of speech analogous to that of music, and possessing equal elements of growth and perfection.

From even so brief a review of the salient features of this author's discoveries, I think the reader will be able to see that the syllabic concrete was the simple key by which he unlocked the supposed mysteries of the speaking voice.

In the process of developing the subject by a farther and more practical treatment, it will be shown how this vital element of speech-sound, in all its forms and modifications, is but the natural outcome or result of the laws governing the mechanism of the vocal apparatus, as well as of those controlling the relations existing between vocal sounds and corresponding mental conditions; and that its intelligent exercise and application in the cultivation of the voice and ear, will place within the student's reach those processes of art by which he may reproduce all the seemingly subtle effects of natural speech. Dr. Rush has clearly demonstrated, in his illumination of the subject, how, by an imitated execution, in the processes of vocal training on elements and syllables, of the vital constituents of expression in the human voice (included in the several stresses, the equable concrete, and the various degrees of concrete and discrete pitch), an intelligent mastery is to be obtained over all the powers, graces, and discriminations of force, quantity, and quality of which language is capable, and which mark its emphatic or significant uses in intelligent or expressive language.

After having discovered all these attributes of the voice in speech, Dr. Rush succeeded in recording a description and explanation of them by employing a definite and intelligible nomenclature, and also a simple form of visible notation. Many objections have been made to the former, on the assumed ground that it involves the subject in too many technicalities and complexities, while the latter has been condemned, in cases of misapprehension of its real intent and purpose, as calculated to create an artificial or mechanical manner in reading or speaking, by applying the line and rule of measurement to what should be an apparently spontaneous exhibition of natural effects. Let us consider the subject in its true bearings. The want of clear and precise ideas, as affixed to the terms used in scientifically treating any subject, must always be the source of much error. The remedy can only lie in employing terms that will convey definite perceptions to the mind, by the aid of which it may reflect upon the principles that are presented to its consideration, and discriminate as to their truthful application.

In the record and treatment, then, of every art or science, there is a necessity for adopting a language of unchangeable meaning, by which its principles may be definitely explained and communicated, and thus placed beyond the possibility of any perversion through misapprehension or individual caprice.

Rush fully realized this necessity in the scientific handling of a subject, and acted upon it in undertaking his exposition of the speaking voice. Until his time this precision of terms had not existed in the treatment of elocution; for the knowledge of the vocal attributes being in itself indefinite, the descriptive nomenclature could not be otherwise. Hence, the loose and figurative employment of terms, both in writing upon and in teaching this subject.

Take the generalistic terms, "fervent expression," "modulation," "tone of feeling," etc. In seeking to employ them to direct a definite effect, the consequence too often is that, owing to their indeterminate and figurative character, and their consequent confusion or looseness of acceptance, a general and unsatisfactory result alone can follow. "We seem not to be aware," says Rush, "that no describable perceptions are associated with such terms until required to illustrate them by some definite discriminations of vocal sounds." In this connection, he adds that, "upon taking up the subject, the words quick, slow, long, short, rise, fall, and turn, indefinite as they are, included nearly all the *discriminative terms* of elocution," and so truly adds that, "the studious inquirer has long wanted a *language for the meaning of the voice he has always felt.*" "The fullness of nomenclature in an art," says Rush, "is directly proportioned to the degree of its improvement, and the accuracy of its terms insures the precision of its systematic rules. The few and indeterminate designations of the modes of the voice in reading, compared with the number and accuracy of the terms in music, imply the different manner in which each has been cultivated."

His idea, therefore, in adopting a more accurate nomenclature, was to describe the vocal constituents of speech, and the principles of their application, with a precision that might enable instruction to be systematic, and as definite in this as in many other branches of science. This object he accomplished by adopting those terms from the kindred science of music that are applicable to similar phenomena in speech, and the uses of which have long been fixed with scientific exactness, and are, therefore, free from all ambiguity; *but rejecting, entirely, such musical terms as suggest, in their application to speech, only a vague analogy to the functions they describe in music.* Also, by adding terms of his own invention to these, to describe such vocal phenomena, or their modifications, as could not be designated with precision by any already in existence; for, as he very justly remarks, "when unnamed additions are made to the system and detail of an art, terms must be invented for them, and even when its known phenomena are exhibited under varied relationships, the purpose of description is less perplexed by the novelty of terms than by an attempt to give another application or meaning to former names." Such scientific precision in treating the subject, certainly does not imply complication nor unnecessary elaboration, except to those who expect to purchase a knowledge of the principles of elocution through means and methods different from those employed in any other art to whose requirements they must conform.

Chapter VII.

Rush's System of Notation.

Now to consider Dr. Rush's use of a visible notation to indicate the movements of the voice in speech. The necessity for a set of graphic symbols to serve as a guide for the reproduction of the intonations of the speaking voice had long been felt, since the punctuative points, although serving their purpose to render written language clear and intelligible, were no indication of the vocal properties of syllables, words, phrases, and clauses, as employed in spoken language. Walker, in attempting to create such a visible notation, borrowed the acute, grave, and circumflex accents from the ancients.

But these borrowed symbols served only, as we have seen, to indicate the general direction of a few undefined movements of vocality; and, in the words of Rush, were "but vague and meager representations of the rich and measurable variety of the voice." Mr. Wright went a step farther than Walker, and made use of the musical staff, with certain symbols, for the purpose of measuring the positive extent of accentual and emphatic slides, and gave a number of obscure hints concerning the movements of the voice through various degrees of pitch; but he, in common with Walker, failed to distinguish the *syllabic movements* of pitch (the slide having been regarded, as we have seen, by both these writers as the attribute of whole *words* instead of syllables), and was also unsuccessful in his attempt to accomplish a definite notation, of speech.

Steele's system of visible notation of speech intonation was, however, in many respects, very satisfactory, as were also his symbols marking the rhythmical progression of language, both proving beyond question the value of the graphic art in its relation to speaking sounds.

Having discovered the measurable degree of intonation, as applied to the simple and familiar diatonic scale, it was not a difficult matter for Dr. Rush to develop the idea of graphic symbols by adopting a form of notation for spoken language, to mark these varied degrees of pitch, similar to that so successfully employed in music, but with certain necessary modifications to adapt it to the peculiar characteristics of the former.

In notating music, a simple dot or circle is placed upon each degree of the staff of lines and spaces; but, in order to express in its form the peculiarity of the upward and downward character, or concrete pitch of the syllabic slide, in contradistinction to the *level line* of pitch in the musical note,—Rush employed a symbol to represent it, which, commencing on one degree of the staff is continued to another, either in an upward or a downward direction, or in both combined, indicating the wave; these *notes of speech*, in their successions on the staff, marking the melody.

His notation is thus intended to describe only the *intonations* of the voice, or its progress through the concrete and discrete intervals of pitch. The attributes of *quality* and *time*, he does not attempt to express by symbols, leaving their proportion and kind to be described by his clear descriptive nomenclature. As regards force, however, he furnishes some symbols of the stressed concrete which are of much value as aids to the ear through the eye. By means of this simple notation, the student has afforded him the tangible instrumentalities by which the measurements of the vocal concrete are rendered appreciable to the eye, and therefore capable of serving as a guide to their exact reproduction by the voice, both singly and in their successions in melody.*

Although this author's notation by no means represents a perfected system, such as we find in music, it is complete as far as it goes, and quite adequate to the purposes it was designed to serve.

In many cases the connection of speech symbols with the study of speech has presented a twofold difficulty,—one, however, greatly exaggerated. In the first place, many students of elocution have no

---

* Illustrations of the notation employed by Dr. Rush do not come within the scope of the present volume. In my practical work, which follows, it is fully illustrated and described in detail in its practical application to the study of the sounds of the voice.

particular knowledge of music or taste for it as a study, and therefore can not see its value as an aid to an understanding of the art of expressive speech. On the other hand, many, and I am inclined to think the greater number, consider the *letter* of the work only, and thus look upon the notation as arbitrarily restricting the movements of the voice to the precision of a musical execution, thereby confining the reader and speaker to the strict observance of an unalterable melodic progression of sound, and hence liable to induce a mechanical style of utterance.

To the first it may be replied that in order to understand the kinship existing between the art of speech and that of music, an extended knowledge of the latter is not necessary.

An understanding of its most rudimentary principles, and a general apprehension of its scope as a science, is amply sufficient, since its niceties and exactitudes of execution are not involved in the application of the same principles to speech; and, as regards the latter difficulty mentioned, it should be expressly understood that the object of Dr. Rush is not to set notations to be arbitrarily followed in reading any prescribed matter, but to present a system of visible marks, by which the learner, as a process of discipline, may be able to note or follow the progressive syllabic steps of the voice, as it moves through the utterance of a group of words or sentences on the speaking scale. Thus the student is enabled to repeat the movements, by following the indications of the symbols, as often

Rush's System of Notation. 83

as he desires, *until he is master of the principles involved.*

The notation of song is made by a musical composer, and is to be strictly followed by the singer; therefore, all singers will follow the same intonations in the execution of the same composition. With the reader it is different. The notation, in his case, serves its purpose, first, by suggesting appropriate modes of expression, as to the feature of intonation; and, secondly, by giving him command, through the practice it affords, over the different vocal movements it indicates. Having, then, by means of the latter, brought the various effects of pitch and other modifications of sound represented in the prescribed notation under the control of the mental faculties and the vocal organs, he possesses the means wherewith to apply the knowledge and skill thus acquired to the creation of his own melody, according as his own judgment, taste, or fancy shall dictate. Thus, although the movements of pitch, indicated by the speech notation, are susceptible of almost the same exactitude in their execution as those of song; and although it is desirable to observe this precision in elementary practice, still, in the final execution of the speech melody, it is not to be aimed at, since the visible marks, after having served their ends in the processes of disciplining and cultivating the voice and ear, are suggestive and relative, rather than positive and absolute, serving as a general outline of direction and proportion.

The notations of Rush are not calculated to make

a reader adopt a method of dealing with language by which his own tastes and conceptions are set aside or rendered inoperative. The principles which the notations illustrate are positive, but the notation itself only suggestive of the means of attaining the desired end of natural effect in the utterance of premeditated language.

Perception and perseverance will, in time, give the student command over all the natural forms of vocality. His ear, cultivated to an appreciation of sounds it had not observed before, will become his only preceptor; and his tongue, from habit and practice, will move in subjection to his will when, from the mere observer, he has become the disciple of nature.

One of the greatest advantages of this whole system of notation and nomenclature, lies in the fact that the teacher, by its means, is enabled to impart to the mind of the pupil a distinct picture, as it were, of the processes employed in producing certain effects, thus making him familiar, in the initiatory steps of his studies, with those principles so necessary to an intelligent progress in the more advanced stages of instruction.

The lack of such an aid, universally accepted, has long been a stumbling-block in the way of earnest and intelligent teachers. Oftentimes the pupil, after having been drilled into something like a successful imitation of the teacher's reading of a given passage, produces, perhaps on his own part, an effect that discovers some vital point of expression, natural and appropriate, but which had not been either in the teacher's own mind or voice, and hence not aimed at in his instructions. "Right!" he cries in approbation; but, in striving to produce the same point of effect in the delivery of another pupil, he finds himself at a loss for definite means by which to direct the latter in its reproduction. The successful performer is then called up to illustrate, by a repetition of his first reading. But, alas! the feeling which brought out the latent beauty has fled, and with it all ability to repeat the same form of expression. The teacher having no means to record or define it by a language of definite and unchangeable significance, the expressive effect and the principle it illustrates are lost both to himself and his class. On the other hand, the well disciplined student of Rush would not only be able to note all such expressive utterances upon paper or the blackboard, and then explain them to his class with the additional aid of well understood terms, but would also be able to preserve them as matters for study and reflection.

That the system of Mr. Walker, popular as it was in England and in this country, for many years, did not, according to the author's own acknowledgment, succeed in making good readers and speakers, is largely attributable to the failure of his visible notation to indicate the vocal effects it was designed to illustrate; for his symbols, not being definite, but only general indications of upward and downward slides of no describable extent, were liable, in their use, to create other results than those desired by the student or intended by the author.

In a grammatical point of view, Mr. Walker's notations are clear and intelligible, and can still be used with the modifications imparted to them, or rather the light shed upon them, by a knowledge of the measurable degrees of intonation described by Dr. Rush, and applied to the management of the voice at minor pauses and periods.

However the fixed habits of study, therefore, may incline him to the system of Mr. Walker, the intelligent elocutionist or student can not but become interested in a study of these principles, upon learning that, through a knowledge of the character or philosophy of the concrete and discrete functions of vocality, the method of Walker's inflections will become at once more intelligible, and more practical.

Many who have condemned the system of speech notations and descriptive nomenclature of Dr. Rush, have proceeded upon the assumption that the variations of syllabic pitch, and other modifications of the syllabic utterance, can not be appreciated by the common ear, and therefore are not susceptible of measurement. Of course, to deny the possibility of measuring the speech sounds, and of perceiving their other modifications, is logically to preclude any possible means of visibly representing or technically describing such phenomena. Indeed, we have just noted this as the reason that the English writers failed to accomplish any thing definite in the way of notation and nomenclature — because of their indeterminate knowledge of the vocal attributes they were designed to symbolize.

Objections upon this ground can only be made, however, by those who have not tested the measurable character of speech tones by actual observation, experiment, and experience; or, by those who have formed their opinion as a foregone conclusion, based upon the established prejudices or popular errors concerning the impossibility of arriving at any definite knowledge of the movements of the speaking voice, and who will not, therefore, give Rush's treatment of this subject that fair, practical investigation which could not fail to lead them to a conviction of the truth of his principles. An eminent actor and elocutionist, after attempting to read a few passages for me, notated after the manner of Dr. Rush with regard to the different movements of syllabic pitch, exclaimed, "Dr. Rush must have been a fool to think that any one could be aided in the study of reading by any such perverted use of the musical staff and its note signs!" The secret of the matter being that he saw something that was unintelligible or meaningless to him simply because·he had not taken the trouble to understand it. To realize the strength of that prejudice, arising from the lack of a true insight into this matter, we have but to reflect that reading itself was looked upon, in its infancy, as a supernatural gift, the illiterate having no conception of words independent of sound, not being able or willing to comprehend that language could be represented to the eye by means of written symbols or letters,— the few who were masters of the art being even regarded as magicians.

What should we think of the opinion of a person if, simply because he lacked a knowledge of musical notation, he should condemn it as unintelligible or absurd; or of the man who, not having a natural or cultivated ear for musical sounds and their appreciable qualities and measurement, should deny that they possessed any such attributes. And yet, such is exactly the logical—or rather, illogical—attitude in which those persons place themselves who deny that speech-sounds are capable of measurement in pitch and its visible representation, or of analysis as to other properties, without having brought the powers of their intellect and of their sense of hearing to test the matter by experiment. I fully realize the fact that it is no easy matter for the ear to intelligently follow these vocal movements, without the most close and careful habits of observation and analysis; for we are so accustomed to accept the significance of these sounds, which we never fail to recognize, that the very familiarity of the phenomena renders us unobservant of its exact character or producing cause. One unconsciously, however, takes the form and measurement of vocal sounds by this recognition of their significance; and all that is needed is to direct the mind to the conscious *observation* of the same phenomena. Rush did not attempt to analyze these movements in *their rapid flight* through speech, but by slow and patient observation *of individual utterances;* and it is only through such gradual means that the student can hope to obtain a disciplined knowledge of their properties which will guide him

Rush's System of Notation. 89

to their correct recognition in the varied combinations of language. Dr. Rush, in commenting upon this point, says:

"The inscrutable character, as it is affirmed, and the fancied infinity of the vocal movements, together with the rapid course and variation of utterance, are considered as insuperable obstacles to a precise description of the detail and system of the speaking voice. We may here ask if there is no other opportunity to count the radii of a wheel, but in the race, or to number and describe the individuals of a herd, except in the promiscuous mingling of their flight? Music, with its infinitude of detail, must still have been a mystery, could the knowledge of its intervals and of its time have been caught up only from the multiplied combinations and rapid execution of the orchestra. The accuracy of mathematical calculation, joined with the sober patience of the ear over a deliberate practice in its constituents, has not had more success in disclosing the system of this beautiful and luminous science, than a similar watchfulness over the deliberate movements of speech will afford for designating its hitherto unrecorded phenomena."

Steele says: "Language is an art that we learn (to speak in a vulgar phrase) very naturally; that is, by rote. Many people learn music nearly in the same manner, especially singing; and both those who talk by rote, and those who sing by rote, are often proficient in practice, without knowing that those arts are capable of rules and of very subtle analyzation, any more than a child of five years old comprehends or can explain how he stands or walks."

In addition to gradual and deliberate processes of study in the beginning, the constant habit of watching the movements of the voice in its impulses and drifts under entirely natural and unpremeditated excitement, as well as its more studied effects in the exercise of professional functions, has brought me the conviction that the most minute vocal movements of speech can not only be measured and described, but that the truth of this has been clearly demonstrated in "The Philosophy of the Voice."

Elocution may, then, be taught with results, if not as certain as those of an exact science, at least with such approximate results to certainty as are necessary for its development as a fine art. To use the words of Dr. Rush:

"It may be remarked, in anticipation of what may be shown hereafter, that the art of speech, in three of its important modes; namely, *time*, with its measurable movements; *intonation*, with its measurable intervals; and *force*, with its measurable degrees,—though not admissable within the pale of exact calculation, is yet upon its border, and when, through future cultivation, it shall take its destined place among the liberal arts, it will be found at least beside architecture and music,—those beautiful associations of taste with mathematical truth,—if, indeed, from its principles of intonation being broadly and strictly founded in nature, it may not claim to be before them."

Chapter VIII.

Rush's System.—Continued.

I HAVE spoken thus at length upon this matter of Rush's notation and nomenclature, and the end the author designed them to serve, as aids to elocutionary instruction, in view of the fact that so many have stumbled upon the mere letter of the work, and have thus failed to grasp its true and liberal spirit.

From the discipline of the organs of speech, which is a necessary result of working with nature, together with the sympathetic effects of discrimination and taste, the student of elocution can not but obtain from a study of this system advantages of the highest importance in his art.

Before concluding these introductory remarks upon the subject of Dr. Rush's work, I would have it clearly understood that it is not claimed that he has demonstrated the art of speech to be capable of the same perfection of results, or rather the same unvarying precision of effects, that we find in music.

For, as Rush himself has said, "The full development of an art, in all its practical bearings, can be effected only by the united labor of *many*, and of *their lives.*"

So general and so deep-seated was the conviction, at the time of Dr. Rush's first publication, of the impossibility of detecting and recording in detail the various modifications of the tones of speech, owing to their brief and evanescent character, that the publication met with the most unfavorable criticism, or, perhaps, one might more properly say, with the opposition of hasty and prejudiced opinion, for no book, probably, ever received, upon its first entrance before the public, so little criticism, in its real sense. To quote Dr. Rush's own witty résumé of the opinions of some of the early critics (?) of his work:

"One says it is a sealed book; another, that it might as well have been written in Hebrew; an eminent leader of opinion on this side of the water says it is not worth reviewing; while, on the other side, one of the very highest rank in British periodical criticism, declares, in the frank confession of an ineffable superiority, that it quite surpasses his comprehension. One, not contented with his own single incompetence, takes the author into his company by saying that he does not understand it himself; while, to a high-placed medical proferssor, the work was altogether so unintelligible that he recommended one of his friends to read it, as a fine example of 'the incoherent language of insanity.'"

I mention these circumstances of the early reception of the book, merely, as Rush himself states, after giving the above summary,—"'as minor chronicles, collateral to the early history of the philosophy of speech," and to show that the history of Dr. Rush's discoveries forms no exception to those of many other benefactors of mankind, whose labors have been undertaken in the cause of truth, and for truth's sake only. How many facts of science, now established without cavil or controversy, and on which much of popular knowledge depends,—how much of the present scientific information (which marks the advancement of the age) would have remained neglected if the *superficial verdict* as to its value or availability, had been necessary to secure its recognition and adoption? When difficulty appears in the way of a ready understanding of a subject not under popular acceptance, there is always a disposition to consider such a matter as either visionary or at least not available for the purpose of general utility. With regard to the "Philosophy of the Voice," it is, and, from the nature of the subject, necessarily must be, a work which requires not only intellect, but patient application and observation, to comprehend its details; and, where these have been given, it has always resulted in acknowledgments of its superior value. It is now more than fifty years since the first publication of the work, and it is with pleasure I testify to the liberal and progressive spirit of the time by stating the fact that a very different opinion now prevails with regard to its merits as a contribution to the scientific study of spoken language. The French have sufficiently considered and appreciated the work to call forth an indorsement of its merits,—the record of the French Academy of Sciences bearing honorable witness to the author's exposition of the vocal organs, and their peculiar functions in the production of those elevations and depressions of the voice, technically known as pitch.

Many of the principles of Dr. Rush's system have met with the corroborations of later science, both from the stand-point of anatomy and acoustics, the discoveries in both these branches of science made by Helmholtz, Lunn, and others simply serving to confirm the correctness of Dr. Rush's vocal methods in the production of sounds, and the results in quality or kind.

The theory for a special vocal culture for speech has been confirmed by Weiss, the German writer on the voice in song and speech, and by later writers on the same subject, who insist, as the former expresses it, upon the necessity of "conscious technical effort," in the artistic use of the voice in speech, as in song.

Dr. Rush's philosophy of the relationships between certain mental causes and peculiar vocal effects, as exhibited in the varieties of intonation, qualities of voice, etc., has been confirmed by no less a modern scientific light than Herbert Spencer, who explains the correspondences between mental and vocal phenomena on the ground of the direct relation existing between mental and muscular excitement. Still, while the principles of "The Philosophy," are thus confirmed, both directly and indirectly, no writer of any nationality has given us so copious and complete an analysis of the vocal functions in their relations to the expression of speech.

In England, several popular and valuable books on delivery bear unmistakable evidences of the fact that their educators have not only read the "Philosophy of the Voice," but have adopted many of its principles; and a recent elocutionary work, of high authority with the English public, in recommending the works of most value on the subject of elocution, says:

"I would name particularly, in addition to the authors to whom I have already referred, the great American work, written on the voice, by the celebrated physician Dr. Rush. It is well worthy perusal by those who wish to study the subject in all its minuteness of detail."

In our own country, this work, since the time of its publication, has furnished material for the greater part of the elocutionary books and systems subsequently issued; and yet, with but a few notable exceptions, the greater number of those who have undertaken to handle the principles embodied in the original work, have either illiberally interpreted, or imperfectly understood and reproduced, them in their various manuals of elocution. Many have selected only the elements of force and abruptness, giving them an undue prominence, to the neglect of other points of as essential value, producing "barkers," as some of the ancient orators have termed it, instead of discriminating and elegant, as well as forcible, readers and speakers.

Others have re-named the various original points, and thus, by unnecessary diversity of nomenclature for one and the same idea, have created confusion, resulting in an obscuring of the ideas themselves.

Again, not a few have chosen to interpret Dr. Rush according to their own conceptions of the kind and value of his principles, and their practical relations to elocution, rather than in accordance with the author's true spirit and intent. Such have selected only those points of his system as came within reach of easy and immediate application to their own purposes, ignoring or rejecting what to them, as superficial students or seekers after knowledge through easy ways, appeared to be hard to understand, and, therefore, too difficult for the demands of teaching. Valuable features of the system, thus detached from the modifying influences of the remaining parts of a complete whole, have been, in many instances, misinterpreted in their application or exaggerated in their functions. I have in my mind, in this connection, one who, for many years, occupied a prominent position in the public eye as lecturer and writer on elocution. While using the Rush system in many of its more mechanical details, he evidently avoided any exposition of its true merits with regard to the melody of speech, or to the true meaning of the philosophy of the formulas by which the vocal organs should be disciplined in order to bring the voice under the speaker's control, without physical injury, and yet to accomplish the greatest amount of vocal effort and endurance. The specialty he developed and made the "feature" of his teaching, was the *special and voluntary control* of the abdominal muscles and the diaphragm. This I give but as an illustration of the tendency amongst those handling the subject of elocution, either as writers or teachers, to give prominence to some peculiar "method," announcing it as the "only open sesame" to the treasures of vocal culture and the supposed *mysteries of natural speech.*

I do not make these statements with any desire to detract from whatever good work has been done in the cause of elocution; but I desire to state facts exactly as I know them to be with regard to the matter in question, in order to show how, from a desultory and imperfect or unfair manner of dealing with a work of minute analysis and profound research, its broad and comprehensive character has not been thoroughly understood, nor its large spirit, as the system of a universal nature, thoroughly grasped, by the public. Such facts clearly explain why there has been, thus far, *no uniform elocutionary development from a source which bears within itself all the essential elements for the accomplishment of that result,* and why there is, as yet, *no established artistic standard of excellence and taste in elocutionary study and execution, which would be the natural outcome of such development.*

Chapter IX.

Reception of the Rush System.

Dr. Rush was not an elocutionist, but I feel assured that, had the pressure of professional duties permitted or circumstances compelled him to become a practical teacher of his system of principles, and to have established an institute for the exposition of his vocal theories, under his own direction, his philosophy would be to-day — what of right it ought to be — the governing power in the study of spoken language among all English speaking people, and of all who use the audible forms of speech for public address.

Dr. Rush always regretted the absence of that unanimity among teachers of elocution, with regard to the vital principles of their art, which prevented their formulating one general plan of instruction, after the custom prescribed for teaching other branches of education. When the book first appeared, the doctor was at particular pains to interest teachers of elocution in its reading and study. He took every fitting opportunity of explaining any point of doubtful meaning to which his attention was called. He was willing and ready to compare notes with those who might entertain preferences for their own theories or practices. He never objected to a friendly presentation of the merits of the old systems, and freely entertained whatever of objection might be raised against his own by those who showed a proper spirit of discussion. To *controversies*, however, he objected strongly, thinking they generally ended in doing harm, rather than in promoting the good of the subject.

The Doctor's ideas concerning the spirit and letter of teaching were entirely novel and original, and not at all suited to the wants of public schools, being better calculated to teach students and teachers the principles which should underlie the forms of instruction they were to create and use. Until one general plan could be determined on, made up of the best points of the best experiences, to be blended into one great whole for the guidance of all, "The Philosophy of the Voice" was to be an exclusive text-book, and in the hands only of the tutors. The blackboards and charts, with the teachers' vocal exemplifications, were to be the means of instruction until the elementary studies should be completed.

In the case of teaching in a more advanced sense, Dr. Rush was of the opinion that teachers should work out the proper results with their pupils, in small classes or singly, by means of practical expositions of the governing principles, illustrated in detail by special examples, not requiring the pupil to commit rules to memory, but to study their meaning and try to apply the principles to sentences or lines dictated by the teacher.

Though utterly reckless of ignorant and pretentious opposition, Dr. Rush was yet generously frank in his desire to receive a sympathetic acknowledgment of the importance of his work, and the assistance of all those who could bring an intelligence, earnestness, and enthusiasm adequate to the necessities of the case. Most prominent amongst the few who succeeded in contributing such aid to the cause was Dr. Jonathan Barber, a member of the London Royal College of Surgeons. He had been a lecturer on the subject of elocution, in conformity with the laws of rhythmus as set forth in the work of Sir Joshua Steele, and of physiology, before the publication of "The Philosophy of the Voice." Upon reading this work, he was so struck with the truth of its principles that he gave the subject a special study, and was the first to acknowledge its superiority, both theoretically and practically, over all other works on the subject of the voice in its relation to speech.

He began to teach the new system, and made so favorable an impression upon the educators of the period that he was afforded the opportunity to introduce his elocutionary training into some of the Eastern colleges.

Yale College was early favorable to the system, but the University of Cambridge, by appointing Dr. Barber to its department of elocution, was the first chartered institution of science in this country that gave an influential and responsible approbation of the work.

One of the features of the system of artistic study

advocated by Dr. Rush, and enforced by Dr. Barber in his teaching, is a preparatory training, for the purposes of disciplining both voice and ear, on the vocal elements of language, in connection with the alphabetic elements and their syllabic combinations.

This study of vocal elements, however, in the exercises preparatory to more advanced studies in declamation, was not congenial to young men who thought they had passed beyond the alphabetic stage of their language, and, by its seemingly unnecessary enforcement, created opposition, which finally led to ridicule. Dr. Barber, in consequence, resigned his position, and, as far as colleges were concerned, the matter fell into neglect. It was, however, continued in some quarters, and with more or less success.

The following letter from America's popular orator, Wendell Phillips, is in itself sufficient comment upon the efficacy and value of Barber's treatment of the Rush principles, and their appreciation by those who, in the simplicity of true greatness, inclined their ear to what they recognized as the teachings of nature:

"BOSTON, MASS., *March* 23, 1878.

"MR. JAMES E. MURDOCH:

"*My Dear Sir*,—You ask me to tell you something of my acquaintance with Dr. Barber, the elocutionist. I had the good fortune to be his pupil, at Harvard College, in a class which fully appreciated the value of his lessons and system. I think I may say we were his favorite class. W. H. Simmons, afterwards teacher of elocution, etc., at Harvard College, enthusiastically devoted to training his rare powers,* Motley, who, had not literature drawn from public speech, would have been one of the most eloquent and finished of American speakers, were of our class, and, with a dozen others, were deeply interested in Dr. Barber's system. It is little to say that we all thought it the best ever offered to any student. Based on Rush, the Doctor's system was at once philosophically sound and eminently practical. I am sure he taught me all I was ever taught, except by a schoolmaster [Withington], whom I lost at ten years old. Whatever I have ever acquired in the art of improving and managing my voice I owe to Dr. Barber's system, suggestions, and lessons. No volume or treatise on the voice, except those of Rush and Barber, has ever been of any practical value to me. The Doctor's reliance on principle, and comparative disuse of technical rules, seem to me a great advantage over all the other systems with which I am acquainted. His teachings tended to make good readers and speakers, not readers or speakers modeled on Barber. It brought out each pupil's peculiar character of utterance and expression, without attempting or tending to cast him in any mold. After leaving Barber a pupil had no mannerism to rid himself of before he got full possession of his own power. Of how few teachers can this be said.

"It is useless to waste words on any man ignorant of the vast power of agreeable and eloquent speech in a republic. You can in no way contribute more to its cultivation than by doing justice to Rush and Barber, and calling attention to their system. For the sake of the public, as well as your own, I wish you the largest success in your effort.

"Very cordially yours,

"WENDELL PHILLIPS."

---

* Mr. W. H. Simmons, the elocutionist, was the *favorite Shakesperean reader* of Boston. He showed decided talent for the stage, and made a successful appearance in several first-class characters; but, being unwilling to submit to the drudgery of stock acting as preparatory to a permanent success, he abandoned the profession.

He was highly educated, and a most agreeable person in society. The most intellectual people of Boston were his auditors,

The quoted letter from Mr. Phillips was written in reply to a request I had made of him for information concerning the peculiar treatment Dr. Barber had received from the students, and which had compelled him, from a sense of self-respect, to abruptly resign his position as professor of elocution at Harvard College. Mr. Phillips told me that his class was the only one which did not show a disposition to ridicule the Doctor's mode of conducting his exercises in speaking and gesture. It would have been well for the cause of what Demosthenes considered the all in all of oratory,—its "action,"—had the faculty and the students of Harvard been better disposed towards a study, the practice of which would have given the country a few more such orators as Wendell Phillips.

The following just tribute to the worth of Dr. Rush's work, speaks for itself.

Mr. Wm. Russell, that eminent educator who did so much to elevate the standard of education in New England, says, in speaking of Rush's "Philosophy":

"Had its author lived in those times when eloquence was cherished as an attainment almost divine, and they who contributed to facilitate its acquisition were rewarded as distinguished benefactors of mankind, neither statue nor votive wreath would have been wanting to his honor."

The following, expressing the same appreciation, is from Dr. Jonathan Barber to James Rush, M.D.:

---

with whom he was a general favorite. Mr. James T. Fields spoke of him as a model reader. He was before the time of Fanny Kemble or Charles Dickens.

"*Dear Sir*,—The treatise which you published in 1827, entitled "The Philosophy of the Human Voice," was the first work that ever presented a true and comprehensive record of the vocal functions. Physiology is a science, the details of which are discoverable only by observation and experiment.

"The history of the functions of the voice is a legitimate department of that science, and you have investigated it in the only true method. Your work is strictly inductive; its philosophical *principle* is, therefore, correct. It combines, at the same time, such fullness of detail, with such an orderly classification of the vocal functions, as to entitle your views of the subject, on the ground both of the comprehensiveness of the particulars and the felicity of the arrangement, to the denomination of *a science*. Much less originality, depth, and accuracy of investigation, devoted to some art which mankind in general have been taught to consider profitable, would have brought you a more immediate recompense of fame,—not, however, perhaps, a large portion of ultimate glory. As to the practical tendency of your treatise, I would observe that it satisfied my curiosity as to the elements of the art which I teach, and enlarged to so great an extent my resources as a teacher, that the advantages I am constantly deriving from it of themselves prompt me to a full and grateful acknowledgment of its merits.

"Your sincere friend and servant,
"JONATHAN BARBER.
"CAMBRIDGE, *October*, 1831."

Amongst the names of others besides Dr. Barber, who wrote justly and intelligently upon the Rush system, may be mentioned those of Prof. Wm. Russell, Samuel R. Gummere, Weaver, and a few others. Their works, however, except in the case of the first mentioned author, are now neglected and some of them out of print.

Chapter X.

The Author's Early Experience.

I THINK it will not be considered an obtrusion of my personal history upon the reader if I here give a passing glance at my early experience with regard to elocutionary study, in order to show how the necessities of my profession led me from the imperfect systems of the old school to the study and adoption of the system of Dr. Rush.

My early choice of the stage as a profession led me to seek the aid of Prof. Lemuel G. White, a well-known elocutionist of Philadelphia, whose instructions, based upon the routines of the old school, were of great benefit to me in the amateur part of my career. After going on the stage, the colloquial use of the voice, in the lighter parts of theatrical representation, was in itself a kind of elocutionary training. But I found, upon attempting the heavier parts of tragedy, that the powers of my voice did not enable me to realize my ideal of the effects I desired to produce, and that I had yet much to accomplish in the way of vocal discipline, my previous studies having been rather a training in articulation and emphasis (in the ordinary sense of force) than a development of the qualities of the voice, or a study of the expressive elements of spoken language.

Although I may safely affirm that the general opinion of the dramatic profession, in our own country and Great Britain, is not favorable to special elocutionary training for dramatic purpose, the late Mr. Forrest (who had been a reader of Dr. Rush, if not a strict follower of his principles), in giving me, a mere tyro, some friendly advice, observed, "While you are paying so much attention to distinctness of utterance and to the inflections of your voice you neglect the modulation of your tones, in consequence of which you tire by uniformity. I should advise you to read Dr. Rush's 'Philosophy of the Voice.'" I was somewhat surprised to receive such a hint from the great tragedian. It however caused to me to recollect that while studying with Professor White he had taken me to see Dr. James Rush, the author of the Philosophy, etc. I remembered, too, that the very instructive conversation I heard on that occasion had impressed me with the idea that the Professor and the Doctor did not agree on the subject of voice cultivation. At the time I speak of I was playing, at the Arch Street Theater, Philadelphia, subordinate parts, at a mere bread-earning salary. I had been but recently married, and my entire time was occupied in the laborious work of memorizing the words of the characters allotted me— sometimes four or five during the same week—the star system, then in vogue, making the stock actor's life a mere drudgery.

The Author's Early Experience.

In consequence of such a constant study of "words, words, words," it may be seen that I had no fitting time to devote to the reading of such an elaborate work as "The Philosophy of the Voice."

The subject therefore passed out of my mind, and I went on acting, it may be said, from mere "instinct." I mention this to show that such studies should be accomplished "in the apprentice days of youth, while the faculties are quick and time accordant."

In spite of adverse influences, however, I still kept an open ear to the vocalities of my profession. Upon a chance occasion I received, in the course of a discussion on the subject of expression in speech, a most useful lesson from a vetern actor, Mr. Dwyer, an accomplished comedian of the old school, whose voice had been trained by long practice upon the stage, and under the influence of such high exemplars as Mrs. Siddons, John and Charles Kemble, and Charles Young. One thing that deeply impressed itself upon my mind, and gave me a new idea of the expressive possibilities of reading, was his recitation of Byron's Waterloo. The heroic sentiment and the pathos of the subject depicted in the tones of voice were as sensibly impressed on my mind as if I had been an actual observer of the scene described by the poet. I then said to myself, "Here are certain movements of voice and expressive effects in utterance which I can not command." His execution had nothing of what might be called the hard hammering of emphasis when expressed only in the percussion of force, or puncturing ictus of merely accentual stress. Nor had it the jingling effect so apt to be received from the system in which expression is regulated by the grammatical structure of the sentence.

It was this circumstance that led me to reflect upon the necessity of some means by which such vocal effects might be intelligently reproduced, for I found that my merely imitative efforts fell very far short of the end desired, my voice degenerating into what is called a stage tone, or executing, from a sense of modulative necessity, certain undulating movements very unpleasant to the ear. This finally determined me to reconsider my style and methods, and to take up Rush instead of Walker as my guide.

It was afterwards (in changed circumstances) my good fortune to become intimately acquainted with Dr. Rush, and to receive from him, rather in the capacity of friend than of professional teacher, a practical exposition of the underlying principles of his "Philosophy of the Voice." Whenever I called upon the Doctor he would draw my attention to certain points regarding the production of sound, by means of certain muscular movements peculiar to the larynx and the vocal chords. The familiar examples he gave, illustrative of important principles, were a revelation to me; and afterwards became of the most inestimable value, in enabling me to gain control over syllabic utterance in its relation to quality and quantity,—the two great essentials of a perfected elocution. In my effort to reproduce, in his presence, the vocal points he executed, he required me to repeat only a line or two of some appropriate dramatic language. He would then comment upon the manner in which I struck or sustained the tone of my syllables, singly or in groups; after which he would execute like movements in imitation of some popular speaker, or after the style of Mrs. Siddons, whose elocution he considered as a model of artistic speech.

By following his mode of organic action in the production of vocal effects, I was enabled to produce the desired sounds and to vary them at pleasure. In this connection I would state that Mr. White's method of teaching was directly opposite to the manner in which Dr. Rush conveyed the information he gave. The former arbitrarily dictated the accent and emphasis, pitch and force, of every sentence to be read or recited. There was no analysis of the elementary principles of the producing causes. They were, so to speak, treated in the lump, by illustration in the teacher's mode of reading or reciting some extract, the pupil imitating, as closely as possible the effects exhibited to him, having previously committed to memory certain rules concerning inflection and pauses, which he applied after the manner prescribed as he could remember.

The insight gained into the subject of Dr. Rush's system of principles, through his own direction, was so much benefit to me, in connection with my profession, that I entered upon a thorough study of the entire work in order that I might test the practical value of its principles to their full extent.

In the course of events circumstances induced me to exchange the profession of the actor for that of the elocutionist, and, in 1840, after special preparation for the purpose of lecturing on the Rush system and teaching its details, I opened, in connection with Prof. Wm. Russell, a school of elocution in Boston. Here it was that, during three years of incessant labor, I not only fully developed the powers of my voice, and thus assured myself of a vastly increased ability to deal with the most difficult elements of dramatic expression, but also tested beyond question the superiority of this vocal system for the purpose of thorough, effective, and intelligent instruction. in the art of truly artistic and expressive reading and speaking.

Although results in the matter of training pupils were all that I could have desired, and many eminent men (amongst whom were Horace Mann, Dr. Humphrey Storer, John A. Andrew and others, some literary and some medical) gave their influence and generous sympathy to the undertaking, other circumstances did not justify a continuation of the work.*

The main cause of the failure of the enterprise was an announcement made in the high schools, to

---

* In connection with the institute for the culture of the voice, I established and conducted a gymnasium for physical training generally, but with special reference to the development of the muscles of the arms, back, and chest, so closely related to the proper culture of the more delicate organs of the voice. The building occupied was large and well adapted to the purposes of an institute of vocal and physical culture. The appliances were extensive and costly, and the staff of assistants numerous and efficient.

this effect, as well as I can remember: "The boys who take lessons at Murdoch and Russell's Institute will not be permitted to contend for prizes in declamation." The reasons given being as follows: "Other boys, who are debarred from such advantages, or it may be can not devote time to training, outside of the elocutionary teaching of the schools, are thereby placed at a disadvantage in competing for the honors of delivery."

This order was brought to our attention by the pupils dropping off, and the reference made to it by parents as the reason for withdrawing their children from the institute. I was, in consequence of such an unexpected "set-back," impelled to retire from the field of elocution and renew my relations with the stage.

In addition to my former list of comedy characters, I appeared for the first time in parts of Shaksperean tragedy, such as Othello, Hamlet, and Macbeth, and whatever degree of public approbation I was fortunate enough to secure then and since, either upon the stage or platform, I believe to have been founded upon the results of the vocal training I had passed through in accordance with those modes of voice cultivation consonant with the laws of physiology and vocal expression laid down by Dr. Rush. I think I may venture, therefore, without either egotism or vanity, to say that if the results of such systematic elocutionary training, as expressed in my own case, may be adduced as an argument for the same, it may not be inappropriately instanced for that purpose. Although engaged in the active duties of the dramatic profession at certain intervals during a period of thirty-five or forty years, I have always found time to devote to my first love — elocution; and I am convinced beyond a doubt that the only hope of a thorough and comprehensive method of instruction in vocal culture, and the expressive and correct use of language for the purposes of art, depends upon a just, intelligent, and practical development of the principles contained in "The Philosophy of the Voice." I regard it, therefore, as the only system of principles universally capable of meeting a great public want, and of insuring the future of elocutionary advancement; for with the equivalents of a fair trial, reasonable time, and patient application, to every one possessing ordinary intelligence, imagination, and feeling, it supplies the means by which pleasing and forcible effects in reading and speaking may be attained — effects which, though produced by the aid of art, exhibit all the beauties, forces, and graces of nature.

The following will show how even a hasty, and consequently an imperfect study of the system may contribute to an improvement in the manner of delivery, where the teacher has proper principles to impart and the student intelligent perceptions and application to practice them:

About 1841, Mr. George S. Hillard was to deliver the *Phi Beta Kappa* oration at the college celebration at Cambridge. About two weeks previous to the occasion he called at my rooms in Boston with a view to "get up his vocal forces," as

The Author's Early Experience. 113

he said, and gain a few practical points in delivery.

Never having paid any attention to such matters when a student, and, being somewhat depressed in his physical condition from a recent illness, he was fearful of a failure in his oratorical effort. I suggested to him a course of vocal gymnastics, such as his case required, and the shortness of the time for preparation allowed.

On his first appointment he brought his manuscript with him, with the idea of making it the subject-matter for the vocal drill; and was much surprised when I told him that it would be better to confine the mode of instruction and practice to elementary exercises in syllabic intonation and stress — together with quality and force, varying in kind and degree. Such a process, I assured him, after a proper understanding of the principles involved, and a reasonable amount of daily practice (the better if in the open air), would enable him, with perfect ease, to give effective audible expression to his own language without subjecting it to the dictation of another conception. Mr. Hillard accepted the proposition, and carried out the details in a spirit of earnest study, visiting a convenient point at the sea-side for occasional "readings," with proper application of the principles explained in the lessons received under my direction. The oration was a marked success, and a surprise to his auditors, on the score of delivery, Mr. Hillard's previous manner never having exhibited any particular points of emotional expression, although noted for elegance and refinement, with all the graces of rhetorical diction. The frequent applause which greeted the orator bore witness to the newly-acquired power of the disciplined speaker. At the close of the exercises Mr. Hillard remarked that, instead of being fatigued, as he had so often been on previous occasions, he felt so much exhilarated by his effort that he believed he could repeat the oration then and there with more ease and comfort to himself than he had just realized in its first presentation.

Mr. Charles Sumner was, at that time, Mr. Hillard's law partner. Calling at their rooms the morning after the delivery of the oration, Mr. Sumner said to me, "Why, Mr. Murdoch, you have gained honors from George's performance yesterday,— for we all tell him that the *delivery* was yours,— though the *matter* was his *own*." I responded by saying that this was not doing justice to Mr. Hillard,— inasmuch as I had never read a word of the composition, and never heard it until it fell from the lips of the orator of the day. Mr. Sumner was greatly surprised when I told him that the instruction I had given Mr. Hillard had been confined to technical elementary exercises, irrespective of any consecutive composition, and especially of that which had won such golden opinions from the scholarly audience before which it was delivered.

Mr. Sumner frankly confessed that, when he heard the author had taken elocutionary lessons from me, he had supposed, judging from the methods pursued in his college days, that his inflections, emphasis, and other expressive effects, had of course been a matter of dictation on my part.

Chapter XI.

Reasons for the Neglect of Elocution.

HAVING already briefly spoken of the position elocution occupies to-day as a branch of general education, and of the limited amount of didactic matter contained in the popular elocutionary text-books, I shall now point out the reasons for the existing state of affairs in this regard.

As the fact became apparent that the old system of teaching elocution did not develop the latent powers of the young speaker, so as to enable him to overcome that artificiality in vocal effect which was owing to the imperfections of the inflective system, teachers became anxious to find a remedy for the existing evil.

But the only system of elocution which could meet the requirements of instruction (that founded on the Rush philosophy), was rendered unavailable with the mass of teachers from the lack of both time and facilities on their part for acquiring a working knowledge of its principles; therefore the Walker principles retained their supremacy.

Again, the introduction into the schools of many new branches of study, much more satisfactory in their results, proved so exhaustive of the time of both teacher and scholar that elocution gradually lost whatever footing it had as a regular branch of disciplined instruction. The easiest and most available methods for immediate results, were therefore accepted for imparting such an amount of elocutionary training as would enable the aspiring scholar to make an effective appearance upon the platform, but leaving him to depend, for the most part, upon the promptings of the moment through the uncertain impulses of his feelings or imagination.

In such a condition of affairs, the teacher could do little else than employ the imitative method of instruction, by which the pupil is taught to read simply according to the dictation of his exemplars—the learner having no time to ask the "reason why," nor the instructor any time "to render a reason."

Suffice it to say that the popular text-book of the schools at the present time is composed chiefly of selections for reading, while the amount of practical direction for their study and execution bears very much the same proportion to the selections themselves as the mouse did to the mountain in Æsop's fable, and the result for good to the learner is in about the same proportion. In many cases, indeed, especially in class instruction, what didactic matter there is, is allowed to repose undisturbed, while the student becomes either a good or a bad reader through the accidents of a good or a bad model, and great or small natural aptitude on his own part; or of superior ability on the part of his teacher in the way of individual or original modes and methods of illustration and instruction.

A Plea for Spoken Language.

While, in justice to a subject demanding the most impartial consideration, I state facts as I know them to exist, yet respect for teachers and their vocation induces me to say that my object in such statements is by no means, to disparage the ability of the former, but to call attention to the fact that educationally elocution occupies a subordinate position, and that where imperfections or faults exist with instructors, they are, in the main, more those of omission than of commission.

It is a well-known fact that in our colleges, and those of Great Britain, with but a very few exceptions, the instruction in elocution is given, not by a professor fitted by especial ability and training—as in other branches of study—to deal with the subject, but by a tutor, selected usually from among the most advanced students in rhetoric; elocution being thus merged in a subordinate way into the chair of rhetoric. The consequence is that while the latter is taught with ability and effect, the former is merely looked over, or, in its broadest sense, overlooked.

Rhetoric, in its present acceptation, is the study of words or language as the symbols of ideas, and is a mental process only. Elocution is the study of those written symbols as the medium of the *vocal expression* of the thoughts or emotions which the symbols signify or represent.

While a knowledge of the written forms of language and their governing laws is essential to a perfect elocution, still a mastery of rhetoric does not by any means involve a knowledge of the vital principles of elocution, as embodied in vocal expression, any more than the ability of the artist to outline exquisite forms on canvas, includes the power also to infuse into them the glowing colors of rounded life. Indeed, this exemplifies the relation elocution bears to the study of the written forms of language. One supplies the form,—perfect, but dumb and lifeless; the other breathes into this form the soul and throb of life itself.

Sheridan gives some valuable suggestions with regard to the relation existing between the two, in substance as follows:

"To those who have not given any especial reflection to the subject it is at first difficult to realize that there is no natural affinity between written and spoken language, but only that connection which custom has established. They are communicated to the mind through the medium of different senses: one through the eye, by means of arbitrary characters; the other through the ear, by means of articulate sounds and natural tones. But these two kinds of language are associated in the mind so early in life that it is difficult ever after not to suppose that there is some natural relationship existing between them. And yet it is always well to bear in mind that the connection of the two in our mind is only that arising from an habitual association of ideas. This is obviously shown in the case of men born blind or deaf. The former may be masters of spoken language, and the latter of written, though neither can form any conception of the communication of ideas through the sense they respectively lack; and we have already alluded to the fact that the illiterate person possessed no other idea of language than that received through the ear. In such cases, also, we generally observe that the person uses a variety of tones in speaking, according to the sense or the emotions expressed by the words; while a deaf man, when taught to speak, always delivers his language with one unvarying monotony of vocal effect. We are very apt to find also, that the reading man, in proportion as he gives attention chiefly to the written or to the oral forms of language, either approaches nearer in his delivery to the monotony of the deaf man, or to the variety of the illiterate. Thus it is so often the case that writers or men who devote themselves almost exclusively to letters are remarkable for their indifferent and ineffective delivery."*

---

* Dryden, though one of the first harmonizers of our language, was so indifferent a reader that when he brought his play of Amphitryon to the stage, Cibber, who heard him give it the first reading, says: " Though he delivered the plain sense of every period, yet the whole was in so cold, so flat, and unaffecting a manner, that I am afraid of not being believed if I should express it."

Southern says of Congreve, "that when he brought a comedy of his to the players (Dr. Johnson believed it to be the Old Bachelor) he read it so wretchedly ill that they were on the point of rejecting it, till one of them good-naturedly took it out of his hands and read it, when they were so fully persuaded of its excellence that for half a year before it was acted he had the privilege of the house."

On the first reading by Addison of his Cato in the greenroom he succeeded so ill that he would not attempt it a second time. He therefore consigned that task to Cibber, who acquitted himself so much better than the author that the latter requested he would perform the part of Cato. But Cibber knew his own talents too well for this, and he yielded the part very judiciously to Booth.

Isaac Bickerstaff recited in a voice so thick and a manner seemingly embarrassed as rendered him not only incapable of giving variety to his tones, but at times was scarcely intelligible. In reading his comedy of 'Tis Well It's No Worse (since cut down to the farce of The Panel) to a small circle of friends, he laid most of them asleep.

"Dr. Goldsmith read so slovenly, and with such an Irish brogue, that it was sometimes difficult to distinguish his poetry from his prose. He was sensible of this himself, and used to say, 'I leave the reading of my pieces and the punctuation of them to the players and the printers; for, in truth, I know little of either.'"— *Foote's Anecdotes*.

"Amongst Coleridge's accomplishments good reading was not one—he had neither voice nor management of voice. This defect is unfortunate in a public lecturer, for it is inconceivable how

One great detriment to the advancement of spoken language — that is, as to its cultivation for artistic purposes in the art of reading and delivery — in Sheridan's time (and it holds, though in a less degree, at the present time), he found to exist in the all-absorbing preference given to the study of the dead languages over that of the living native tongue — that noble state and essence of sound represented in the early and later English classics. Sheridan says:

"After the revival of the dead languages, which suddenly enlightened the minds of men and diffused general knowledge, one would imagine that great attention would have been paid to an art which was cultivated with so much care by those ancients to whom we are indebted for all our lights, and that it would have an equal progress amongst us with the rest which we had borrowed from them. But it was this very circumstance — the revival of the dead languages — which put a stop to all improvements in the art of reading, and which has continued in the same low state from that time to this. From that time the minds of men took a wrong bias. Their whole attention was employed in the cultivation of the artificial to the neglect of the *natural language.* Letters, not sounds; writing, not speech, became the general care. To make boys understand what they read, to explain the meaning of the Greek and Roman authors, and to write their exercises according to the laws of grammar or prosody in a dead language, were the chief objects of instruction; whilst that of delivery was so wholly neglected that the best scholars often could not make themselves understood in repeat-

---

much weight and effectual pathos can be communicated by sonorous depth and melodious cadences of the human voice to sentiments the most trivial; nor, on the other hand, how the grandest are emasculated by a style of reading which fails in distributing the lights and shadows of a musical intonation."—*De Quincey.*

ing their own exercises, or disgraced beautiful composition by an ungracious delivery."

In our own day is it not alike painful and humiliating to see the best years of youth spent, during the usual academic and collegiate course of instruction, in the study — seldom the acquisition — of the dead languages, to the comparative neglect of our own, as well as that of other spoken tongues? A most valuable treatise on the subject of the amount of time devoted to the Latin and Greek in the English schools and universities, with suggestions for a reform in this regard, published in 1825 by Geo. Jardine, F. R. S. E., then professor of logic and rhetoric in the University of Glasgow, contains the following caustic though truthful observations:

"If the study of language be such an essential to the development of the adolescent mind, why," says he, "should not living languages be acquired instead of dead ones? They have, at least, the additional value of being spoken as well as *read*, and they would be studied with far more delight by the young, because they could daily witness the *use* and *force and see the end of such acquisition*. But we are told that we must cultivate the classic languages, because thus only can we acquire taste, literature, poetry, oratory, grammar, etymology, and heaven only knows what more. All these things, be it remarked, not as they relate to the two languages in question, but as they relate to our own. In this process, also, be it again remarked, we are neither compelled to cultivate our grammar nor our own language, with all these and whatever categories are involved in it. In fact, our own language and its authors, are not only neglected, but excluded*.

---

* Not excluded now, but still comparatively neglected as far as the relative time paid to them is concerned.

Reasons for the Neglect of Elocution. 123

by the system, and, were it not for our mothers and nurses, we should possess as little language as an orang-outang, since we should understand neither English, Latin, nor Greek.

"But yet we are told that without the dead languages we would have no models for poetry or eloquence. We must, therefore, either deny that the poetry or oratory of Britain can be formed by those of Greece and Rome, or, what is more easily proved, assert that they are not actually so formed; that many of our highest orators and poets have derived nothing from classical models, and that there is no want in the English language or in those of modern Europe, of models to follow or materials to form a taste. . . . . Are we to believe that if the names of Cicero and Demosthenes had never been heard, there would not be, or might not have been, or will not be, great orators now?"

I think this question will be satisfactorily answered by a consideration of the preceding facts in the history of the art of delivery amongst the English.

Read Quintilian and Cicero, says scholastic authority to the earnest seeker for the secret of the expressive powers of speech. But unfortunately when they are read the practical result is very much the same as that in the search for Gratiano's reasons as stated by Bassanio:

"His reasons are as two grains of wheat hid in two bushels of chaff; you shall seek all day ere you find them, and when you have them, they are not worth the search."

There can be no doubt that if but one half of the time were devoted in our schools and colleges to the proper study of our own spoken tongue, in connection with an equal amount of training with regard to the features of its written construction that is given to the dead languages, the practical proof of its capabilities as a vehicle of both beauty and power would soon exist in the artistic delivery, as well as in the ordinary speech, of those who by such study had mastered a knowledge of all its constituent elements of expression.

A knowledge of the classics doubtless disciplines the youthful *mind* for a true understanding and appreciation of English, but does it give the *tongue* the ability to deal strongly and eloquently with the audible expression of that language in which a Shakespeare and a Milton thought, wrote, and spoke?—a language which is destined to be heard and admired when Greek and Latin syllables in their modern sounds shall have become as dusty and obscure as the ruins of the ancient temples and forums which once re-echoed with their true vocalities in the service of classic zeal and manly eloquence.

Chapter XII.

Capabilities of the English Language.

THE English language has been shown to possess, when employed in accordance with those principles which govern its perfect utterance, all the essentials of both musical and powerful effect in speech. An English writer (C. J. Plumtre), in a series of lectures at Kings College, recently published, on the subject of elocution (and which are most gratifying in the substantial testimony they contain with regard to the growing recognition of the value of this study in England among men of eminence), says, in speaking of the carelessness and slovenliness of utterance amongst the English people:

"Hence that unmusical and expressionless 'gabble' which so often pains and wearies our ears in the reading desk, pulpit, and public meeting, which has brought down upon our glorious English tongue—that tongue which the great German philologist, Jacob Grimm, asserts to possess a veritable power of expression and comprehension unsurpassed by any language on earth, whether ancient or modern—the reproach of being harsh and rugged. I say most emphatically, the reproach is not deserved. Our English language has not merely a sufficiency of consonants to give it nerve, energy, and power, but quite a sufficient recurrence of vowel sounds, *if justice is only done them*, to give it full beauty and melody of sound in pronunciation. I give this challenge: Let any one hear a fine passage from Shakespeare, Milton, or Tennyson, for instance, read by an accomplished and refined reader, well endowed with good natural gifts, and capable by study and practice in the art of elocution of conveying all the poet would desire to the senses and feelings of his audience, and then say, if he honestly can, that our English language is wanting either in grandeur or beauty of sound."

Sheridan, who, in the capacity of both actor and scholar, had every means of appreciating the powers and beauties of our spoken language, thus eloquently writes of it:

"Through the want of inquiry into the true genius and power of our own tongue ourselves, we are apt to admit whatever criticisms foreigners are pleased to make on our language, and to acquiesce under whatever censure they throw out. On such an inquiry, it would be found that probably in no language in the world have the vowels, diphthongs, semi-vowels, and mutes been so happily blended, and in such due proportion, to constitute the three great powers of speech — melody, harmony, and expression. And, upon a fair comparison, it would appear that the French have emasculated their tongue by rejecting such numbers of their consonants; that the German, by abounding too much in harsh consonants and guttural, has great size and strength, like the statue of Hercules Farnese, but no grace; that the Roman, like the bust of Antinous, is beautiful indeed, but not manly; that the Italian has beauty, grace, and symmetry, like the Venus of Medicis, but is feminine; and that the English alone resembles the Ancient Greek in uniting the three powers of strength, beauty, and grace, like the Apollo of Belvedere.

"But all the powers of sound must remain in a state of confusion or impenetrable darkness while the custom continues of applying ourselves wholly to the study of the written language and neglecting that of speech. When the art of reading with propriety shall have been established and has produced its effects, a new field will be opened to our writers, unknown to their predecessors, for composition both in poetry and prose, which will display in a new light the vast compass of our language in point of harmony and expression, from the same cause which produced similar effects at Rome in the writers of the Ciceronian or Augustine age. For it was at that period that the Romans first applied themselves to the cultivation of the living language, having before, like us, employed themselves wholly about the written."

"The English language," says one of our own lexicographers, "is peculiarly adapted to popular eloquence, being nervous and masculine, *when pronounced according to the genuine composition of its words.*"

Sheridan tasks the people of England in his day with being a nation of bad readers and speakers in spite of the fact that "in no other country is there greater need or greater occasion for good reading or speaking." Unfortunately, the same may be said of our own people as a nation to-day, and will, indeed, always be true every-where until spoken language takes its proper rank as a branch of education.

Here, in a land where education is so universal, where the power of eloquence is so mighty and so valued; here, in our institutions of advanced learning, from the subordinate position in which elocution is placed, insufficient time is allowed either for the intelligent or artistic study of our spoken language,—the common speech of two of the greatest nations of the earth; while the fountain-head from which all learning springs—the public schools—are without sufficient time or systematic plan for the instruction of our children in the correct employment of the natural *vocal elements* of their native tongue. From this lack of special and intelligent instruction in the early stages of education, children are permitted, as they advance in years, to lose sight of that blessed boon of natural and unaffected speech vouchsafed to a state of childhood. The preservation of this gift of nature from the inroads of bad habits, so easily acquired in the midst of the artificialities of conventional life, demands a more radical and thorough system of instruction,—a system in which the training (upon the natural vocal elements and their significance in speech) in the primary departments, would furnish a foundation for instruction in the higher grades, and thence carry the pupil to the crowning point, which molds *an easy, unaffected utterance* into the forms of a perfected elocution.

The proper place for these last studies would be, of course, in connection with rhetoric in a college course. But as long as the deficiency exists in the early stages of education, irregular and unformed habits of speech will inevitably engraft themselves upon youth, and, becoming matured before the intellectual faculties are fully developed, will produce serious obstacles in the way of the acquisition of a truly natural, graceful, and finished delivery.

Articulation, accent, and correct pronunciation, *purity of tone and pitch of voice*, should be taught as primary points or elementary features of education; that is, before the more advanced stage of expressive reading or of public address is taken up as a special study.

When this is accomplished, the teacher of elocution will have the advantage enjoyed by the teacher of music. His pupils will know, as it were, the *notes of speech*, and he will have but to dictate their use, and direct the learner in their execution in the interpretation of an author's language.

The advantages, therefore, of such a systematized and graduated method of vocal training in our schools, based upon the unchanging laws of nature, as would lead by sure and easy stages to the perfections, not only of oratorical delivery and artistic reading, but to those of eloquent and natural speech, certainly can not be too highly estimated.

Considering the existing state of things from the standpoint I have from conviction been led to take, I feel justified in stating that the subject of elocution, as at present treated in our schools and colleges, possesses neither the characteristics of a science nor the practical enforcement of any such fixed rules and laws as those upon which are founded the formulas of all well disciplined art. Proofs to the contrary no doubt exist in exceptional cases, but I am safe in saying that there is no *generally accepted mode of instruction* in the art of reading and speaking that ought to be, from its intrinsic value, the basis for a standard of authority and excellence. Of the position elocution occupies in relation to instruction, independent of its general treatment in our regular institutions of learning, I shall not speak farther than to say that, owing to the object of both teacher and pupil being, in the majority of cases, and from a popular estimate, *immediate results*, the study is considered, and consequently treated, in too generalistic a sense. Its effects are grasped at, without a due appreciation of the methods and details of vocal discipline necessary to legitimately and artistically accomplish those effects. The tendency, therefore, is towards exaggerations of utterance and crudities of style, and that, too, in many cases, where the same amount of native power and ability in the student, under the direction of developed taste, intelligence, and artistic skill, would produce results of the highest order. This desire to leap rather than to grow into the mastery of bold and strong points betrays the reader or speaker into indiscriminate and excessive uses of voice and action,—such as unmeaning transitions and exaggerations of tone, "full of sound and fury signifying nothing;" abrupt starts. striking attitudes, and overstrained facial expression,—in short, into whatever will succeed in creating a series of startling effects by which to challenge the attention and admiration of the auditor. The result of this "acting out" of the author's language is to defeat the legitimate and primary object of all good reading, which is to present the language through the medium of the reader's vocal art, instead of obscuring the author by an obtrusion of the reader's personality.

I speak strongly upon this point because I can not but believe, though I do so with regret, that the tendency of elocution, as the outcome of existing circumstances, is at the present day rather towards *poor acting* than *good reading*. Indeed, from such inartistic methods in the popular treatment of elocution, the subject itself has come under reproach amongst a large number of persons of good taste and sound judgment, who believe that they are judging the tree by its fruits. Thus, in large measure, may we trace that general indifference to the subject among educational authorities, to which we have already alluded, and which is to be deplored, though it can not be condemned, since we may look upon it, in one sense, as a negative indorsement of the true art when that art and its possibilities shall come to be fully understood and developed. The following, taken from the recent English work we have already quoted, may serve to confirm the justice of the foregoing remarks:

"Let me here stop to inquire why it is that a science and art like elocution,—for I claim that it is both,—and which, in classical times, was so highly valued, should of late years have been comparatively disregarded as part of our education; and yet music, singing, drawing, and other accomplishments have all received their due share of attention,—and most properly so, for I should be the last person to undervalue the cultivation of any one art that tends to promote the grace and refinements of life, and advance the civilization of all ranks of society. But why is it that elocution should have fallen from the position it once occupied in other days and circumstances? Well, one reason, I believe, is to be found in the fact that the word has been made a *bug-bear* of, and has frightened away many excellent persons—persons of taste and refinement—from the pursuit of its study, through a completely erroneous interpretation of its meaning and character. Does not many a man entertain a sort of secret conviction, even if he does not openly express the opinion, that the study and practice of elocution must eventually lead to a pompous, bombastic, stilted, and pedantic style,—a style, in short, in which the palpably artificial reigns predominant over every thing that is pure, simple, and natural? Now, all that I can say is that, if elocution either means, or, properly understood and taught, really tended to, any thing of the kind, I should be the last person to advocate its adoption in colleges, schools, or anywhere else."

It is needless to add my concurrence in this last opinion. Of this "effect defective" in the popular method of dealing with the subject of elocution, I hope to speak more at length hereafter. I mention it here briefly for the purpose of calling attention to a fact that can not be too much deprecated, and that is, that, from the lack of a generally accepted standard of true artistic excellence, and hence of taste, in the matter of reading and recitation, the public too often accepts—nay, applauds—crudities and exaggerations of style in the place of a just copy of nature implied in good reading.

But when the general taste shall have become educated to understand the whole art and its requirements, as in song, then there will exist a standard and a tribunal for the vocal art in speech, from whose decisions there will be no appeal.

I have not set down these things concerning the present state of elocution in the spirit of the Shakesperian lines,

"I am Sir Oracle;
And when I ope my lips, let no dog bark!,"

but in that spirit of impartiality which should mark all suggestions for the general good, and, in the earnest desire for the advancement of the art of spoken language through rational means and on truly scientific and artistic principles.

"Fixed principles in the arts," says the author who has revealed to us those of elocution, "are of the utmost importance, not only because they are the true sources of the intellectual enjoyment which the arts afford, but they are the most effective means for their improvement." With foundations laid in these, what may we not hope for the future of our spoken language.

In the onward march of the American spirit of inquiry and improvement in the science of education, the time must come when the claims of an advanced state of elocutionary training will meet with the appreciation and support of a generous public opinion. Then, as foreshadowed by the eloquence of a Chatham or a Webster, our grand old Saxon syllables, rounded by the developed powers of a *national voice*, shall be heard from ocean to ocean, rivaling in vocal beauty the far-famed honors of the notes of song.

Let those who doubt the great possibilities of the art of spoken language under the combined influences of time, scientific principles, and patient industry, reflect upon what has been achieved in the service of song. Let him reflect, too, upon the fact that the tones in which the primitive singer sought to give expression to his joy or sorrow were only the unheeded sounds of speech, intuitively caught up and expanded or diminished, raised or depressed, and, in exulting loudness or desponding softness, made the echo of the inner life.

How long did such simple intercourse gladden the heart of shepherd and shepherdess, in the responsive notes of pipe and song, before the invention of the lettered page or the noted sheet? And yet, by patient observation and comparison of the various effects of music, by perfecting its symbols and nomenclature, whole nations have been educated into a capacity, not only for the common enjoyment of its highest results, but also for the just criticism of its performances.

The art of music, perfect as it is at present, sprang, then, from the most artless beginnings; nor has its progress always been smooth and uninterrupted. From the time that Hermes strung the shell with four strings, and first created tones through a cycle of ages; from barbaric rudeness to the highest civilization of the classic era, the art of song budded, blossomed, and then faded with the glory it had helped to inspire, until it found a grave amid the ruins of the Roman Empire.

But it rose again at the call of the early church, in the form of its rude chants, till, beneath the fostering wing of religious fervor and inspiration, it acquired those glorious perfections by which Timotheus raised his fellow-mortals to the skies, and the fair Cecilia drew her sister spirits down to sit enraptured at the feet of the mistress of song.

What transcendent talent, what inconceivable time and industry have been devoted to the service of music since that day, while the smiles of kings and princes and the plaudits of the world attest its triumphs and uphold its sovereignty!

The development of the art of speech may be considered of perhaps more intrinsic value to the human race than even the brilliant and captivating department of song. One, at least, in which the highest results appeal, not only to the sensations of the beautiful in sound, but to the highest intellectual and moral faculties.

Says Charles Lunn, a modern scientific authority on voice production, in comparing song and speech: "An orator, for one end, unites the forces found in *emotions*, in *impressions*, and in *ideas;* and he can only do this when he possesses absolute control over the voice."

This writer also speaks of the "downfall of tone" in speech, which accompanies the advanced intellectual standard of the present day, and attributes it most justly to the exclusive attention to *ideas* in the uses of speech, and the consequent neglect of the *sound values* of language. He adds, in this connection: "Purely as a question of health, the voice should be cultivated. Collaterally with the culture of words, both spoken words and vocal tone should grow up together."

The time has come for the American educators to investigate the claims of the art of spoken language in that spirit of progression which so eminently characterizes the age. As long as the public men who are looked to for direction and authority in matters of educational interest remain indifferent to, or ignore, the true principles upon which is based the proper study of audible reading and public address, or fail to acknowledge the practical means by which such principles can be plainly manifested and applied, so long must the vocal perfections of our language remain comparatively unknown, and an immense educational power be permitted to lie undeveloped.

When all narrow and prejudiced opinions shall have given way to more advanced views on the subject of elocution, it will not then be looked upon as a monopoly in the hands of a small number of people known as "Elocutionists," but as a necessary branch of all liberal education.

Part Second.

The Power of Sound in Language.

CHAPTER I.

Power of Voice and Gesture Compared.

NOTE.—It is by no means my design in the present part to attempt a disquisition upon the origin and growth of language, but simply to outline the subject, through the aid of acknowledged authorities, in a manner that will shed light on the study, to follow, of the principles underlying vocal expression in speech. My object, therefore, in the preparation of the pages of this part, has been to touch upon only the most salient features of the interjectional and onomatopoetic theory, as illustrative of the great fundamental principle in vocal expression; namely, the intimate connection existing between sound and feeling, and sound and sense; or, in other words, the peculiar significance of sound in speech.

For the ideas concerning this theory of language, and for many of the forms, I wish to acknowledge myself chiefly indebted to the valuable work of the Rev. Frederick W. Farrar, M. A.

I HAVE stated the fact, in the preceding part, that the relations existing between the various states of mind and the speaking voice constitute the basis of the true philosophy of the latter, and hence the great value of Dr. Rush's discoveries. In the following pages, I think I shall be able to show that these mental and vocal relationships are more intimate and more easily traceable than may be at first supposed.

This great fundamental principle should, then, be regarded as one of primary consideration in a proper study of elocution.

Writers on elocution, both ancient and modern, previous to Rush, recognized the existence of such relationships in a general sense, but a knowledge of their exact character or specific features, as existing in the varied forms of vocal expression, seems not to have been perceived, or, at least, not developed in any writings before those of this author.

Sheridan, who has treated the subject more extensively than any of the other early writers, wrote upon it with great ability and correctness as far as he went; and it is upon the grounds established by him that Dr. Rush proceeded in his analysis of the vocal sounds for the purpose of discovering their elements of significance and power. Sheridan says most truly:

"The mind, in communicating its ideas, is in a continual state of activity, emotion, or agitation, from the different effects which these ideas produce in the mind of the speaker. Now, as the end of such communication is not merely to lay open the ideas, but also the different feelings which they excite in him who utters them, there must be some other marks beside words to manifest these, as words uttered in a monotonous state can only represent a similar state of mind, perfectly free from all activity or emotion. As the communication of these internal feelings was a matter of much more consequence in our social intercourse than the mere conveying of ideas, so the Author of our being did not leave the invention of this language, as in the other case, to man, but stamped it himself upon our nature in the same manner as he has done with the animal world, who all express their various feelings by various tones. Only ours, from the superior rank we hold, is infinitely more comprehensive; as there is not an act of the mind, an exertion of the fancy, or an emotion of the heart, which have not their peculiar tone or note of the voice by which they are to be expressed, all suited in the exactest proportion to the several degrees of internal feeling."

No writer on elocution, I believe, has attempted to explain the reason of this correspondence between the mental state and the vocal sign, beyond the fact that the mental agitation or excitement has, by observation, as in Sheridan's case, been found to produce certain effects; which effects have farther, in the case of Rush, been analyzed and classified in detail, in accordance with the psychological condition primarily producing them. But we have in addition a most satisfactory elucidation of the subject from the stand-point of physiological science, from the pen of Herbert Spencer, in his valuable article on "The Origin and Functions of Music," in which he also treats of speech, and shows that music was but an outgrowth from the original vocal sounds of spoken language. The following are a few extracts upon the point under present consideration:

"All vocal sounds are produced by the agency of certain muscles.* These muscles, in common with those of the body at large, are excited to contraction by pleasurable and painful feelings, and therefore it is that feelings demonstrate themselves in sounds as well as movements; therefore it is that Carlo barks as well as leaps when he is let out; that puss purs as well as erects her tail; that the canary chirps as well as flutters. Therefore it is that the angry lion roars while he lashes his sides, and the dog growls while he retracts his lips. Therefore it is that the maimed animal not only struggles but howls; and it is from this cause that, in human beings, bodily suffering expresses itself, not only in contortions, but in shrieks and groans,—that in anger, and

---

* That the vocal chords are a muscular organism, and that the act of breathing is also performed by muscular agencies, are well-known physiological facts.

fear, and grief, the gesticulations are accompanied by shouts and screams,—that delightful sensations are followed by exclamations, and we hear screams of joy and shouts of exultation. We have here, then, a principle underlying all vocal phenomena. The muscles that move the chest, larynx, and vocal chords, contracting like other muscles in proportion to the intensity of the feelings; every different contraction of these muscles involving, *as it does, a different adjustment of the vocal organs;* every different adjustment of the vocal organs causing a change in the *sound emitted;*—it follows that the variations of voice are *the physiological* results of variations of feeling; it follows that each inflection or modulation is the natural outcome of some passing emotion or sensation; and it follows that the explanation of all kinds of vocal expression must be sought in this general relation between mental and muscular excitements."

After having illustrated this point by a number of valuable instances of the various modes of vocal expression, which it will be more directly to our purpose to quote hereafter, he proceeds:

"Thus we find all the leading vocal phenomena to have a physiological basis. They are so many manifestations of the general law that feeling is a stimulus to muscular action — a law conformed to throughout the whole economy, not of man only, but of every sensitive creature—a law, therefore, which lies deep in the nature of animal organization. The expressiveness of these various modifications of voice is, therefore, innate. Each of us, from babyhood upwards, has been spontaneously making them, when under the various sensations and emotions by which they are produced. Having been conscious of each feeling at the same time that we heard ourselves make the consequent sound, we have acquired an established association of ideas between such sound and the feeling which caused it. When the like sound is made by another, we ascribe the like feeling to him; and by a further consequence we not only ascribe to him that feeling, but have a certain degree of it aroused in ourselves: for to become conscious of the feeling which another is experiencing, is to have that feeling awakened in our consciousness. . . . . . All speech, then, is compounded of two elements,—the words and the tones in which they are uttered,—the signs of ideas, and the signs of feelings. While certain articulations express the thought, certain vocal sounds express the more or less of pain or pleasure which the thought gives. Using the word cadence in an universally extended sense, as comprehending *all modifications of voice, we may say that cadence is the commentary of the emotions upon the propositions of the intellect.* This duality of spoken language, though not formally recognized, is recognized in practice by every one; and every one knows that very often more weight attaches to the tones than to the words."

From this stand-point, then, that "mental excitement of all kinds ends in excitement of the muscles," and that the muscles of the vocal organism are subject to this universal law, Spencer furnishes us with the intermediate link, so to speak, between the primary cause already recognized in the state of mind and the ultimate effect as expressed in vocal phenomena. As an expression of the ideas of the ancients on this point, we have the words of Cicero:

"Every passion of the heart has its own appropriate look, tone, and gesture; and a man's whole countenance, his whole body, and all the voices of his mouth, re-echo like the strings of a harp to the touch of every emotion in his soul."

Thus man may be said to be gifted with two forms of natural language, the one appealing to the eye, and the other to the ear, both expressive, and, when used together, powerful beyond compare. The flash of the eye, the contraction of the brow, or its sudden lifting, the pallor or flush of the countenance, the compressed lip or open mouth, the varied movements of the hands and arms, the positive indications of the fingers; the various attitudes of the body, all aid in conveying, in a certain sense, a significant expression.

In moments of extreme passion the disturbing thoughts may be mutely expressed, and with great power and effect, by these alone; but we have innumerable proofs that the soul is more nearly reached through the ear than through the eye, therefore the language of sound is far superior in its range and power of expression to those mute indications of the state of the mind, embodied in look and gesture.

The following quotation from Canon Farrar, in which he embodies the opinions of Heyse, Charma, and Herder, strongly illustrates the point under discussion :

"It is, however, easy to see that gesture could never be a *perfect* means of intercommunication. Energetic, rapid, and faithful, it is yet obscure, because it is sylleptic; *i. e.*, it expresses but the most general facts of the situation, and is incapable of distinguishing or decomposing them, and wholly inadequate to express the delicate shades of difference of which every form of verbal expression is capable. The flashing of a glance may belie years of fulsome panegyric; a sudden yawn may dissipate the effect of a mass of compliments poured out during hours of simulated interest; an irrepressible tear, a stolen and smothered sigh, the flutter of a nerve, or the tremble of a finger, may betray the secret of a life which no words could ever have revealed. The veiled and silent figure of Niobe may be more full of pathos than the most garrulous of wailing elegies. The wounds of the victor of Marathon, or the maimed figure of the brother of Æschylus, the unveiled bosom of Phryne, or the hand pointing to the Capitol which Manlius had saved, may have produced effects more thrilling than any eloquence; but such appeals were only possible at moments of intense passion, or under a peculiar combination of circumstances. The ancient orators, well aware of the power which lies in these mute appeals, made them gradually ridiculous by the frequency with which they employed them; and the introduction of a weeping boy upon the rostrum would produce but little weight when many of the audience knew that weeping may express a wide variety of emotions, and when an injudicious question as to the obscure cause of these moving tears might elicit the malapropos complaint, 'the master flogged.'

"In moments of extreme passion, then, a language of gesture, a language appealing to the eye rather than to the ear, is not only possible but extremely powerful, and one which will never be entirely superseded. And possibly some natures may be so sensitive, some faces so expressive, that even during the most peaceful and equable moments of life, the passing thought may touch the countenance with its brightness or its gloom. But this could never be the case with any but a few; and even with these, what attention would be found equal to read and interpret, without fatigue, symbols and expressions so subtle and so fugitive? Moreover, to the blind, and to *all* during the darkness, and whenever an opaque body intervened, and whenever the face was turned in another direction, such language would instantly become impossible. It is incapable of representing the distinctness and successiveness of thought; it is limited on every side by physical conditions; it requires an attention too exclusive and intense; it would reach a shorter distance, *and appeal to a less spiritual sense*. For, though *both* sight and hearing are ideal senses, as distinguished from the inferior ones of touch and taste and smell, hearing is more ideal in its nature, and reaches more nearly to the soul than sight. It is the clearest, liveliest, and most instantaneously affected of the senses. That which is seen is material, and remains in space; but that which is heard (although as permanent and as corporeal), yet, to our blunt senses, has a purely ideal existence, and vanishes immediately in time. Hence, sound is especially adapted to be the bearer, and the ear to be the receiver of thought, which is an activity requiring time for its successive developments, and is therefore well expressed by a succession of audible sounds. Juxtaposition in *space*, appealing to the eye, could only remotely and analogously recall this succession in time. Moreover, hearing requires but the air, the most universal of all mediums, the most immediate condition of life; whereas, the eye requires light as well, and is far more dependent on external accidents. The fact that even a sleeper is instantly awoke to consciousness by the tremor of his auditory nerve under the influence of the voice, is a proof of the impression and immediate adaptability of sound to the exigencies of the intellectual life; so that hearing is the very innermost of the senses, and stands in the strictest and closest connection with our spiritual existence. The ear is the ever-open gateway of the soul, and, carried on the invisible wings of sound, there are ever thronging through its portals, in the guise of living realities, those things which of themselves are incorporeal and unseen. Wonderful, indeed, that a pulse of articulated air should be the only, or, at any rate, the most perfect, means wherewith to express our thoughts and feelings. Without its incomprehensible points of union with all that passes in a soul which yet seems so wholly dissimilar from it, those thoughts and emotions could, perhaps, have no distinct existence—the exquisite organism of our hearing would have been rendered useless, and the entire plan of our existence would have remained unperfected."

Rush divides spoken languages into two kinds— instinctive or natural, and artificial or verbal—shows us that a union of the natural and verbal gives the most exact and impressive vocal representation of the logical and the passionative states of the mind.

First, let us see what is the full meaning of the expression natural language. To quote Sheridan again in this connection, he says:

"In the beginning, barbarous nations have nature only for their guide in their speech, as in every thing else. With them, therefore, all changes of the voice and the different notes and inflections used in uttering their thoughts, were the result of the acts and emotions of the mind, to each of which nature herself has assigned her peculiar note. In a calm state of mind the notes of the voice, in unison to that state, are little varied, and the words are uttered nearly in a monotone.* When the mind is agitated by passion, or under any emotion whatever, the tones expressive of such passion or emotion spontaneously break forth, being unerring signs fixed to such internal feelings by the hand of nature, and common to all men and universally intelligible, in the same manner as the sounds and cries uttered by different animals."

It has been said that by one of nature's laws nearly every thing that is struck rings, and that so it is with the human being. The passions and emotions, striking, as it were, upon our sensitive or nervous nature, force from the lips certain involuntary cries or other vocal utterance, as the tones of the bell ring out in response to the stroke of the clapper.† The sounds of the voice in spontaneous utterance, expressive of love, grief, hatred, and the other emotions and passions, are natural operations, therefore, of the voice, and not only intelligible in every language and understood by all of our own species, but also by the lower animals.

---

* This last assertion is too sweeping, but the idea as to the psychological cause for corresponding vocal effects is well stated.
† In the words of Canon Farrar, *expression*, by a law of nature, is the natural and spontaneous result of *impression*.

Speaking in reference to this point, Sheridan says:

"The horse rejoices in the applauding tones of his rider's voice, and trembles when he changes them to those of anger. What blandishments do we see in the dog when his master soothes him in kind tones; what fear, and even shame, when he changes them to those of chiding. By those the wagoner directs his team and the herdsman his flock. Even animals of the most savage nature are not proof against the collective tones of the human voice; and shouts of multitudes will put wild beasts to flight who can hear, without emotion, the roarings of thunder. The circumstance is singular, that the ear, from the influence of tones, should excite and strengthen compassion so much more powerfully than the eye. The sigh of a brute animal, the cry forced from him by bodily suffering, brings about him all his fellows, who, as has often been observed, stand mournfully round the sufferer, and would willingly lend him assistance. Man, too, at the sight of suffering, is more apt to be impressed with fear and tremor than with tender compassion; but no sooner does the voice of the sufferer reach him than the spell is dissolved, and he hastens to him—he is pierced to the heart."

Indeed, so closely are the tones of voice connected with corresponding mental conditions that the most impressive effects may be produced by the voice sounds alone, independent of words.

There are certain cries that are the natural and even necessary expression of the stronger impulses or sensations of the mind — certain inarticulate bursts of feeling to which men give utterance when, in the vehemence or suddenness of some pain, affliction, or passion, they seem to return to a state of nature, losing, for the moment, the conventional or verbal forms of speech. These cries are retained in all languages unchanged (except as modified in degree and quality of sound by the prevailing national temperament), and used alike by all races of to-day. Says Sheridan again:

"The tones expressive of sorrow, lamentation, mirth, joy, hatred, love, pity, etc., although usually accompanied with words, in order that the understanding may, at the same time, perceive the cause of these emotions by a communication of the particular ideas which excite them; yet, that the whole energy or power of exciting analogous emotions in others, lies in the tones themselves, may be known from this: that whenever the force of these passions is extreme, words give place to inarticulate sounds. Sighs and murmurings in love; sobs, groans, and cries in grief; half-choked sounds in rage; and shrieks in terror are then the only language heard. And the experience of mankind may be appealed to whether these have not more power in exciting sympathy than anything that can be done by mere words."

To give a familiar illustration of this expressive character of inarticulate sounds, I was once waiting in the ante-room of a dentist, when my attention was suddenly arrested by a loud cry from the next room, which, after continuing for a moment or two at the utmost altitude of pitch, suddenly dropped to the lowest audible sound, and terminated in an extended groan or grunt. The two extremes of vocality were so expressive as to require no explanation of their meaning. The shrill scream said more plainly than words, "Oh, how terribly it hurts!" While the groans into which the cry suddenly changed was quite as clearly expressive of "Oh, thank heaven, it's over!" Instances of a similar character could be multiplied indefinitely, all illustrating the expressive power of sound in the speaking voice. In all languages may be found a large number of interjectional words, traceable to these instinctive cries, expressive of fear, anger, pleasure, astonishment, sorrow, compassion, disgust, and other similar feelings, and produced by impressions received from without chiefly through the senses of sight and hearing. However merely animal in their nature these interjections may have been originally, they were most probably the first to acquire the dignity and significance of speech, since these utterances must have expressed so distinctly and vividly to the hearer, by the association of ideas, the feelings or sensations of which they were the energetic and spontaneous expression. In the language of Herder, "They were the sparks of Promethian fire which kindled language into life." They form, in the truthfulness and simplicity of their characters, one of the chief glories of language, and have added a singular force and charm to the impassioned utterances of poetry. Many an exquisite passage owes its beauty and pathos to these earliest elements of speech, as in the following lines from Wordsworth:

> "She lived unknown,—and few might know
> When Lucy ceased to be;
> But she is in her grave,—and oh,
> The difference to me!"

It is related of the celebrated preacher Whitfield that he threw a world of pathos and meaning — pity for the unconverted sinner, and sorrow for his hardness of heart — into such interjectional expressions as "Ah, my friend!" and "Oh, my brother!," which gave him a power over the human heart that was wonderful. It was the appeal of the natural man to the natural man, as it were, through the universal medium of sympathetic communication.

Chapter II.

The Development of Language.

In view of the preceding facts and statements, it is not difficult to believe that sounds without verbal or conventional forms were the first means of communication between man and man; and that these first utterances must have consisted in the expression of emotion and passion, since the conventional language of ideas was necessarily a gradual growth, not disconnected, as we shall see, with the natural language, but more independent of it than the language of feeling and passion.

However men may disagree as to the modes and means by which primal man attained to the almost fabulous achievement,— a starting-point in the progressive stages of intelligent speech,— all will agree that the vocal organs of the human being were created for the purposes of language; so we may conclude that the intelligence of man prompted him, by untiring efforts, to consummate the vocal effects which the mechanism of the voice was created to produce. It has been said that each man is in all things an epitome of the race. Following this idea in the matter of language, take the infant in the cradle, or before the period when he seeks to

Development of Language.   153

express himself in articulated sounds, and we have the type of the infancy of language, while inarticulate sound was as yet the primary means of communication between human beings. Here we see the expressive vocality as exhibited in a natural effort to attract sympathetic attention or to communicate wants, and the power of vocal utterance, independent of fixed verbal forms; for the mother understands the cooing, whining, or droning of the babe, or its iterated particles of sound, its spasmodic sobs or more extended sighs or wails, as natural signs of the state of the quiet mind or excited feelings. In the more advanced stage of development, these vocal signs become involved with the verbal or conventional, and, as life progresses, their combined effects are used in the communication of thought or the expression of emotion or passion.

The subject of the growth of language—or, rather, of the principles underlying its growth—is one, not only of interest to the student of elocution, but also of the greatest importance; as, by going back to the origin of conventional or verbal forms, it reveals the many close ties that unite sound and sense in our speech, as well as the resemblance to be found between the latter and the various sounds throughout nature. Its study will thus teach him to observe the great value of sound as embodied in the vocal forms of spoken language, and thus enable him to trace its vitalizing character as an agent of expressive effect in reading, and in dramatic or oratorical speech. The constitution and materials, then, of the living, breathing *word* becomes a subject of the first importance. We have seen that the real or vocal elements of language were provided, by divine law, in the nature and instincts of the primitive man. His emotional and imitative cries furnished the means by which he was enabled to express his own sensations, and to recall the most striking objects and influences that surrounded him.* All the sounds of nature were called upon to contribute their share to the growing speech. The voices of living animals; the rustling and whispering of the forest leaves; the booming of the surging sea upon the shore; the howl and shriek of the voices of the storm; the boiling, seething, rushing, and roaring of the cataract; the rippling murmur of the brook; and the sighing cadences of the wind;—all were adopted by man for his use in the art of articulate language: and all the senses, the memory, the understanding, the will, were ac-

---

* These interjections, intimating generally a desire to command, or to convey significant meaning to some other person, have been called by the German writers *lautgeberden* or *begerungslaute*, vocal gesture or sounds of desire. They are found in the utterances, st! sh!, and were called vocal gestures because they are often connected with gestures, and can be represented by them; as, "sh!", with the finger on the lips, and "st!", an equivalent to "hark," with the finger beckoning or raised to the ear. Being mainly consonantal, they approach nearer, in their origin to the complicated articulations of speech than the class of interjections first alluded to, in which the consonants play a very subordinate part; and they differ from them in being, not merely the expression of a passive feeling, but the energetic utterance of will, while they also correspond to an important step in the advance of human intelligence. Hush! hist! hark! ahoy! hallo! and all similar cries belong to this class of words, besides all the isolated monosyllables or longer words by which we invite or repel the approach of others, or encourage or check their efforts.

tively engaged in giving form and growth to this important art. The merely interjectional and imitative cries, or verbal impulses, that were originally employed to express the feelings or recall numberless objects and influences of the outward world, received positive syllabic form and outline from the articulative modifications that are ever at work in language.*

Of course the impulsive imitative effort to reproduce sounds in the formation of language, was not to make identical representations of the original sound, but an effort to reproduce the impression such influences made upon the mind. Thus each race, possessing different mental and temperamental characteristics, would differ in the verbal expression

---

* "It is a curious and interesting fact that even among uncivilized nations we find what appears to be a trace, mythologically expressed, of this same conception; viz., that it was the mighty diapason of nature which furnished man with the tones which he modulated into articulate speech. The Esthonian legend of the kettle of boiling water which 'the aged one' placed on the fire, and from the hissing and boiling of which the various nations learned their languages and dialects, mythically represents the Kesselberg, with its crests enveloped in the clouds of summer steam, which they regarded as the throne of the thunder-god; and the languages which it distributes are the rolling echoes of thunder and lightning, storm and rain. They have another and still more beautiful legend, of a similar character, to explain the origin of Long or Festal speech. The god of song, Waunemunne, descended on the Domberg, on which stands a sacred wood, and there played and sang. All creatures were invited to listen, and they each learned some fragment of the celestial sound; the listening wood learnt its rustling; the stream its roar; the wind caught and learned to re-echo the shrillest tones, and the birds the prelude of the song. The fish stuck up their heads as far as the eyes out of the water, but left their ears under water; they saw the movements of the god's mouth, and imitated them, but remained dumb. Man only grasped it all; and therefore his song pierces into the depths of the heart, and upwards to the dwellings of the gods."—*Farrar.*

of these impressions as the national characteristics and circumstances of climate, etc., differed. In addition to this change from the original sounds attendant upon an imitated impression, there was also another produced by the operations of the vocal organs,— the sounds of nature being inarticulate, but in speech becoming articulate. This point may be illustrated by the fact that a little child may readily learn to imitate the crow of a cock by making use of but one capacity of his voice; but he is more apt to articulate the impression he has received of the cock's crow, and cock-a-doodle-do becomes the sign of the sound that he thus imitates. The varied forms which many words have assumed in different languages, and which are yet all directly inspired by the imitative principle, shows that "what the eye sees, and the ear hears, depends in no small manner upon the brain and heart"; or, as we have before suggested, upon the mental and temperamental alembic through which impressions pass before their reproduction by the voice. The imitative crow, before referred to, of "cock-a-doodle-doo," is changed, in other languages, into "hicken-hoe" and a variety of other articulated forms; and yet, in all of them, it is a merely imitated impression. We are told that, during the time of the enthusiasm among the French people, upon the return of Bonaparte from Elba, the sound of the cock-crow became to their ears a distinct exclamation, and they confidently believed and declared they heard every cock shout distinctly, "Vive l' Empereur!"

Development of Language.

The spirit of spoken language is so far lost in its printed reproductions upon paper, that it is sometimes difficult to discover the close sound resemblance of imitative words through their changes of form in different languages. Bang in English, and *pouf* in French, are both imitative of the sound of a gun, and yet how much unlike they seem when written. Though, in this case, the English word probably imitates the sound of the explosion, and the French the flash from the powder, showing how in one language one impression connected with a certain thing may be the object of imitation, while in another, a different feature of the same thing may have made a deeper impression, producing a totally dissimilar result in its verbal form of expression. Coleridge speaks of the nightingale's tone as it "Murmurs, musical and sweet, jug, jug;" while Tennyson writes, in the person of a peasant woman, "Whit, whit, whit, in the bush beside me, chirrupt the nightingale." And the Turkish poet, still trying to reproduce the same sounds, calls the bird a "bul-bul."

The sounds produced by the mass of inanimate objects generally indicate clearly to us their character and properties. The clang of the various metals, from the deep reverberations of iron to the tremulous shiver of steel, and the sharp tinkling of brass and tin; the whisper and splash of cohesionless liquids; the crackle and blare and roar of flame; the ringing resonance of stone and marble; the creaking of green boughs; the ripping of splintered wood; the chink of glass, and the dull thud of soft and yielding bodies; the discontinuous rattle of their dry substances, and the flap and rustle of woven fabrics in the wind;—all of these sounds, and thousands more, are capable of articulate imitation, and have been adopted into language in the form of words, whose sounds are indicative or suggestive of their meaning.

Sheridan has, perhaps, amongst the whole range of writers on the subject of words most thoroughly combined a theoretical and practical knowledge of their vocal properties. Perhaps better analyses of the mere alphabet have been made by others, but the value of letters in their combinations has not been so thoroughly investigated, or so completely explained by any other writer within our knowledge. He says:

"As the nature of syllables depends upon the nature of the letters whereof they are composed, some coalescing with ease, and others not mixing without difficulty; so the nature of words depends upon the same principle; and they are harsh or smooth to the ear in proportion as each subsequent syllable is with ease or difficulty pronounced after each preceding one. Their strength or weakness also evidently depends upon those properties in their component syllables."

He then refers to the imitative or mimical words, the sound of which is indicative of the sense, as derived from the cries of animals or from sounds in nature. He tells us that among vowels, the *a* (awe) was borrowed from the crow; the *a* (hate) from the sheep; the *a* (bat) from the goat; the *o* (prove) from the dove; the *o* (note) from the ox; the *ow* from the dog, etc. Of the consonants, we

Development of Language. 159

borrow *b* from the sheep; *k* from the crow; *m* from the ox; *s* from the serpent; *th*, in thistle, from the goose. Of inanimate objects, *f* resembles the sound of the wind blowing through apertures; *v*, the rapid movements of spinning-wheels; *sh*, the sound of rockets previous to explosion; *s*, the flight of an arrow; *ng*, the terminal sound of a bell. The mutes and short vowels are best filled to express short sounds; the semi-vowels (liquids) and long vowels, sounds of continuance. The semi-vowels, the clear; the mutes, the obtuse sounds. The aspirated letters in combination, the strong; the simple, the weaker sounds. Thus we have glide, grow, tap, pat, slap, kick, pit, mink, but, stop, stab, step, quit, back, break, tall, leap, move, loiter, groan, gloat, lead, alive, gurgle, murmur, enduring, ring, bright, clear, laugh, bell, light, sheen, glimmer, liquid, lively, little, dark, third, throb, knock, plant, pack, dump, knot, abut, despotic, harsh, hiss, firm, stiff, sheet, shout, fetter, horrible, weak, loft, flow, steam, smooth, sing, sweet, lure, easy.

There is also an expressive power in words which represent ideas that come into the mind through the other senses (beside that of hearing), and which, though from the nature of things they can not have the least similarity to those ideas, yet have a certain congruity with them, which makes them fitter to represent those ideas than words of a different construction. To illustrate, words beginning with the consonants *str*, signify force and general exertion of force.

Strong, strive, struggle, stretch, strenuous, stress,

strike, stroke, string, strew, strict, strangle, stricture, straggle.

As will be seen by these examples, the first letter in this combination is formed by the sharp force of the breath in a hissing sound, which is interrupted by the pure mute *t*, that borrows its sound, not from a vowel, but from the semi-vowel *r*, with which it unites itself with difficulty, and therefore occasions the harsh sound of the roughest and strongest of the consonants to be heard in full force. When the *r* is omitted, and *st* only begins the syllable, it is still expressive of strength, but in a less degree and without so much exertion, as: stand, stay, steadfast, sturdy, stiff, stagger, stamp, stanch, stare, steer, and a few nouns which do not so exactly express the idea of the others. *Thr* marks violent motion; as, throw, thrust, throng, thrive, throttle. There are but few words of this composition.

Sw marks a silent agitation, or a gentle and more equable motion, as swim, sway, swell, swath, swift, sweat, swerve, swagger, swaddle, sweep, swash, swab, swan. Apparently swear, sweeten, swindle, and sword do not answer the conditions. *Sp* denotes a dissipation, or expansion, and generally a quick one; as, spit, sputter, speak, spread, spell, sprinkle, spin, split, spear, splash, sparkle, spoil, spade, spike, spangle, spank. In the word sparkle, *sp* denotes dissipation; *ar*, accute crackling; *k*, a sudden interruption, and *l*, a frequent iteration. *Sl* denotes motion, but of a more equable kind; as, slow, slant, slur, slice, slobber, sliver, slouch, sling, slacken; and, doubtfully, slap, slander, sleek, slave, slumber, slay.

Ash, as a termination, indicates something acting nimbly and sharply: clash, slash, gash, crash; while *ush*, similarly used, implies acting forcibly, though not with such nimbleness or smartness; as, crush, rush, gush, flush, blush, push. *Ing*, terminal, implies the continuation of a motion or tremor, at length indeed vanishing, but not suddenly interrupted; as, swing, sing, sling, sting; while *ink*, closing with a pure mute, indicates a sudden ending; as, clink, blink, wink. If there be an *l* added to those terminations, there is implied a frequent iteration of the acts: jingle, tingle, mingle, tinkle, sprinkle, twinkle. But still the acts expressed by *ing* are not so sudden or evanescent as those by *ink;* jingle expresses longer duration as well as something more forcible than tinkle, mingle than sprinkle, tingle than twinkle.

The close connection existing between the different senses is constantly making itself felt in this imitative language of nature, and in what may be regarded as its highest expression, the impassioned utterances and the figures of poetry. Thus the analogy formed in our minds between the phenomena of light and sound gives us the corresponding words of *sheen* for *clear*, *brightness* for *sound*, *reflection* for *echo*, and *glimmer* for *noise;* *glow* and *clang* seem but one word; and not only does tone correspond to color, but all the different colors seem to have their corresponding tones. There is a familiar instance in the story of a blind man who, upon being asked what idea he had of scarlet, replied that it was like the sound of a trumpet. A deaf mute has been known also to liken the note of a trumpet to scarlet. In like manner, Gardiner, in his "Music of Nature," has characterized a number of musical instruments by colors, classing them thus: clarionet, orange; oboe, yellow; bassoon, deep yellow; flute, sky blue; diapason, *deeper* blue; double diapason, purple; horn, violet; violin, pink; viola, rose; violincello, red; double bass, deep crimson red. Akenside speaks of tasting the fragrance of a rose, and Byron of "*inhaling* an ambrosial *aspect.*" The adjectives nice and sweet, which properly belong to taste alone, are indiscriminately applied to all things that are pleasing; and the adjectives soft, sharp, mild, rough, smooth, and hard, are used to describe objects, not only of feeling, but also of sight, of taste, and of sound. Leaving out the merely animal cries and the interjections, we append a list of words where the sound is suggestive of the sense, in a greater or less degree:

Flap, roll, gouts, whizz, rumble, shout, pop, thwart, bang, lull, crack, twirl, rush, moan, whistle, shatter, jostle, jangle, clink, shout, pour, slam, thump, peal, smooth hiss, wrinkle, bluster, puff, hurry, climb, grope, strick, stagger, brawl, squall, shudder, clatter, log, buzz, lisp, romp, sputter, clap, dreary, crackle, swathe, crash, rub, quick, glide, daub, pull, yell, scream, smash, dash, break, tear, grate.

The same principle that employed the sound received, through the one sense of hearing, to illustrate all the various impressions made upon the brain from without, was adopted in naming the more spiritual and intellectual phenomena of the mind. These, though intangible, are none the less really felt, and a resemblance to the other operations of the mind having been discovered in them, they were represented by means of self-suggestive symbols, chosen and combined from among the imitative and interjectional words of language. The growth of language must at all times have been gradual and slow, and though the imagination, so warm and strong in the primitive man, was actively engaged in creating the resources of speech for the wants of the growing intellect, it is probable that long periods passed by before it was called upon to exert its sway over the higher realms of speech. A high degree of cultivation was required to enable the mind to give distinct shape to the more abstract ideas or principles, and thus name them.*

---

* "But although at first the intellect be but a passive and dormant faculty, *it is there*, and it is the sole clue wherewith we disentangle the myriad raveled intricacy of sensuous impressions, and thus the senses become the gateways of knowledge; and a man born without the capacity for external sensations would also be of necessity soulless and mindless, because, though not the *single source* of all our thoughts and faculties, the senses are yet the necessary condition of their development. Thus it is that the senses, during the earliest days of man's existence, act the part of nursing mothers to the soul, to which afterwards they become the powerful and obedient handmaids. They are the organs of communion between man and the outer world; they place him *en rapport* with it, uniting man to the universe, and men to one another. Thus they baptize man as a member of the moral and physical cosmos, and awaken thereby the intellect, which would otherwise remain infructuose, like an unquickened seed."—*Farrar*.

In the early progress of language, the imagination was predominant at every step. Nothing was too small, nothing too great, for it to exercise itself upon. The busy and wandering soul attributed a portion of its own life to every object surrounding it, and it seemed impossible to regard any thing as entirely without life. To many ancient nations, "the earth itself," says Farrar, "was a living creature; the stars were divine animals; and the very rainbow lived, and drank the dew."

In the Scriptures we find remarkable instances of personification, arising from the vivid imagination so apparent in the olden languages. These tendencies of early language to attribute an active life to surrounding nature, and a sympathy with the joys and sorrows of man, are reproduced by the poetic instincts within us, and find their expression in our language of poetry; but, in the ordinary uses of speech, we are no longer under the dominion of the imagination and fancy.

Metaphors and figures, which gave so much picturesqueness to early language, are, in too many cases, comparatively lost in the refinement of style attending civilization. They belong now almost exclusively to the poet. In Shakespeare, eminently our poet of nature and imagination, the metaphors crowd upon each other with such richness and profusion that he has even been reproached for such luxuriance; but it is this that makes the glory of his style; it is this that appeals to every heart still alive to the sweet kinship between man and nature, that, for our own pleasure and happiness, should never be lost sight of in our communication with each other. Metaphor is universal in language; and, in the more ancient tongues, such as the Hebrew and the Arabic, the sway of fancy and imagination is to be seen in words, "each of which," says Farrar, "is a picture, whose colors are still bright and clear." But as civilization advances, and the more extensive and frequent intercourse among men renders clearness of style, in signifying their meaning to each other, the chief object of attention, the fancy which gave birth to a word is forgotten, the picturesque coloring which gave it meaning in its birth is lost, and the word too often is allowed, by ignoring its imitative origin, to become a mere arbitrary symbol, having no connection with the thing it represents, save that established by custom and use. We are all constantly using, in the most ordinary employments of language, metaphors and other figures, of which we are unconscious, that had their poetic origin when the imagination of man was more active. One of the characters in a well-known French comedy is surprised to learn that he has been talking prose all his life without being aware of it. A glimpse into first use of words and phrases may surprise some of us still more by the discovery that we have been talking poetry all our lives without knowing it. Indeed, it is a necessary matter for the artistic reader to discover this poetic element, if he would give to language its full force, fervor, and power, when the requirements of his author's language demand such expression.

To sum up briefly Sheridan's masterly views on the subject of the development of speech, he states that by the growth of language through the intelligence of man, and the more active exercise of his higher faculties, the mere animal rudeness of natural sounds became modified by their association with the conventional forms, and new vocal beauties and graces were consequently developed; but that, through all these changes, the natural significance of the sounds of the voice has been largely preserved.

Herbert Spencer expresses the same idea in his treatment of the subject, showing that, while the higher intelligence has refined upon the simplicity of nature, making the forms of communication between men more complex and comprehensive than in the beginning, still the natural language of sound retains, through all changes, its original attributes.

Sheridan assumes that in the transition stages of a language, from the early natural sounds to the polished utterance of high civilization, the tones of the voice were, out of caprice and a natural love of variety amongst mankind, given fantastic, and hence unmeaning, forms; which tones, in the further progress of intelligence and judgment, gave way, in their turn, to the original expression of nature; chastened and modified, however, by the many affecting influences of civilization or cosmopolitan intercourse, but still having as much, if not more, vocal significance than the original language. He accounts in this way for the peculiarities of intonation to be found with people of different provinces of the same country, who, when fused into one society at any center, lose their peculiarities of habit in vocal utterance, and return, more or less nearly, to the simplicity of nature. Be this as it may, a practical observation can not but assure one of the fact that in the sounds of the voice, or the vocal signs, in the language of civilization, lies the vivifying, active principle ever accompanying the signs of the intelligence, and equally, if not more vividly, descriptive of the varying states of the mind.

Gummere, whom we have already mentioned as being an able writer on the Rush philosophy, has the following apt remarks illustrative of this point:

"Those who speak the English language use a certain set of sounds to communicate any idea, while the French, the Spanish, or the Germans will not only use different sounds from ours to convey the same idea or thought, but each will use different sounds from all the others. The language of emotion or passion does not thus vary according to the nationality of the speaker. If you hear a person speaking under the influence of emotion, such as sorrow, anger, or scorn, you have no difficulty in recognizing that emotion, although you may not understand a word that he utters. . . . . We must therefore conclude that the languge of emotion is co-extensive with our species."

So, language becomes, in an advanced stage of development, such as our own represents to-day, equally an exponent of intelligence, of feeling, and of imagination. The tendency of our education seems to be to consider it chiefly as the vehicle of intelligence, but we can not fail to see that by so doing we are ignoring the vitalizing and spiritualizing essence which was first breathed into it from the heart and imagination of man. We are still nearer to the language of nature than we realize, even in the most polished and elegant of tongues. The bond which unites the feeling, the imagination, and the intelligence into one irresistible power in the living spoken language, is too vital a matter to be ignored in the development of its full perfections, and too strong a tie ever to be severed in any language spoken by a race of intelligent, imaginative, and emotional beings. As a proof of the last assertion we have but to instance the utter failure on record of those who have attempted from the stand-point of intellect alone to invent a philosophical or purely arbitrary language, appealing only to the intelligence, as in the case of Bishop Wilkins, Leibnitz, and others.

CHAPTER III.

Significance of Sounds.

Rush tells us that it is "the union of an arbitrary verbal designation of a state of mind with its natural vocal sign, that constitutes the true and essential means of expression in speech." As each word therefore is indicative of some idea, so each vocal sound accompanying its utterance has also a special significance of its own. Every idea, emotion, or thought having its generic vocal sign, — a level line of sound has its peculiar meaning; a leap of the voice, either in altitude or depression, has its own signification; a wave of the voice, either in the graceful flow of its movements or its swelling fullness of sound, has its varying degrees of expressive effects. An abruptness of voice has a meaning of its own; a prolonged loudness has a certain fitness; a vocality of continued softness possesses a purpose of its own. Slowness and rapidity of utterance are opposite effects of extreme conditions; fullness and force of sound are equally so. All of these and other natural modifications of vocality, Rush has clearly described and classified under the heads, or divisions, of Force, Time, Pitch, Abruptness, and Quality, which include all the forms and modifications of the vocal concrete, and which will be fully explained hereafter.

The conventional form of words, as Sheridan's analysis of their constituent elements may have suggested, has much to do with their power to take on the various natural attributes of expression embodied in the varieties of the above forms, as the student will be better able to realize after a careful study into the individual elements which go to make up syllables and words.

A glance again into the intimate connection between the sound and the sense, in their articulative formation, will give a general explanation of this, and a specific realization will come to the student, as we have said, after he has mastered the varied forms of expression in stress, pitch, etc., and is able to see how words are adapted by their peculiar, articulative form, to take on their specifically appropriate modes of expressive vocality.

He will find that the forms of audible language take their impressive character from the peculiar and appropriate actions of the organs by which they are uttered, as well as from the state of mind or of feeling which they are intended to represent. The English language, from its abundance of Saxon elements, whose origin bespeaks a simple and childlike imitation of nature, contains many evidences of the tendency to represent our ideas by their resemblance in sound. The resemblances in the Latin and French elements of our language, having been more subject to the modifying influences of time, are less obvious. The native force and freshness of the Saxon is exemplified, however, by a wide range of words whose sounds correspond in vivid analogy to the ideas and feelings they represent.

All emotions which are recognized as calm, quiet, gentle, tender, winning, or melting, find their natural expression in softened, prolonged, and flowing sounds devoid of all semblance of force. In Dryden's Ode we have an illustration of this in the lines:

> "Softly sweet in Lydian measures
> Soon he soothed his soul to pleasures";

and Milton's well-known and beautiful numbers:

> "With many a bout of linked sweetness long drawn out."

These passages tell with a soothing effect upon the ear and heart, which make us regard the charm of vocal sound as akin to magic itself. The tranquil and gentle emotions in their enunciation glide softly to the ear upon prolonged vowel quantities, and liquid consonants. In the utterance of harsh and abrupt emotions we perceive, on the other hand, the instinctive tendency of speech to assume a corresponding harshness and abruptness in its expressive elements. Thus, when the poet of the Seasons describes the downfall of the oak, the monarch of trees, he represents it as

> "Rustling, crackling, crashing, thundering down."

Fierce, angry passion seems to choose, by some subtle law of instinct, harshness in its elements to give a corresponding fierce effect to its utterance.

The words of heroic ardor in the almost fierce intensity of command burst forth in such passages as:
"Down, down! your lances down!
Bear back both friend and foe!"

The character of action is suggested in such words as heaving, swaying, prancing, darting, lagging, twittering, glancing, glowing, glittering, frittering, quick, cut, crawl, bawl, plunging, etc.; splashing, stuttering, spattering, clatter, etc. Passion or emotion is expressed in words like brawling, braggart, hence, avaunt, dastard, begone, blasting, blighting, blistering, hateful, spiteful, wicked, go, dare, dart, break, etc. A gentle expression seems naturally to belong to such words as softly, calmly, slowly, meekly, sweetly, mildly, smoothly, gently, lowly, lovely, lingering, graceful, love, tenderness, etc. Calm quietude breathes in such utterances as balm, peace, dream, stream, hope, mercy, murmur, melancholy, etc. Grief expresses itself to the ear as readily as to the mind through the medium of such words as alas! oh! ah! woe, groan, weeping, wailing, woeful, sobbing, warning, wasted, etc. Joy and triumph cry out in huzza! ha, ha! hurrah! It also makes itself felt in such words as gladly, gaily, gleeful, brightly, etc. Then we have words exemplifying bold and forcible utterance, as: big, brag, stab, bad, brave, dread, dive, thunder, drive, dare, do. Quickness or rapidity of movements, as: brisk, frisk, quick, bit, wit, pat, rash, rapid, vivid, torrent, etc. Sublimity of emotion, as: grand, growl, bald, hurl, hold, bold, brand, dive, die, dead, dread, dared, etc.

The effect produced upon the imagination by language is largely due to these vocal resemblances, and the most skillful of our poets are indebted to them for their most celebrated passages; the language of true poetry being ever the language of nature. An article from Johnson's Rambler on the subject of "Sound to Sense," says, with regard to this felicitous use of words by writers:

"The adumbration of particular and distinct images, by an exact and perceptible resemblance of sounds, is sometimes studied and sometimes casual. Every language has many words formed in imitation of the noises which they signify. Such are *stridor*, *valo*, and *beatus*, in Latin; and in English, to *growl*, to *buzz*, to *hiss*, and to *jar*. Words of this kind give to a verse the proper similitude of sound without much labor of the writer, and such happiness is therefore to be attributed rather to fortune than to skill."

Should it not be attributed to the poetic gift which instinctively recognizes and seizes upon the sounds most appropriate for expressive purposes?[*] He continues:

"Yet they are sometimes combined, with great propriety, and undeniably contribute to enforce the impression of the idea. We hear the passing arrow in this line of Virgil:

"'Th' impetuous arrow whizzes on the wing,'—

and the creaking of Hell-gates, in the description by Milton:

"'Open fly, with impetuous recoil and jarring sound,
The infernal gates, and on their hinges grate
Harsh thunder.'"

---

[*] "Poetry reproduces the original process of the mind in which language originates. The coinage of words is the primitive poem of humanity, and the imagery of poetry or oratory is only possible and effective because it is a continuation of that primitive process which is itself a reproduction of creation." *Bunsen.*

A Plea for Spoken Language.

The following is a familiar example from the same author:

> "Arms on armour clashing brayed
> Horrible discord; and the madding wheels
> Of brazen fury raged."

We have also an equally vivid sound picture of another kind in the following lines of the same author:

> "And heaven opened wide
> Her ever-during gates, harmonious sound,
> On golden hinges turning."

Again, the following lines from the "Voice of Music" (by Mrs. Hemans), illustrate the wonderful adaptation of the word forms to express a picture of the idea:

> "Thine is the lay that lightly floats,
> And mine are the murmuring, dying notes
> That fall as soft as snow on the lea,
> And melt in the heart as instantly."*

In the following impressive description by Thomson, we readily perceive the effort made by the poet's mind to reproduce, in vocal sound or forms, the ideas of force and sublimity embodied in a contemplation of the storm:

> "'Tis listening Fear, and dumb amazement all;
> When to the startled eye, the sudden glance
> Appears far south, eruptive through the cloud;

---

*The expressive character of poetic numbers, as will be seen later in Sheridan's treatment of the verse, is effected by the peculiar succession of sound in the metrical arrangement, as much as by the individual character of the words themselves.

Significance of Sounds. 175

And, following slower, in explosion fast
The thunder raises his tremendous voice.
At first, heard solemn, o'er the verge of heaven
The tempest growls; but as it nearer comes,
And rolls its awful burthen on the wind,
The lightnings flash a larger curve, and more
The noise astounds; till over head a sheet
Of vivid flame discloses wide, then shuts
And opens wider; shuts and opens still
Expansive, wrapping ether in a blaze,
Follows the loosened aggravated roar,
Enlarging, deep'ning, ming'ling peal on peal,
Crashed horrible, convulsing heaven and earth."

We have spoken before of a tendency to grow away from the original imaginative and expressive forms of utterance in our ordinary careless language of daily intercourse. The changes by which the significance of sound in words has been so greatly disguised as to be scarcely distinguishable, do not consist alone in the various modifications of their original forms in the different languages, but also in the quick clipping modes of their utterance in ordinary speech, by which the value of the vocal elements that compose them is largely ignored. It is only by a return to the emotional language of nature, as it is often exemplified in the speech of children, before they have caught the artificialities of those surrounding them, that we are able to discover the power and meaning of which the imitative sounds of words are capable. These imitations may be followed through all the various forms that words have assumed in different languages, and when they are brought out and made prominent by means of the intonations and perfected enunciations of expressive speech, they give a power and beauty to words which are entirely lost in the familiar, and what may be termed *pinched up, utterance* of those who, following the general tendency of the day, study words rather as printed symbols for the eye than as sound pictures, if I may so call them, for the ear. Let us take, for instance, the word *break*, as it is usually pronounced. The imitative sound which gives it so much vigor and expression is lost; but if it is uttered with the full oral effect of which it is capable, the imitative character becomes at once apparent. Now if you will trace this word *break* through the many different forms given to it by the spirit of different languages (and this can readily be done by simply turning to it in Webster's quarto dictionary), you will find the same clearly distinguishable imitation in all of them, when they are pronounced in a full and impressive manner, and with a proper observance of the holding power of their articulative construction. In giving attention to the sound power of words, however, as an expression or suggestion of their sense, one thing must be observed in this regard and strictly complied with in the practice of the student of elocution, and that is, *to resist the tendency to carry such imitations to extremes*. The old axiom, that there is but one step from the sublime to the ridiculous, may be well applied in this connection. Thus, on the stage, the low comedian often makes use of this exaggerated, imitative expression to heighten his comic effects.

The idea, then, of adapting sound to sense in

the utterance of imitative words (especially fashionable at present), must by all means receive such a modification of its accepted literal significance as that embodied in the remark of Sheridan on this point, that the sound used in the utterance of such words should be a suggestive comment merely on the meaning, rather than a mechanical imitation. For example, the words buzz, hum, rattle, hiss, jar, are obviously *imitative* words, but their sounds inappropriately exaggerated, would only occasion ludicrous associations of the idea. Words, as we have seen, receive their expressive sound-power, not only from their articulative construction, but from the vocal form and character accompanying this articulated utterance in the intonation, quality, and other vocal attributes of all syllabic sounds; but, as we have before suggested, *these two elements of expression are closely dependent upon each other, since the peculiar articulation or elemental arrangement of a word determines, in great measure, its capabilities for taking on the various appropriate, expressive powers of intonation and its attendant modifications.**

The reader or orator, then, must learn to combine the different appropriate sounds that give expression to the emotions with the verbal forms of his language in such a manner as not only to present a full and clear meaning of these words to the minds of his hearers, but also to awaken a

---

* Sheridan, in speaking of the capabilities of expression in a large number of words in our language, says: "Whoever will examine such words closely will find that every letter in them contributes to their expressive power."

lively and active sympathy with the various feelings or passions they express. The demand upon the elocutionist is therefore imperative for *a fitting adaptation of his tones* to the spirit of the language of which he becomes the vocal interpreter. The application of art in giving expressive vocality to words is, then, so to speak, to clothe them in their most appropriate and descriptive sound colors; and this tone-shading in speech is very consistently described by the phrase, "word-painting." Without insisting, then, upon words being made an echo to the sense in every case, we do affirm that there are circumstances in speech, under strong emotion or passion, especially where the subject is poetic, when the speaker is required to give some imitation of the characteristic qualities, in action or condition, of the objects or ideas his words are intended to represent. In such cases, the taste and trained skill of the artistic reader or speaker will enable him to produce an echo to the sense without marring his effects by an excessive material effort of imitation, thus lowering the matter to mere mimicry.

We have simply taken the preliminary and somewhat cursory view of this subject, for the purpose of leading the mind of the reader to reflect upon the full value of sound in the expression of language, and of its intimate connection with the various mental and emotional conditions of mankind; and also to impress him with the importance of a correct and appreciative knowledge of those expressive movements of the voice by which nature,

Significance of Sounds. 179

with such graphic power, distinguishes all the various feelings and emotions that accompany our mental operations. To dissect, study, and recombine these natural vocal movements, are the means by which the student of elocution may be enabled to avail himself of all the impressive effects of oral function in reproducing his own thoughts, or reading those of others. These properties of the voice may not be caught in their full perfection solely by the mere inspiration of genius, nor by the imitation of some favorite speaker. It is only by taking nature as a guide and studying the revelations she has made that we may follow, through art, the different expressive effects she has supplied. Although in many cases it has been denied that these subtle vocal agencies can be measured in natural speech, it has been made manifest to our intelligence that they were both conceived and executed by man in his infancy, and made the basis of the whole art of language. We certainly ought, then, to be able to so far perceive and study such sounds as to reproduce them in the utterance of the words to which they gave birth and character. Dr. Rush's systematized mode of elementary and syllabic analysis takes us back, as the careful student will learn, to the very beginning of speech, and carries us, by progressive study, through all the various modes of oral expression, until we finally attain a full knowledge and command of the various shades and niceties of tone and emphasis that give power and effect to spoken language, thus enabling us to reproduce, by means of art, a faithful transcript of all those unmistakable and significant modes of expression by which nature portrays the various inner workings of the soul.

It is most probable that the Greeks and Romans were acquainted with these vocal elements, for without their study they could never have attained that wonderful degree of excellence in oratory for which they have been so distinguished. It must be supposed that, with that true insight into nature which characterized them in their studies of art, they made themselves masters of expressive speech by an analytic measurement of all its varied forms of sound.

But sound, unlike the productions of sculpture and painting, is evanescent as the dew. The classic languages are dead because their tones, that which constituted their soul, are lost forever. Let us, then, set to work in earnest to supply the deficiency. The materials are around us. Our perceptive faculties are as quick and penetrating as those which existed before us; our industry, proverbial; and our enterprise, surely as great. Then let us be willing to learn those good things which others found it possible to acquire in the school of nature, and by which they made their own schools produce such results as helped to create the Greek and Roman glory. Let the student of elocution be, above all, the student of nature. Let him listen to her voice as expressed in his own untrammeled utterance of emotion and passion; study the notes of the birds and the tones of the animals around him, listen to the many voices of the winds and waters, until his ear becomes familiar with all known sounds, and his heart attuned to the vocal beauties of nature, and thus learn how they all conform to the laws of natural expression. He will find many of these sounds in nature are tunable,—that is, musical,—while others are untunable, or merely noisy. An opportunity for the observation of such sounds may be had, for example, at a wharf where ships are moored during a storm. There let any one stand and listen as the wind whistles through the rigging and shrouds, then contrast the shrieking pitch of such sounds with the loud blow of the steam pipe; the groaning of the ponderous timbers of the wharf chafed by the weighty vessels; the angry splashing of the waves breaking against the many obstructions; the clatter and clanking of chains; the complaining of cables strained to their utmost tension. Again, let him stand on the sea-beach near to some bold promontory, and his ear will be filled with sounds of another kind,—the heavy boom of the tempestuous sea; the swollen tide as it falls crashing on the beach; the thunder and roar of waves as they hurl themselves against or sweep over opposing rocks. In such concerts as these, which nature invites us to hear and admire, we may recognize the voices of grief and pain; the vocal signs of petulance—fretting and moaning; the hurtling sounds of anger, rage, and ferocity; and the deep, loud vocality of awe, sublimity, and grandeur.

In reading, it requires the skill of an artist who has studied his subject in detail to be able to employ the vocal signs corresponding to the verbal forms which express the ever-changing states of mind represented in the language he assumes. Yet, how often do we observe in the tones of an untrained speaker's voice an indiscriminate employment of certain vocal signs where there is no warrant for their especial use in the matter he is enunciating, with no other definite or intelligent purpose than what arises from a vague notion of the necessity for a variety of vocal effects. In our unpremeditated or spontaneous utterance, the vocal signs expressive of the changes from one state of mind to the other are born, so to speak, simultaneously with the verbal form; but, in reproducing the language of another, the most consummate skill is necessary to reproduce the ever-changing variety of tone, or, in other words, to employ, with perfect naturalness of effect, vocal signs appropriate to the natural expression of such language. By introducing a mere unmeaning variety — that is, by employing vocal signs for verbal signs of an entirely opposite character — do many speakers and readers confound all the real vocal distinctions of language and the varied shades of thought and feeling. It must be apparent, then, that a study of such expressive agencies in their individual character is absolutely necessary in order to apply them in their true significance in the combined effects of artistic speech, just as the painter must become familiar with the primary colors, and then with their combined effects in light and shade, before he can portray in their combinations a true counterfeit of

Significance of Sounds. 183

nature. Such a knowledge of the vocal signs as discipline and industry, close observation and faithful practice will give can not be overestimated, since, as the reader will not fail to see, from the view we have had of the close connection between the varying states of the human mind and their expression in vocal sound and verbal forms, it must constitute the master key to the true art of elocution.

Before passing on to a specific view of the subject as treated by the author who has made a detailed study of these vocal signs of thought and passion a possible matter, it would be as well to have his position with regard to the subject clearly defined in his own words, and thus, perhaps, to remove a misconception which is apt to be entertained concerning the apparently unlimited extent of such a study. He tells us, and demonstrates the fact, also, that each natural or instinctive vocal sign, represented by certain forms of stress, time, quality, pitch, etc., is used in its various degrees to indicate more than one state of mind, since words or verbal signs, as descriptive agents, are more numerous — being the result of the growth of intelligence — and thus that many of these states generically represented by the same natural sign, have their specific difference marked by the artificial sign or conventional language that describes them. He says:

"By the use, then, of a *comparatively limited number of vocal signs*, together with the assistant means of conventional language, the *apparently infinite forms of expression in speech are produced.* A specification of these signs and numerical limitations of the terms of their nomenclature, at once afford an observer the means to survey, through the composure of a classifying reflection, the whole extent of this supposed infinity, and thereby to change a vulgar and distracting wonder at immensity into an intelligent admiration of the obvious combinations and endless intermutable variety of a few distinguishable constituents."

He then adds, and we can not better close this general review of this phase of the subject than by these words:

"He who has a knowledge of the constituents of speech, and of their powers and uses, is the potential master of the science of elocution, and he must then derive from his ear, his sense of propriety, and his taste the means of actually applying it with success."

Part Third.

Elocution as a Fine Art.

Chapter I.

Popular Errors Regarding Elocution.

BEFORE entering upon a detailed consideration of the vocal signs of thought and passion, and their varieties of expression in the utterances of speech, which constitute a large part of the working material for the study of the true art of spoken language, it has seemed to me expedient to meet some erroneous ideas and objections which have long been, and still are, advanced by many concerning the matter of a disciplined and artistic study of elocution,—ideas and objections which, judging from the similar attitude of the public mind toward all subjects that have not been thoroughly investigated, and hence, in many cases, unfairly represented, are founded more upon a certain popular prejudice than upon a plain, rational, and unbiased view of existing facts.

I think I am perfectly safe in stating that it is affirmed by a large class of thinking people, and even by persons of influence in educational matters, that the ability to read and speak well is a special, natural gift, bestowed only upon certain favored individuals. The "natural reader" is, therefore, supposed to be endowed with the capacity to exercise the functions of expressive, premeditated speech, without especial study or preparation; to deal spontaneously, as it were, with his subject-matter, the intellectual and emotional attributes of which often require it to be lifted to the highest plane of dramatic delineation or oratorical eloquence. There needs no stronger corroboration of this statement than the fact before spoken of; namely, the modern tendency toward a contraction in didactic matter in our books of reading, which stands but as an acknowledgment of the belief that detailed and practical principles and rules of instruction in this branch of education are of but little avail.

I have in my mind in this connection a characteristic example of this "natural reader" idea, contained in a reading book published by a popular reciter in Philadelphia a few years ago, boldly enunciating the theory that rules and principles were not only not necessary to make a reader, but rather stumbling-blocks in the way of the learner, and summing up the requirements of the latter in substance, as nearly as I can remember, as follows:

"The selections contained in this book abound in fitting expressions of thought, emotion, and passion, and, as such, are calculated to excite in the reader corresponding feelings; all, then, that remains for him is to enter fully and strongly into the spirit of the language, and deliver the words as if they were his own, expressing them in such tones as he would use himself were he in the same position as the personage represented by the author."

The extreme simplicity and "naturalness" of such instructions may be well placed with the profound assertion of Dogberry that, "to be a well-favored man is the gift of fortune, but to read and write comes by nature." And yet we have grave authorities for this same theory.

This oft-repeated injunction to make the language your own and then utter it naturally, is, however, by no means wrong in itself, but, on the contrary, is, in its full significance, as we shall see hereafter, an epitome of all the requirements of the most studious and artistic reader. But, taken as constituting the *sum of instruction*, it is no more a key to the end desired than the title page of a book to the detail of its contents. It contains simply a statement of something to be accomplished which involves all that is to be effected in reading, and, moreover, the necessity of a knowledge how to do it. To expect a person to be guided by such a direction alone toward excellence in reading would be as logical as to state a difficult proposition in arithmetic or geometry, involving all the principles of mathematics, and then require the student to solve it without any previous instruction in those principles. In other words, it is simply offering as a rule to guide one to a desired end that which is only the result arising from principles properly applied.

In the first place, to enter into the author's thoughts and make them one's own, means not only an apprehension through the intelligence of the sense conveyed by the grammatical structure of the language, but a further apprehension of the feeling, passion, and imagination which led to its creation, and of which it is the tangible expression. This must necessarily imply a close and analytic study of the written forms, not only with the searching power of the intellect, but with that of the heart and imagination. This accomplished, what remains? By far the most difficult part—"to express it," we are told, "as if it were our own, naturally."

"To be natural" means, of course, to employ such vocal signs or modes of expression as nature has invariably assigned to certain states of the mind for the expression of the language which is the exponent of such mental conditions,—since it has been established that the ordinary tones and movements of the voice which we employ in our intercourse, either in simple, unimpassioned communication, or the more earnest vocal forms peculiar to argument, narrative, vivid description, or passion, are the gifts of nature, formed originally, as we have seen, upon the inarticulate voices of primitive man.

But can being natural, in the absence of the immediate impulse of instinct, be other than being able to imitate successfully the same vocal means we would employ to produce a corresponding unpremeditated utterance? And can such means be successfully imitated, in all their manifold variety, unless the reader be consciously aware of them, and possess a control of them at will? Rush says:

"In looking for a rule of excellence in the art of elocution, we are always referred, as in the other fine arts, to nature. But nature is, when shut out from the light of analysis, an *unassignable pattern.* .... But it is the belief of those who can not perceive the application of analysis and precept to elocution that the power consists in the wonder-working of 'genius,' and in proprieties and graces beyond the reach of art. So seem the plainest services of arithmetic to a savage, and so to the slave seem all the ways of music, which modern art has so accurately penned as to time and tune and momentary grace. .....

"Now genius, as it appears from its productions, is only *an unusual aptitude* for that broad, reflective, combining, and persevering observation which perceives and readily accomplishes more than is done without it, and is, therefore, in its purposes and uses, not altogether removed beyond a submission to knowledge and rule."

Thus admitting that even genius needs the aid of art toward the full development of its powers, how much more are those dependent upon art's enlightening assistance who are not possessed of transcendent gifts!

As before suggested, every thing in reading will depend primarily upon the ability of the mind to perceive and realize the author's meaning, not only in the root, as it were, of the ideas and sentiments, but also in the various modifications and qualifications which spring from and cluster round the main current of thought and feeling. When the reader has fully conceived and mastered the text mentally, then, how much depends upon what may be called the simply physical ability to deal with it in natural utterance. Just in proportion to the reader's ability to vary and intensify his modes of expressive utterance in consonance with nature's own varied methods of appropriate expression for her thoughts and feelings, will his effects be commensurate with the demands of an intelligent and demonstrative interpretation of the author's language. For it must be plain that, if the *exact and appropriate* expressive vocal character of the thoughts, emotions, and passions be not given to the words by which they are represented, the reader must fail in transferring the workings of the mind and soul of one intelligence to another. The sounds of the spoken language can in such case only serve to obscure the thought and to deaden the spirit of the written language, which it is their real province to illuminate and vivify. The undisciplined effort to be natural in reading, without knowing just how to go about it, further than to enter into a sort of general understanding of the feeling to be expressed, results, in the majority of cases, in the formality of a certain "reading tone," unlike any expression of nature or of art,—a tone which becomes, through custom, confirmed by the unreflecting habit of treating expression, as one may say, "in the lump."

Who has not frequently been struck with the pretentious, not to say pompous, display made by some uncultured aspirant for elocutionary honors, in reading "naturally" from a newspaper, the mixed material of a narrative, dramatic, and descriptive character, contained in the report of some exciting article of the day? And can we not all call to mind the chanting or droning sentimentalism of the "natural" reading of some favorite poem, or, as a more familiar matter, the reading-tone by which the language of some inspired hymn has fallen upon the ear in sounds calculated to banish all sentiment or feeling suggested by the words?

"There is nothing could put the difficulty of reading properly in a stronger light to any man than his attempting to read aloud a scene of a comedy; in which, though there are no tones to be used but what are known to him, and which he acknowledges as such when used by others, yet can he by no means command them at his pleasure; and he must be obliged to own that to *conceive and to execute* are two different things."—*Sheridan.*

In allusion to the precept before stated, and so often proposed as the key to natural expression in reading, Rush justly observes:

"Teachers have sometimes varied their old and imperfect rule of teaching by imitation, to something like the system of nature, as they think, by requiring their pupil not to imitate another, but figuratively, as it were, to imitate himself. Such a direction, in assuming to be the rule for a just and effective elocution, only requires a pupil to speak as he pleases;—that is, as his own particular ideas prompt him,— for, by the direction, he is to make the ideas of the author his own; but having, as implied by the necessity of the direction, no previous *rule*, he is left to utter them only as he pleases, by an assumed rule of his own. I have more than once seen among aspirants of the stage the pitiable results of what was supposed to be a representation of the truth of nature by thus affecting to become identical."

How often, indeed, when the student undertakes to feel what he reads and read naturally, as the *sole* guide towards achieving the end of proper expression, does the following occur: He at once finds himself manufacturing such tones of utterance (in remembrance, perhaps, of what he may have heard from the pulpit, stage, bar, or platform) as his imagination, entirely independent of judgment or previous training in the distinctive value of vocal sounds, leads him to suppose are suited to the subject. The excitement attendant upon the situation carries him away, and his feelings, rushing on from point to point, compel him to an utterance in which all the various shades and outlines of emotion are blended into a confused mass,—or, more plainly, into one continuous tone,—and finally, after fatiguing his hearers, he concludes his discourse or composition with exhausted lungs and irritated throat, *entirely unconscious of the process employed*, save that he has *felt his* subject and *tired himself*. And indeed, if such an unregulated and perverted use of the voice is persisted in for any length of time, the vocal organs become diseased, the lungs and bronchial tubes perhaps affected from their relationship to such disorganized members, and the citadel of life itself slowly but surely yields to such fatal encroachments. This is no exaggeration, as the many cases of broken health amongst men who are called upon to use their voices professionally, without previous training, will testify.

Dr. Rush, speaking on this point, says:

"Let us, however, suppose this rule of self-imitation might serve for commonplace ideas on every-day occasions. On the other hand, suppose the art of reading to be exerted in representing the utmost force and delicacy in dramatic character and of imaginative creation by the poet. How, with the great crowd of mankind, will this rule of substitution meet

Popular Errors.

the case? .... It is a prevailing opinion that persons who speak their own states of mind in social intercourse always speak properly, and that transferring this 'natural manner,' as it is called, to formal reading, must insure this required natural propriety. This idea has arisen from ignorance of the functions which constitute the beauties and deformities of speech. Without a knowledge of causes and effects on these points, teachers have been obliged to refer to the spontaneous efforts of the voice as the only assistant means of instruction. Setting aside here what we might insist on, that no one should pretend to say what the right or natural manner is before he knows the principles that make it so, we will admit that the 'natural manner,'—or any body's manner, or, rather, no manner at all, from our being accustomed to it, and having, it may be, a fellow feeling with the faults,— is less exceptionable than the *first attempts of the pupil in reading*. Still, the faults of ordinary conversation are similar to those of reading, though they are less apparent. Perhaps the common opinion is grounded on the belief that a just execution must necessarily follow a full perception of the thought and passion of discourse, for these are supposed to accompany colloquial speech. No one indeed can read correctly or with elegance if he does not both understand and feel, as it is called, what he utters; but these are not exclusively the means of success. *There must be knowledge derived from peeping behind the curtain of actual vocal deformity still hanging before the just and beautiful laws of speech, and there must be an organic faculty well prepared in the school of those laws for the representation of thought and passion*. Were it certain that this pretended 'natural manner' truly represents the proper system of vocal expression, we would no more require an art of elocution than an art of breathing; and the whole world, in reading and speaking, as in the act of respiration, would always accomplish its purposes with a like instinctive perfection. Yet, far from uniformity, there are wide and innumerable differences in what now, with individuals and schools, pass for the proprieties, as well as in what are the acknowledged faults, of speech."

There is one point, therefore, with regard to this theory of a "natural manner" which we should carefully consider; namely, that what we call natural in the matter of unpremeditated speech is, after all, an acquirement with each individual, the result of life-long exercise of the organs of speech, where the intelligence, working with nature or under her promptings, produces habits which become apparently purely instinctive. Indeed, it is this power of progression beyond the merely animal cries that marks the intelligence of man as distinguishing him from the brutes, whose utterances, being the result of instinct alone, can not advance to those varied vocal acquisitions which accompany intelligent articulate communication. All the natural and seemingly purely instinctive functions of the body that are subject to the will, though fashioned to certain uses, still await the training of education to adapt them to the purposes for which they are by nature unquestionably fitted. The hands, feet, and limbs of the child are adapted to their several purposes by a slow process of education, and the analogy holds throughout all the operations of the body, subject to the will, the organs of speech amongst the number. To quote Rush again:

"Man's whole executive purposes are directed by his thoughts and passions, the same agents that direct his speech, and as far as history and well grounded conclusions inform us, the just designs of nature, in his moral, his political, and his vocal condition, were found to be already crossed or perverted when he first began to look into her laws and to turn an eye of philosophic inquiry and comparison on himself."

The whole possibility of perfection or corruption of the art of elocution lies in this capability of education in the vocal organs, and the capacity for acquiring habits, good or bad, as they may be directed, either by earnest intelligence or self-satisfied and indifferent ignorance. Thus, many habits of utterance, though seemingly "natural," are in reality not natural, because they are the result of a violation of nature's laws of proper and complete utterance, for this latter is always and only that which accords with the most perfect functions of that vocal mechanism which nature has provided. This is plain from the fact that the voice is always strengthened and beautified by exercising it in the evident line of nature's intent. Sheridan says, in speaking of pronunciation,—and the remark applies with double force to intonation,—that it is an indisputable truth that the *sounds which are most easily uttered* by the organs of speech are *most pleasing* to the organs of hearing, and that this is the very best rule by which the pronunciation of any language could be formed.

"In speaking, as in other arts, the useful and agreeable are almost always found to coincide, and every real embellishment promotes and perfects the principal design."—*Walker.*

"Thus instinct, even when dignified into genius, seems to be nothing more than an organization prepared by nature to receive the impression of directive causes, which, therefore, act necessarily to excite the organic power, limited as it may be, and to exercise it to its end."—*Rush.*

In coming to study the details of nature's laws, we are compelled to acknowledge the fact that:

"There are individual instances of vocal deformity presented by 'nature'—with sacrilege, so called,—and daily suffered to pass without remark because we are engaged at the moment with other thoughts and designs, which we perceive only when the voice itself, as a subject of taste, is the exclusive object of reflective and discriminating attention."—*Rush*.

Many persons also acquire, by different and various means, certain habits of speech by no means natural in sound to the ear of persons unaccustomed to them, and which are but a misuse of vocal movements and forms of expression correct and agreeable in their own place or province, but misapplied through the accidents of ignorance or carelessness, or it may be caprice.*

Another point to be considered in the matter of naturalness is that temperamental peculiarities beget, in the natural utterance, certain vocal peculiarities, and though these need not be faults of utterance, still they represent but one phase of a varied nature, in addition to which is a large unconquered territory in the field of natural utterance, every inch of which the reader must be familiar with in order to be able to traverse it at his will in the representation of the varied expression common to all. To illustrate,—a dramatic reader must be able, in "making the language his own," and speaking it "naturally," to utter it in the manner natural, not to himself, but to the person of whose temperament and personal characteristics it is the ex-

---

* To illustrate,—the circumflex movement of New England is certainly not a natural one, although custom has caused it to seem natural to those persons by whom it is heard daily.

pression, and this he will not be able to do with any degree of perfection until he learns *how* through an analysis and practical mastery of the true causes of varied natural effect.

The evil of much that is false or imperfect in utterance, lies in the earliest education of children, where the visible sign, or skeleton of speech, is taught in the faith that the flesh and blood, or the vitality of sound in proper intonation, etc., will follow naturally; and how does it follow? Certainly not in accordance with the proprieties, melodies, and harmonies existing in the vocal attributes of nature, but too often through the example of those crude, slovenly modes of speech, those sharp, discordant qualities of voice, which jabber, scream, mumble, or mutter in the streets, the play-ground, and often in the home life,—those places where our children's voices are molded after the fashion of the vocal impressions which become familiar to their ears, and which, in so many cases, override or obscure the more delicate, tender, and agreeable forms of vocal expression.

"Amongst those bred at the university, or at court, as well as amongst mechanics, or rustics; amongst those who speak in the senate house, pulpit, or at the bar, as well as amongst men in private life, we find stammerers, lispers, a mumbling, indistinct utterance; ill management of the voice, by pitching it in too high or too low a key; speaking too loud, or too softly as not to be heard; and using discordant tones, and false cadences. These being, I say, common to all ranks and classes of men, have not any marks of disgrace put upon them, but, on the contrary, meet with general indulgence from a general corruption."—*Sheridan.*

Our feelings are no longer sufficiently simple and natural to distinguish the real without the help of a knowledge of these universal and unchangeable principles which, though they can neither create talent nor supply the place of it, can yet furnish it with aids, and with such aids we may avoid much that is false, though sometimes accepted as nature, and much that is injurious.

"The practical ends of elocution, as an elegant art, are to convey our thoughts and passions, with truth, propriety, and taste, and consequently without the error and deformity of awkwardness or affectation. When, therefore, by analytic knowledge of the constituents of an art, principles or classifications of its facts for some effective purpose are framed, these principles become, as it were, the *scientific instinct* of the new and more complicated organization of the mind in its state of acquired knowledge; just as, in its own way, the original and more simple organization of nature exercises its limited and merely animal instinct."—*Rush*.

To read naturally, therefore, must not consist in reproducing any mere accidents of expression, so to speak, but the ability on the part of the reader to draw from the great heart of nature that vocal power and meaning which thrills through language, universally recognized and always simple, appropriate, strong, and beautiful.

This idea of expressing the language of an author "naturally" is, however, with a large class of people, interpreted to mean in the reader's familiar and colloquial manner of speech,—that is, in his usual or ordinary conversational mode or habit of expressing himself. The rule indeed is sometimes given, "Read as you talk." Assuming this familiar utterance to be perfect of its kind,—that is, serving its own end faultlessly,—it can not even then meet *all* the requirements of a truly natural or appropriate expression in reading and oratory. In many respects, of course, a familiar, "natural" manner, as it is called, possesses claims upon our attention. But let it be remembered that, while suitable in certain forms of reading and speaking, such a style of utterance is not the language of exalted imagination or heroic ideas. We must not only contemplate, but reproduce, such language from the standpoint of one who conceived it in the white heat of inspiration,—the fervor and glow of kindled genius. We may, indeed, by uttering such language colloquially and familiarly, express ourselves in a manner natural to ourselves in the ordinary affairs of life, but it will certainly not be expressing the author naturally.

Does not naturalness of effect in all expression mean a fitness or congruity, an adaptation of the proper means to the desired end? Admitting this, it must follow that, in order to be able to express the thoughts of a writer as if they were our own, implies, in many cases, the necessity of rising in our vocal utterance to modes and forms commensurate with the beauty or grandeur of the ideas of the creative spirit, and the verbal mold into which they are cast, instead of dwarfing them into the familiar, the commonplace, and even the flippant. Poetry, for example, is the medium by which men seek to give utterance to fullness of feeling and emotion too great for the limited expressive effect of language in its ordinary every-day use. It is an attempt to excite a sympathetic realization of the sublime or the beautiful, in minds of a congenial nature, by means of a figurative, exalted language, that soars above the regions of commonplace expression required for the practical affairs of life. It is always suggestive, not literal. Its utterance, therefore, requires vocal modes which must excite in the mind of the hearer something beyond the impressions he receives in matter-of-fact recitals, or dry statements of mere intellectual comprehension.

The tones employed in reading poetry must, therefore, be something more than the ordinary range of utterance,—the same in kind, but more extended in degree. They must be natural, but yet in nature's happiest vein, her most elevated mode of expression. The same is true of the higher drama, of elevated prose,—in short, of all that language of genius and inspiration which represents the finer and nobler part of man.

There is, unfortunately, a strong tendency in the drama, the public speaking, and the reading of the present day, to dwarf the ideal, the heroic, and the classic into a conformity with the limited interpretation of this term "natural," of which we have spoken. A great actor of the present time (Jefferson) speaking in deprecation of the tendency toward the familiar, colloquial treatment of the language of Shakespeare's tragic heroes, for example, once said to me, "They are not men merely six feet high, but sixteen;"—a copy of nature indeed, but on a grand colossal plan; and the effort to reduce them to the ordinary unidealized pattern, by a familiarity or flippancy in the utterance of their language, is only to produce an incongruous effect, often amounting to absurdity. Let this popular idea of naturalness be followed in reading much of the Bible or of Milton and Shakespeare, and we sin against the author and the language by robbing the latter of its beauty, sublimity, and power.

It is of vital importance, then, in the proper treatment of language in reading, to reflect in all cases what is a truly natural, in other words, a congruous and appropriate, manner of treating our subject; for the least reflection must show us that to treat a sublime, heroic, or finely poetic subject familiarly or in the colloquial manner, is as much a violation of the unchanging fitness of things as it would be for the artist to paint a Prometheus in the garment of a modern drawing-room, or to represent a Psyche directing domestic affairs. The reverse, of course, holds equally true. To clothe an author's thoughts, therefore, in vocal forms commensurate with the beauty or grandeur of his ideas, as well as in the lighter and more colloquial forms necessary at times to their expression, should be the end of the truly *natural*, which means the truly artistic, reader.

CHAPTER II.

The Principles of Elocution.

IT has been before stated that, in the art of reading or premeditated speech, naturalness of effect can only be accomplished by a successful imitation of the varied vocal forms corresponding to similar mental conditions which nature employs in unpremeditated utterance; and yet, to obtain a model for such imitation representing the best and purest expression of nature, we must look higher than to the spontaneous expression of any one individual.

"Although a compensating nature, still holding her regards over the wayward errors of the human voice, may not, under its corruptions, deign to show us a single instance of the fitness and beauty of her laws, she has, as an indication of her means of perfecting the vocal powers of the individual, diffused throughout the species all the constituents of that perfection. A description of the true character and wise design of these constituents, and the gathering-in of their scattered proprieties and beauties, furnish the full and choicest pattern of imitable nature; which, reduced to an orderly system of precept and example, must constitute the proper and elegant art of elocution. If, then, nature's excellencies are scattered throughout the species, art must ordain her canon by collecting them in one faultless example. The canon, so called, of statuary in Greece, which represented no singly-existing form, but which was said to contain within the rule of its design all the master principles of the art, was the deliberate work of observation, time, and careful experiment on the eye, in the very method of reflection and discriminating selection we here claim for elocution."—*Rush.*

Perfection in the art of elocution, also, is the adroit blending together of diverse beauties to produce that pleasing effect which is most nearly allied to that which we are pleased to call nature. Or, more accurately, it is the province of the art to seek out completeness by the means nature has placed within reach, and through the suggestions she has given of her own possibilities, if unthwarted in her original designs.

A French critic, in speaking of Shakespeare, has beautifully said: "What Shakespeare desired above all was the living reality,—a reality which he enlarged and exalted to the ideal." In this single sentence we have the summing up of this whole matter of naturalness in the art of elocution. We want, indeed, the *living reality*, but we would have true natural expression idealized into its highest possibilities of beauty, grace, and power. To illustrate: All the strong passions of the mind communicate themselves, as we have seen, so suddenly and irresistibly to the body that vehement gesticulations and impassioned tones are the result. These tones and gesticulations are, no doubt, natural, but they are not always the most perfect or graceful expressions of nature. The untutored extravagancies of the ignorant and uncouth under the impulse of violent emotion, though they are perfectly intelligible and strongly expressive, will often excite, in the uncultivated mind, a feeling of repulsion that prevents a full sympathy with the passions so coarsely expressed.

Thus nature may readily run into deformity, and it must be the purpose of art and cultivation to conceal or remove all deformities, for art is called in, not to pervert, but to refine and exalt nature. Nature, it is true, will accomplish much without art in all human operations, and art will be of no avail without nature; but it is only by a combination of the two that we can produce perfection in any thing that is the workmanship of man.

If we take a view of all the elegant arts,—music, architecture, painting, dancing, etc.,—we can find no one exactly as it was when first invented. Cultivation and improvement have carried them far beyond their original limits. The rude and uncouth have been made to give way to the beautiful and graceful, and an ideal perfection has been achieved far beyond that found in the first, simple imitations of nature, imperfect as all our untutored efforts in that direction must necessarily be.

In the art of elocution, the two great principles are force and grace,—the one derived chiefly from nature, the other from art. United, they mutually assist each other; alone, each loses a portion of its effectiveness. Force of speaking may excite emotions and convictions; grace or artistic intonation pleases and excites the imagination. There is no agreeable sensation we receive from language but is capable of being heightened by the power of agreeable, harmonious, or measured sounds; hence the pleasure we receive from poetic numbers, and even from the less apparent and looser measure of prose. Deprive poetry of its figures, its metaphors, its measured numbers, and it becomes the plain, unvarnished expression of thought; deprive speech of its graces, ornamental attributes of tone and measure, and it becomes the short and sharp action of every-day conversation. In order, then, to please as well as impress, we must imitate the beauty and vigor of nature. To choose these from among all her forms, requires an *improved taste*, made perfect by long and continued study and exercise. For all qualities of execution are dependant upon a knowledge and discrimination of the truth.

"All fine arts are essentially *arts*—each the offspring of a fruitful alliance between knowledge and intellectual facility— the high accomplishment of the work by the artist, and the reflective enjoyment of its truth and beauty by the votary, being purely the result of close observation, extensive comparison, enlightened choice, and harmonized combination of the scattered constituents of propriety, unity, expression, grandeur, and grace."—*Rush.*

The spirit of genuine art should be the life of all speech. It should breathe through and animate language, as the soul animates the body, or the vital principle permeates the trees and plants, building up their trunks and extending their branches to the sun to blossom and bear fruit.

Ease and grace of execution in any art, that of speech among the rest, can come only from a disciplined practice, founded upon a correct knowledge of the principles of the art, and under the guidance of an educated taste.

"We maintain, against the admirers of natural faults and the decriers of artificial excellence, that it is not natural to do any thing well which is liable to disturbance from ignorance and the irregularity of the will."—*Barber*.

In the first place, it is false to suppose that, because the voice is a natural gift, we must leave its development to nature alone or unaided. Like most natural gifts, it comes to us with marvelous capacity for improvement, and the full expansion of its powers depends upon their intelligent exercise. We may, it is true, read well, and even sing well, "by ear" alone, but it is only by a truly scientific cultivation, aided by discerning judgment and good taste, that a thoroughly artistic and effective use of the vocal organs may be acquired. A knowledge drawn from a correct observation of the working powers of the speaking voice, enables the speaker to discipline his organs to a fitting obedience to the dictates of his will and the prompting of his mental powers, in giving vocal impress and character to the language he deals with, whether poetic or matter-of-fact, premeditated or extempore.

It can not be denied that the ability to effect this is sometimes possessed as a special gift. But, while allowing that such exceptions exist, the rule is,— the prevalence of undeveloped powers. In the study of elocution, then, nothing is more important than the method to be employed in developing or building up the voice, and imparting to the student at the same time a natural style of delivery; that is, a style in accordance with nature's own workings. The two, indeed, if proper means be employed, must, of necessity, go hand-in-hand; for, in the beautiful economy of nature, the principles of natural expression, properly applied; are those which develop the organs in the very line of action which nature has marked out for herself.

Thus, the same principles to which we are indebted for the ultimate perfection and polish of accomplished oratory, are those by which, also, we are to detect and remove the peculiarities of the foreigner, communicate the gift of speech to the mute, and give fluency to the convulsive stammerer. The intimate connection between correct theory and successful practice in the art of elocution, and in other arts also, is well expressed by a poet, who used the lines for another object, but who, unconsciously, has made them applicable to our immediate purpose:

"Truth and good are one,
And beauty dwells in them, and they in her,
With like participation."—*Barber*.

In all efforts, then, to develop the latent powers of the vocal organs, and to improve, by cultivation, the quality of the speaking voice, the greatest care should be taken to follow where nature leads, otherwise mannerisms and affectations of voice are apt to be acquired,—sometimes from a restricted mode of utterance, arising from an affectation of extreme nicety or elegance in pronunciation, and again from adopting tones which are not, as it were, a free-will offering of the organs of speech, but the result of their restraint or subjection. This is, of course, in all cases, to create a style of objectionable peculiarity; and such effects, which must arise from employing inherently bad means of oral communication, can not fail in time to deprive the reader or speaker of all ease and freedom of speech, impair the vocal organs, and cripple the beauty and power of audible language.

CHAPTER III.

Necessity of Training the Voice.

THE members of the human family possess in common certain organs for the purpose of speech in all its diverse forms; but, though alike in kind, they differ with different individuals, not only in their degrees of strength and flexibility, but in the peculiar character of their tone-qualities. Thus each individual is possessed of a voice by which he is distinguished from other human beings as much as by the personal identities of feature, form, etc., — certain expressive characteristics distinguishing the one from the many. As the mechanical appliances employed to develop muscular power, and to secure grace of action in the limbs and easy carriage of the body, improve and develop the physique of the gymnast without rendering less distinct his physical personality, so does proper vocal culture enlarge the powers and refine the qualities of the voice of the student, and yet, at the same time, does not alter its identity as an individual expression of a distinct personality. Under training, therefore, properly begun and carried to its results, there is no danger of creating an artificial mode of expression, nor of imparting to the student a mechanical style of utterance,— both of which objectionable features, however, do so often mar the premeditated forms of spoken language where the student has not worked with nature,— the only method of true art,— or rather, through nature back to accomplished art. When these facts are accepted and properly reflected upon, the necessity will be apparent for such a training of the voice as will enable the reader or speaker to distinctly and effectively mark the differing states of mind, so as to make the hearer fully sensible of the changes from one state to another, and of the special characteristics of each as they pass before him in the panorama of vocal expression.

There is no one of the faculties with which the Creator has endowed humanity which is subject to such extremes in its development as the faculty of speech. In singing, the most rigid compliance with formulas established on fixed principles is required of the learner, together with an almost slavish exactitude in practice and an unlimited degree of patient labor. While, in the cultivation of the voice for the purposes of expressive utterance in speech, how much is left to the natural *instincts* alone! Indeed, special cultivation of the vocal organs for reading and speech may be regarded as the rare exception, and not the general rule.

The vocal organs in speech are exercised to a certain extent by daily practice, and in proportion as the ear becomes cultivated or sensitive to sound-impressions, and the taste refined, we speak plainly and agreeably. But the daily use of the voice employs but a limited range of its powers, and hence it will be obvious that when a person wishes to exercise or exhibit the power and variety necessary in almost any varied composition, he finds himself at a loss for that scope and control of voice necessary to meet all the demands of the case. Let us run through the gamut of requirements in reading and speaking: To enliven the social circle by a pleasant and animated rendering of some favorite author; to read aloud in a public assembly any article or address devoted to an earnest and forcible exposition of some popular theme; to read the impressive, eloquent, and sometimes impassioned essays of the pulpit; the harangues of the bar, the senate, or the rostrum; to give utterance to the brilliant fancies and burning thoughts of the poet and dramatist upon the platform or the stage. All these oral presentations demand of the reader a more extended vocal ability than is furnished by the ordinary conversational use of the voice, or by its only occasional bursts of emotion or passion. The more important and impressive effects of artistic public delivery especially require for their cultivation a more positive and energized exercise of the constituent members of the voice-making power. Says Boutain, an able writer on this subject: "The kind of voice adapted to the exercise of public speaking is not the voice of ordinary conversation; it is a larger utterance."

What shall I say, then, of the necessities of vocal culture and the requisites of refined and regulated taste and judgment? How shall I describe the rich store of expressive means which should be, above all, at the command of the public speaker; the clergyman depicting the terrors of the final judgment or the unutterable love of the Creator; the orator denouncing the public enemy; the lawyer pleading for the triumph of justice; or the actor, inspired by language of a Shakespeare, swelling with the grandeur and power of kings, or sighing in the tender tones of the lover? These are situations, indeed, in which the ordinary instincts of the voice will not serve, in their uncultivated and merely impulsive efforts, to impart the soul of thought and passion to the language.

Now, if expressive and intelligent vocal agencies are employed by nature to give effect to her myriad colored pictures of thought and feeling, will not the man who observes and studies these agencies, for the purpose of bringing them within the control of his will for imitative purposes, as well as for the purpose of developing his vocal powers,— will not such a man possess, in reading, a vast advantage over one who has only the power to exhibit to his hearers the tones of mere conversational habit, and *that* enfeebled still more by the absence of the exciting impulse of spontaneous feeling? The latter will seldom be able to attain to any thing beyond a shadow of earnestness or a semblance of feeling, and hence will fall short of the ability to create in his hearers a sympathetic realization of his intended effects. His conception of the author may be perfect, but the mechanism of execution not being at his command, these conceptions can not be realized. He will only misinterpret himself through the distracting effects of untrained effort. Just in the same way, the fluent and eloquent talker or speaker who is unaccustomed to express himself in writing will, when he attempts to give his thoughts expression in this form, lose the fervor and glow of his inspiration, and become stiff and mannered in his style. How often do we see an accomplished student or writer who is called upon, professionally or otherwise, to stand before his fellow-men to impart to them the thoughts and feelings that have burned in his own mind and heart with an almost inspired fervor, deliver them in such a deformed condition that they are utterly lifeless, and fail to convey one spark of that which animated him! And this simply because he has never been trained in the mechanism of delivery, so to speak, by which the powers of natural utterance are voluntarily exercised and artistically controlled in the use of premeditated language, as he has been intellectually developed with regard to the powers of its expression in written forms. Walker, speaking of this, says:

"Reading may be considered as a species of music;—the organs of utterance are the instruments, but the mind itself is the performer;—and therefore, to pursue the similitude, though the mind may have a full conception of the sense of an author, and be able to judge nicely of the execution of others, yet, if it has not imbibed the habit of performing on its own instrument, no expression will be produced. *There is a certain mechanical dexterity to be acquired* before the beautiful conceptions we possess can be communicated to others."

It may be said of the uncultivated voice what Addison has said of the human soul,—that "it is like the marble of the quarry, which shows but a small part of its beauty until the skill of the polisher brings out the colors, makes the surface brilliant as the crystal, and discovers every ornamental cloud-spot running through." In other words, the uncultivated voice is the raw material out of which is wrought the thing of use and beauty.

But, it will be asked, is it possible for all to learn to read and speak well? Not all equally well, as in what art can we find uniform excellence? But where it is possible, for example, for a man to write a good sermon or to compose an effective argument or address, it is just as possible for such a man to effectively deliver it from memory or read it from the manuscript with all the fervor of spirit and force of feeling which enabled him to give fitting expression to the subject through the medium of his pen. For, where there is soul and mind, the vocal means to express them are always attainable. Nothing can stand in the way of such ability but a lack of perfect construction in the vocal organs or a disinclination to undertake the necessary study. A full command at will of all the various movements of the voice in their application to premeditated speech, is as attainable to the student of elocution as force and nicety of touch to the pianist, or as the quick and supple movement of the wrist in the skillful use of the rapier to the fencer. All that is necessary is that there shall be well directed and persistent labor in the discipline of the vocal organs, without which the student can not hope to bring the expressive agencies of speech within his grasp in a cultivated sense.

Discipline may not in every case win the battle, nor practice make the orator, but without them the means of victory are lessened, and the chances are against success. It may be urged that many use their voices successfully in a professional way without the training of which we speak here. This is indeed true, but they accomplish unconsciously, often through the necessities of circumstance,—as is often the case with the actor,—what he might have been taught intelligently, free from the errors that the teachings of accident must necessarily engraft. But even admitting native ability to have a large part in execution, the natural speaker, as he is called, or the man who speaks from impulse only, however great his effects when he is aroused by feeling, finds at times that he can not excite that sympathetic fervor on the part of his auditors that he desires. Here the trained speaker has the advantage, having the arm of art to lean upon when nature fails him,—that is, being familiar with all the modes of expression, and master of the methods of producing them, from an intelligent knowledge of the vocal forms corresponding to the mental states of emotion, thought, and passion, he commands his effects when he will. In order, therefore, to be able to stir the blood, to melt to love or pity, or to rouse to anger or indignation, the speaker must have at his command, not only "wit and worth and words, but action and utterance, and all the powers of speech, 'to stir men's blood.'"

In the commencement of his studies it is necessary, then, that the student of elocution *should be taught every thing* that is comprehended in a perfect utterance of language under its various modifications in speech. Articulation, intonation in all its varied forms, qualities of voice, management of pauses, etc., must all be governed by rules, or at least directed by principles.

"But Archbishop Whately—and his opinion only represents that of a large class—is sure that if a person is taught to read on what he calls 'the artificial system,' he will be constantly thinking of the manner rather than the matter; and will consequently fail to give satisfaction to his hearers. But why does he think so? He has taken great pains to instruct his hearers in the principles of logic and rhetoric. Would not the same objection lie against either of these branches of knowledge? But, he would answer, the student is to become so imbued with the principles of these arts that he applies the rules without really thinking of them at the time, and yet he could not violate them without being at once conscious of the fact."—*Gummere.*

Why should not the same apply to the principles and rules of elocution? Is it reasonable that in this department of education alone all logical deductions should be set aside? It would, of course, be absurd, as I have acknowledged, to deny the existence of superior ability and great natural gifts in the case of some particularly favored individuals, in this as in other arts; but it is equally absurd to deny in this art to the mass of students that which is granted them in every other; namely, the means to double their "one talent," if such it be, or of their five to make ten. I certainly admit that while the rule is present to the mind, the student will be awkward and confused, and the constant fear of mistake will make him more constrained and irresolute than if he were to give way to his habitual manner, for every thing executed by the line and measure of prescribed rules is at first formal, severe, and stiff. But use is second nature. The awkwardness wears off in time, and the proper execution becomes free and natural to him; then it is the mere rule is forgotten, while the principle which underlies it becomes, as it were, fused into the very nature of the artist, for artist he is when arriving at results through such intelligent discipline. The beauty and force thus acquired of accomplished elocution obliterates all the stilted stiffness and measured movements that are to be observed in the processes of discipline and practice.

"*In all art it is necessary to know what is to be done and what means are to be thoughtfully employed to do it well;* to practice its rules, at first, perhaps, awkwardly, in closely and slowly thinking of their application, and thus, by frequent repetition, to enable the act to so far wean itself from the directive thought as to become an *efficacious habit;* and finally to use a full knowledge of the art with almost the unconscious power of what we have metaphorically-called a scientific instinct. The purely acquired human art of swimming, unassisted by instinct, though learned with tedious effort, directed by earnest thought, and only mastered at last by careful attention to every imitative and embarrassing motion, is afterwards, from that attention fading into habit, successfully employed in danger with the thought only of the shore to be reached and the life to be saved."--*Rush.*

The nicety of execution in the initiatory steps of the dancing school leads to the freedom and grace of movement which constitute the poetry of motion; so do the exact and formal elementary exercises of elocutionary training lead to that full command over the powers of the voice which enables the speaker or reader to give constant variety, force, and beauty to expressive language, with perfect readiness and ease. The student of elocution will be no more subjected to the consideration of rules, as rules, after he has mastered their principles and applied them practically to the purposes of speech, than the student of rhetoric or grammar is compelled to have the mere form of his early lessons in his mind's eye, by which to arrange his words or construct his sentences, when he comes to employ language in a practical way. Who does not remember the struggle through which the mind and memory were compelled to pass in order to accomplish the tasks imposed by these studies? And who has not, in his after life, had occasion to wonder at the fact of being so entirely independent of an exactly realizing sense of the mere forms and technical character of his school lessons, in the ease with which he indites a letter or other literary composition, or gives correct oral expression to his thoughts? Is it not plain, then, that our present ability to deal with written language seemingly at the promptings of present instinct and impulse is mainly owing to what we formerly considered the drudgery of the schools, the rules and discipline of which have come to almost imperceptibly perform their functions in compliance with our demands, like the works of the clock, which are hidden from the eye, while the movements of the hands are distinctly marking the flight of time.

So it is with the accomplished painter, who, while making his canvas quick with life, has no occasion to cool the fervor of his enthusiasm in his final execution by stopping to consult elementary principles of the schools. These have been mastered and absorbed by his mind; they have become part, as it were, of his very self, and exercise themselves almost unconsciously in his work, holding him within the limits of truth, propriety, and good taste, but never restricting either his individuality or his genius. These acquired principles, on the contrary, furnish the means through which his ability or genius is to develop itself. The practical details of their application form, as it were, the scaffolding by which he is enabled to advance, stage by stage, to the completion of his structure of perfected art, and which, no longer needed, drops down, leaving no trace of its original unsightliness. Freed from the hampering effects of mere mechanical incapacity, natural ability is enabled to soar into the ideal regions of its own conception. The beholder who gazes upon the works of a true artist, while he enjoys the consummate beauty of the art as expressed in the creation before him, is secure from the obtrusion of any visible appearance of the mechanism by which the skillful master was enabled to arrive at such an exhibition of beauty and truth. Indeed, the artist himself may, in time, even forget these practical details by which his creation was wrought to perfection; but still from these it grew, and, without them, could never have expressed the same result.

In the same way, in elocution, precision and disciplined routine in the *modes of practice*, while the youth is under the eye and direction of the master, become the self-imposed restrictions of the graduated student. The mechanism of execution once perfectly under control, the higher powers of the imagination and the superior intelligence are enabled to work untrammeled, and thus to develop the greatest possibilities of native talent. "All art," says Goethe, "must be preceded by a certain mechanical expertness." This once acquired, freedom of touch and breadth of effect when giving scope to the imagination, and tangible forms to the conceptions of the mind, in obedience to the creative will, are alike the privilege of the painter, the writer, and the speaker.

The individual mode of expression peculiar to each person will, of course, depend, in elocution as in the other fine arts, upon his perceptions and imagination. Each will see and feel, with regard to any object of perception or emotion, according to the nature of his own mind and characteristics; and each individual will therefore have a manner and style peculiar to himself, although, in the main, the style of all persons must be original only within the limitations of artistic truth and taste. In other words, the speaker or reader will always be able to mark his identity in the execution, and exhibit degrees of power and excellence, such as are apparent in all works of art as produced by the many students of the same master and the master himself. For, where cultivated taste and disciplined execution are brought to bear on elocution, they carry with them the capability to produce a variety of effects, while ignorance and the want of skill, on the other hand, narrows reading and oratory down to one mode of presentation. For example, a dozen different orators or readers may deliver the same speech or read the same selection,—and do it well,—in as many different ways, their vocal expression being governed in common only by certain laws of vocal effects, which separate the good from the bad, or the correct from the incorrect; or, the same individual may be able to express the same matter well in a variety of different ways, for the disciplined and intelligent student has a choice of methods, while he who depends upon his natural capabilities alone is too often at a loss to distinguish the available from the unavailable, and hence to express himself in all cases as he would.

Chapter IV.

Art not Opposed to Nature.

There is no doubt that, owing to the fact I have before suggested,—namely, that reading and speaking have not received the recognition due so noble an art,—imperfect results from imperfect means, or incomplete efforts to treat elocution as an art, have been looked upon as conclusive evidence that readers, like poets, are born, not made,—that is, not made with success. As I once heard it expressed, "the student of elocution is too apt always to bear the marks of the chisel." Any half-completed work of art falls short of a counterpart of nature, and hence produces the objectionable effect of artificiality. A statue roughly cut from the native marble, although capable, through the patient labor of the artist, of the most exquisite grace and beauty of outline and finish, if claimed as a work of art before these effects be accomplished, would be repudiated as rude and unnatural. Thus with elocution. For where the student stops short of the full accomplishment of art, and exhibits only its mechanism, stiffness and artificiality are the inevitable result.

This, unfortunately, is too often the case, but

Art and Nature. 225

the art of elocution itself should not suffer from the misrepresentations of those of its advocates who are yet not true to it to the end. A little learning in this direction is an especially dangerous thing, for there is between the spontaneous, or natural, and artistic delineation of emotion and passion, that very delicate and even dangerous ground which is said to exist between the sublime and the ridiculous, and is to be passed over in a single step. That this step is sometimes, nay often, taken, can be no argument against the genuine means of art for arriving at the desired end of true naturalness of effect in speech.

"Art and nature are not opposites; the former is the end of the latter; the latter the means to the former. To be natural does not come by nature, but by art, and art itself is nature. Elocution, therefore, is none the less natural that it must be studied as an art, and the study of this art is not to be condemned, whatever condemnation may be due to the errors of elocutionists."—*Chambers's Encyclopædia.*

Dr. Barber, in his first publication, has the following, which is most appropriate in this connection:

"If it should be suspected that the mode of instruction deduced from the elements accompanying this essay might lead to an artificial and measured formality, it may be answered, that such a mode is founded, not in inventive art, but on practical analysis; that its direct object is to secure that *identical effect which every graceful speaker, in his happiest moments of harmony and fluency, intuitively attains;* that a strict analysis of the inspiring exertions of such moments in a Chatham or a Henry, would elicit the very rules which are to secure a successful imitation. In these opinions I am sustained by high authority.

"'In all these, I am very sensible that the utility of systematical rules has been called in question by philosophers of note; and that many plausible arguments in support of their opinion may be derived from the small number of individuals who have been regularly trained to eminence in the arts, in comparison with those who have been guided merely by untutored genius and the example of their predecessors. But, in all such instances, in which philosophical principles have failed in producing their intended effect, I will venture to assert that they have done so, either in consequence of *errors* which were accidentally blended with them, or in consequence of their possessing only *that slight and partial influence over the genius which enabled them to derange its previously acquired habits, without regulating its operations, upon a systematical plan, with steadiness and efficacy.* In all the arts of life, whether trifling or important, there is a certain degree of skill which may be obtained by our untutored powers, aided by imitation; and this skill, instead of being perfected by rules, may, by means of them, be diminished or destroyed if these rules are *partially and imperfectly apprehended, or even if they are not so familiarized to the understanding as to influence its exertions uniformly and habitually.* In the case of a musical performer who has learned his art merely by the ear, the *first* effects of systematical instruction are, I believe, always unfavorable. The effect is the same of the rules of elocution. But it does not follow from this that in either of these arts rules are useless. It only follows that, in order to unite ease and grace with correctness, and to *preserve* the felicities of original genius amidst those restraints which may give them a useful direction, it is necessary that the acquisitions of education should, by long and early habits, be rendered, in some measure, a second nature.'" (Stewart's "Elements of the Philosophy of the Human Mind," Introduction, p. 59, Part II.)—*Barber.*

The French critic, Gustave Planche, in speaking of a great English actor, gives a beautiful idea of the effect of real and perfected art:

"He did not wait until the eyes of the multitude were upon him to invent the means of moving it. He came upon the stage armed with a foreseeing power, resolved in advance upon determined gestures, upon studied intonations. The magnetic influence exercised over the actor by the two thousand faces over which he was about to reign, did not take him unawares; but with him, as with the great orators, as with Demosthenes and Mirabeau, the will resembled destiny,—it commanded, but while itself obeying a superior power."

It can not be denied that the artist who has made himself familiar, by previous study, with the readings, gestures, and perfected action of the character he is about to personate, may, under the inspiration of the moment, produce effects not resolved upon. The following, from "Oxbury's Dramatic Biography," in allusion to the great English actress, Francis Maria Kelly, may be appropriately quoted in this connection:

"Being generally called 'The Child of Nature,' many persons imagine that she always acts on the immediate impulse of the moment. This is not the fact. A perfect picture is not produced at a sketch; and, whilst we are upon this subject, we shall pause to make a few observations on what is termed 'natural acting.' The majority of persons uphold the system of impulsive acting, or, to be clearer, that school of acting where the performer settles in his mind merely the broad outline of his character, and *fills up* at night, *ad libitum*. The general failing of those who thus act from immediate impulse, is mannerism. Our natures do not vary with the character, or with the night; therefore, acting on impulse, we must eternally represent ourselves, rather than the author, till we tire by reiteration; whereas, a studied actor, having arranged in his mind what he intends doing, goes forth to the stage to represent a creature of his fancy; and though he may, in consequence, be colder in his style than the devotee of the other system, the chances are ten to one that he is more consistent, and more original. Actors from impulse are always unequal. If the excitement they receive from applause be less than usual, they will become flat and insipid in the very scenes that, on a previous evening, they rendered vigorous and inspiring; besides, in the casualties of existence, whatever has in the day operated on their feelings in real life, they will communicate, at night, to the character of the mimic scene. It is only when study degenerates into precision, that it becomes displeasing. The most finished actor may find something occur to him, during the fervor of acting, that would never have been thought of in the closet; as the general may find a maneuver present itself in the field that he did not dream of in his camp. Then, indeed, when impulse aids study, it becomes valuable."

And one of our best writers on Rush, in speaking of what constitutes a truly eloquent man, has well said:

"He will present nothing but what under the circumstances is prompted by nature; nature, not as opposed to a deliberate effort to adopt the best means to the best ends, and to do what is to be done as well as possible—*for this, though in one sense is art, is also the purest nature*—but nature as opposed to whatever is inconsistent with the idea that the man is under the dominion of genuine feeling, and bent upon taking the directest path to the accomplishment of his object. True eloquence is not like some painted window, which not only transmits the light of day, variegated and tinged with a thousand hues, but calls away attention from its proper use to the pomp and splendor of the artist's doings, but it is a *perfectly transparent medium*, transmitting light, without suggesting a thought about the medium itself."

Let it be but once acknowledged that nature does not work without specific laws of cause and effect in the production of vocal expression in speech

Art and Nature. 229

any more than she does in the production of any other natural phenomena, that these laws are understood and may be mastered, and through this means the best effects of nature be reproduced, and we have the requisites necessary for classifying elocution as a true art. And, by learning the secrets of nature through her laws, we come into possession of the key to unlock the mysteries of her ultimate perfection, the possibilities of which then lie within the reach of intelligence and will.

"Established principles are not as the barrier of a flood, which, in protecting from inroad, sometimes prevents the opportunities of further conquest, but as the guide and escort of the arts to acquisitions of wider glory."—*Rush*.

We have seen that the powers and actions of the vocal organs afford an infinity of combinations to effect all the different purposes of speech. To persuade or to command, to express pity or contempt, or irony or indignation; to terrify, to reproach, to applaud, or to condemn,— there is not one single state of the mind that can not find an expressive utterance in the tones and various modifications of the voice. These vocal phenomena, then, having been copied from their highest possible expression in nature and brought within the control of the will through the careful exercise of the organs of speech, familiarized to the mind, and brought into full sympathy with the emotional powers, will *become subservient to the demands of the brain or the heart*.

What is meant here by bringing these elements of vocal expression into full sympathy with the emotional powers (and I speak of this more explicitly because a proper understanding of it must dispel the idea that a mechanical effect must be the result of art in elocution) may be explained as follows: The natural vocal modes of expression which represent certain states of the mind being at the command of the artist to produce, will excite the mind when executed to that condition of which they are the natural result in expression. For just as the natural excitement of feeling produces certain effects in vocal expression, so these effects created by art will at once induce, through the sympathy arising from the inseparable connection between mental state and vocal sign, that state, or those states, of mind which, in spontaneous utterance, would have been their producing cause. Having command, then, at will, through art, of the various vocal signs, we have the key to that real state of mind of which they are the indication; art thus having the effect to arouse and enlist the natural feeling in her cause, and not to create merely a cold and formal result. Walker has well expressed this idea in the following passage, although the imitation of which he speaks is rather that blind imitation which does not imply an intelligent analysis of the vocal characteristics of emotion and passion:

"When the voice assumes that tone which a musician would produce in order to express certain passions or sentiments in song, the speaker, like the performer on a musical instrument, is wrought upon by the sound he creates; and, though active at the beginning, at length becomes passive by the sound of his own voice on himself. Hence it is that, though we frequently begin to read or speak without feeling any of the passion we wish to express, we often end in full possession of it, ... for, by the *imitation of the passion, we meet it, as it were, half way.*"

Le Gouvé illustrates this point in the following anecdote:

"Madam Talma relates in her memoirs that once, when she was acting in the character of Andromache, she was so deeply moved that, not only the spectators wept, but she herself. The tragedy finished, one of her admirers came to her, and, taking her by the hand, exclaimed, 'O my dear friend! It was admirable! It was Andromache herself! I am sure you imagined yourself in Epirus and the wife of Hector!'

"'I!' she replied, laughing, 'not at all!'

"'But you were really moved, for you were weeping.'

"'Yes, I was weeping, without doubt.'

"'But why? what made you weep?'

"'My voice.'

"'Your voice!'

"'Yes; it was the expression which my voice gave to the sorrows of Andromache, and not the sorrows themselves. The nervous tremor which ran through my frame was the electric thrill produced by my own accents. I was at the same time auditor and actress. I magnetized myself.'"

It is hoped that we have now come to a rational understanding of the term "natural" in its relation to the use of premeditated language, which has proved such a Will-o'-the-wisp to many seeking for the right way, and to a realization of the fact that art in speech can never be opposed to nature. Not nature viewed from the limited horizon of one undeveloped individual, but from that grand point of view which takes in all that is best and most beautiful in the wider field of human expression. A point of view from which all narrow impressions that dwarf and contract the sensibilities and confine the mind and soul within the limits of personal conceits, dogmatisms, and assertive excellence will be dissipated, and a wide view and generous recognition of nature in her broadest aspects embraced. The truth expressed in the following beautiful lines of Longfellow apply most forcibly here:

> "Art is the child of nature; yes,
> Her darling child, in whom we trace
> The features of the mother's face,
> Her aspect and her attitude;
> All her majestic loveliness
> Chastened and softened and subdued
> Into a more attractive grace,
> And with a human sense imbued.
> He is the greatest artist, then,
> Whether of pencil or of pen,
> Who follows nature. Never man,
> As artist or as artisan,
> Pursuing his own fantasies,
> Can touch the human heart or please,
> Or satisfy our nobler needs,
> As he who sets his willing feet
> In nature's footprints light and fleet,
> And follows fearless where she leads."

Chapter V.

The Advantages of Methodical Study.

THE student of elocution must master the rudiments of his art before it is possible for him to effect an artistic display of its beauties. But let us see how nearly, in the teaching of this art, the above requirement is met. One of our prominent school superintendents once told me that reading or elocution was taught in the schools as well as it could be. The scholar studied the few rules concerning pause, emphasis, and inflection to be found in the reading books, and then read or recited in accordance with those rules and listened to the suggestive criticism of the teacher. "For the rest," said he, "all depends on the taste, discrimination, and judgment of the pupil." And yet, if I had asked if music should be taught on the same principle, by trusting chiefly to the taste, discrimination, and judgment of the pupil, and to a few uncertain rules, independent of pitch and time, his reply would doubtless have been, "Oh, no; of course the pupil must be taught the elements of music before he can sing." The average pupil does not read well by nature alone, any more than he sings well by nature alone. Every musician who attempts to teach singing will begin with elementary vocalization, and so should it be with instruction in speech, for, as we have said, in order to be able to make use of the expressive graces of language, we must first gain an entire control over them by an assiduous study of their elements. All teachers who realize the truth of this carry their pupils back to the elements of articulation. But the elements of intonation in speech are either so imperfectly understood or considered of so little importance that they are generally omitted or hurried over, in order that the scholar may deal with the more important matter (so considered) of managing words in sentences, or continuous composition. So it results that the pupil of the schools may be a fair reader as far as making the sense of his author clear to the intelligence of his hearers, yet, when he comes to the matter of expressive reading, he too often finds himself unable to adapt his voice to the promptings of emotion or passion, however well the organs of speech may articulate the symbols of thought.

"It is needless to offer arguments in favor of an elementary didactic system to those who, from experience, in acquiring the sciences, have formed for themselves economical and effective plans of study. Let all others be told that one, and perhaps the only, reason why elocutionists have never employed *such a system is that they have overlooked the analytic means of inquiry into the subject of vocal expression*, and have therefore wanted both the knowledge and the nomenclature for an elementary method of instruction. There are too many proofs in science and art of the success of the rudimental method to allow us to suppose the same means

Advantages of Study.   235

would not have been adopted in elocution if they had been known to the master. . . . .

"When an attempt is made to teach an art without commencing with its simple elements, combinations of elements pass with the pupil for the elements themselves, and holding them to be almost infinite, he abandons his hopeless task. An education by the method we here recommend, reverses this disheartening duty. It reduces the seeming infinity to computable numbers, and furnishes us with an unexpected simplicity of means to produce the unbounded permutations of speech. It would be possible, even without regard to the alphabet, to teach a savage to read by directing him, word by word, to follow a master. And thus it has been proposed to teach elocution by a similar process of imitative instruction; but the attentive reader must now know with me, and others may know among themselves hereafter, that the analysis of words into their alphabetic elements, and the rudimental methods of teaching instituted thereupon, do not give more facility, in the discriminations of the eye on a written page, than the means here proposed will afford to a student of elocution who wishes to excel in all the useful and elegant purposes of speech. . . . .

"The human muscles are, at the common call of exercise, obedient to the will. Now there is scarcely a boy of physical activity or enterprise who, on seeing a circus rider, does not desire in some way to imitate him,— to catch and keep the center of gravity through the varieties of balance and motion. Yet this will not prevent failure in the first attempts, however close the natural tie between his will and his muscles may be. For, without trial, he knows imperfectly what is to be done, and, even with that knowledge, is unable, without long practice, to effect it. Thus there are many persons with both thought and passion, who have a free command of the voice on the common occasions of life, who yet utterly fail when they attempt to imitate the varied power of the habitual speaker. When the voice is prepared by elementary practice, thoughts and passions find the confirmed and pliant means ready to effect a satisfactory and elegant accomplishment of their purposes. The organs of speech are capable of a certain range of exertion, and, to fulfill all the demands of a finished elocution, they should be carried to the extent of that capability. Actors with both strong and delicate perceptions, and who earnestly express them in speech, are always approximating toward this power in the voice, and with no more than the assistance of a habitual exercise, which enlarges their instinct, do in time acquire a command over the forms and degrees of pitch and stress and time, without the actor himself being at all aware of the *how* and the *what* of his vocal attainments, or having, perhaps, one intelligent or intelligible idea of the ways, means, and effects of their application. The elementary method of instruction here proposed, being founded on the analysis of speech, at once points out to the actor what is to be desired and attained, and how every vocal purpose of thought and passion should be fulfilled.

"After all that has been said, the best contrived scheme will be of little avail without the utmost zeal and perseverance on the part of the learner. It is an impressive saying by an elegant genius of the Augustan age, who drew his maxims from the Greek tragedy, and illustrated it by his own life and fame, that 'nothing is given to mortal without indefatigable labor,' meaning that works of surpassing merit, and supposed to proceed from a peculiar endowment by Heaven, are in reality the product of hard and unremitting industry. It is pitiable to witness the hopes and conceits of ambition when unassisted by its required exertions. The art of reading well is an accomplishment that all desire to possess, many think they have already, and that few set about to acquire. These, believing their power is altogether in their 'genius,' are, after a few lessons from an elocutionist, disappointed at not becoming themselves at once masters of the art, and, with restless vanity of their belief, abandon the study for some new subject of trial and failure."—*Rush*.

There is, amongst the sayings of Confucius, one which applies most aptly in this connection: "Ambition is the spur of a great mind to great action, but it impels a weak one to absurdity, or sours it with discontent." For the great mind is one that is willing to work, the weak one only expects results without means. It is well-known that the orator celebrated above all others, Demosthenes, had, by nature, neither the voice nor the delivery which he afterwards developed to so high a state of perfection. His eloquence, which was so powerful because so seemingly natural, was, at the same time, largely the result of laborious cultivation.

From "The Arte of Rhetorick," written by Sir Thomas Wilson, in 1551, this quaint and appropriate passage is taken:

"By what means Eloquence is obtained: First, nedeful it is that he which desireth to excell in this gift of Oratorie, and longeth to prove an eloquent man, must naturally have a wit and an aptness thereunto; then must he to his boke, and learne to be well stored with knowledge, that he maie be able to minister matter for all causes necessarie. The which when he hath gotte plentifully, he must use muche exercise, both in writyng and also in speakyng. *For though he have a wit and learning together, yet shall they bothe little availe without much practice.* What maketh the Lawyer to have such utterance? Practice. What maketh the Preacher to speak so roundly? Practice. Yea, what maketh women go so fast awaie with their wordes? Marie, practice I warrant you. Therefore in all faculties, diligent practice and earnest exercise are the only thynges that make men prove excellent."

If there is much time and great application required to master the initiatory and more advanced processes of elocutionary study, it must be remembered that there is an object to be gained of incalculable importance, independent of laying the foundation for an energetic and finished style of public reading and address,— and that is the effect such study, universally pursued, must, in time, have upon the development of spoken language in all its departments of usage, and the reflex influence of such development on the general literary cultivation. In truth, no study can be of greater importance in this regard than the comparatively neglected one of oral language. The proper study of a composition necessary to give it vocal expression leads the student, of necessity, to penetrate more deeply into the intent of the author, as regards both thought and feeling, than a mere silent perusal ever can; for, by a study of the corresponding vocal means necessary to express what the written language embodies, the intelligence, imagination, and emotional nature are quickened and made to perceive a multitude of ideas and intentions that are lost in the dumb language of the printed page. This is well exemplified in the case of the true actor-student, who often arrives, through the necessity of dwelling upon and weighing every word, phrase, and sentence as a condition of giving it fitting utterance, at a much keener realization of the real value of the author's language, than any mere literary analysis of the commentators could alone supply. Indeed, pen can but imperfectly record or tongue describe the vivid revelations of meaning which at times dawn upon such a student, and the hidden beauties of the language which in consequence unfold. And, indeed, such must be the result in all careful study of language for the purpose of oral expression, whether for the stage, the platform, or the social circle. The written language, read silently, may be regarded as but a dim outline of that which it is intended to express; infused with appropriate vocal sound, it stands out as an illuminated picture, in all the beautiful effects of tint and color, light and shade. For it is only by a skillful use of the constituent elements of vocal sound that we are enabled to give full expression to the whole world of thought in all its myriad forms, or to reveal the inmost life of feeling and passion in all its tenderest and finest processes. Legouvé says:

"One of the greatest advantages of reading aloud is precisely to bring to light numbers of delicate shades of meaning sometimes not recognized even by the artist who placed them there. For this reason this art of reading aloud might become a powerful instrument of education. It is as often an excellent professor of literature as a great master of elocution. . . . . The best means of comprehending the *ensemble* of a composition is to read it aloud."

All who have made the matter a subject of study and practical application or experiment have realized this same mutual dependence of the one form of language upon the other. Thus Walker:

"Pronunciation (delivery) and composition mutually throw light on each other. They are counterparts of one operation of the human mind; namely, that of conveying the ideas and feelings of one man to another with force, precision, and harmony."

A more general and correct study of oral expression could not fail, therefore, to contribute to a greater appreciation of the powers and beauties of the written language, and hence to a generally increased love of the best in literature.

In view of these considerations what a foremost rank should the study of spoken language take in the education of a people. It was beyond question the great perfection to which the Greeks brought their spoken language, with the attendant developing and refining influences, that gave them the title to distinction as a type of the highest culture on record; and I feel assured the time will come with us when the condition of our spoken language will be one of the strongest indications of the general intellectual, æsthetic, and even moral standard of our people.

It must be remembered, in this connection, that all culture for reading should not be alone for public or dramatic purposes, nor should all artistic speaking imply declamation or oratory. In other words, dramatic effect and declamation in language must by no means be regarded as the sole ends of elocutionary study. There is a large intermediate territory lying between the flippancy, inaccuracy, and vocal imperfection of every-day conversation and the more formal matter of public reading or address, which comes as legitimately within the province of a true elocution as the latter, and is of as much, if not more, *general* importance. I mention this point particularly, because there is a certain danger that a desire for display and showy effect alone will cause vocal culture and artistic

Advantages of Study. 241

reading, as an elegant social or domestic accomplishment, to be too largely overlooked. But the true art of elocution is more catholic in its scope and spirit, laying the broad foundations in an intelligent and disciplined study of spoken language upon which any variety or degree of effect in utterance may be built, as exigency or propriety in the circumstances or conditions may demand. Weiss says:

> "Not only does the profession of the singer and actor require special efforts of the voice, but there are other callings in life, not immediately devoted to art, that make no less claim on vocal capacity, and often we find those engaged in such calling are, as regards voice, incapacitated to fulfill their demands. To such the question is whether it is possible to develop apparently limited vocal capacities to greater power or duration without danger of injurious reaction."

With regard to the art and science of elocution, as they exist, although we claim much for both, we do not wish to be understood as claiming perfection for either. Many are the works of human effort which, to begin and follow to perfection is rarely granted to one, or, indeed, many generations; so it is and must be with elocution. But where perfection in its highest sense is not immediately attainable, we must rest content with approximate results, always working onward, however, to a supposable consummation, and never permitting the ideal to be reduced to a lower standard in order to bring it within the reach of easier attainment. Thus, an intelligent faith and practiced ability, directed by the light of principles already understood, must eventually, though gradually, work out a final result which will place the study and practice of speech, both private and public, upon solid foundations.

When the various nationalities are fused in the alembic of American unity, when the great heart of the continent shall pulsate with blood whose vitality shall quicken a race "native and to the manner born," of one family and of one tongue, then should the utmost possibilities of the spoken language of so great a people be fully developed. I do not doubt that this result will finally be reached, but it can only come through the intelligent and disciplined study of the uttered forms of our speech being made an essential feature of the national education.

"Language being the great instrument of elocution, if it be not of a good sound and large compass, will never suffer that art to give much delight, nor consequently to make any great progress. But though a nation should be in possession of an instrument, in its construction perfectly fitted to show all the force of harmony; if they never inquire into its powers, nor try what compass it has; if they take no pains to put it in tune; if they learn not the rules of music, nor are acquainted with the notes, they will not be in a much better situation than those who are confined to the poorest. Some, indeed, may learn a few by ear, but the generality will produce nothing but discord, like those who touch the keys of an harpsichord at random."—*Sheridan*.

Again, I would not be understood to claim that the cultivation of the voice, and the system of study here proposed can produce eloquence. A soul, intellect, appreciation,—the essential powers of a speaker or reader,—are gifts of nature that can not be created by any methods; but that they can be cultivated and aroused to life and action, in many cases when they are but dimly recognized by their possessors, I do most certainly believe; and I am convinced that "futurity will probably show that some such system alone can direct, enlarge, and perfect them."

Educated talent gives power to the speaker by increasing his confidence and faith that he can accomplish that which he has undertaken, with credit to himself, and with advantage to the cause in which he labors.

Finally, and above all, the study of elocution must be a labor of love. Daniel Webster, in drawing the line between what is and what is not eloquence, said, most justly, that the schools give the student — or should — the weapon of the orator, keen, true, and capable of the result desired, but that the strength of arm is needed to make it trenchant, and, more than that, the love is necessary to complete the force by which the blow is dealt. Although it is true that in our studies we must invoke the powers of the brain to define and direct the methods and forms of practice and discipline in accordance with the principles which underlie the art, still it is the love of the art which quickens the imagination and emotional nature of the student and blends the warmth and fervor of enthusiasm with the colder promptings of intellectual conception. Principles thus mastered and employed give a soul to what would otherwise be a cold and formal, however correct, delivery.

This love of what is beautiful and eloquent in speech is, without doubt, inherent in our race, and in this fact lies the earnest of the result we have foreshadowed for the art of spoken language; for in this, as in all things, —

> "It is the heart and not the brain
> That to the highest doth attain;
> And he that followeth love's behest
> Far exceedeth all the rest."

Appendix.

Rythmus.—Barber's and Hill's Essay.

Chapter I.

The Principles of Rhythmus.

There is a disposition on the part of some of our modern elocutionists to establish a system of reading poetry by printing verse in the form of prose,—obliterating the usual graphic distinctions employed to mark the blank verse line, the rhymed couplet, the quatrain, etc.

The apparent object of this arrangement of the text of poetry is to divest the latter of any appearance of recurring forms in the measured lines or their terminal syllables, by which the voice may be led, through the eye, to that offensive uniformity or sing-song repetition of sounds, exemplified in the child's reading of nursery rhymes.

There is great danger, however, of such an arrangement of the text inducing the opposite error of the familiar or colloquial style of reading poetry, by which a presentation of the mere grammatical sense of the language is made the primary object of delivery, and the emotion or sentiment left to take care of itself.

While I admit that the sing-song manner of reading verse is too prevalent, and much to be deprecated, still I wish to call attention to the fact that there is a better and surer means of avoiding this evil than that of knocking our poetic forms into *pi*, as the printer has it, and (to continue the figure) setting them up again in the prosaic forms of a daily advertisement.

There is a golden mean to be attained, in the reading of poetry, between the "ti-tum-ti" style and the familiar manner appropriate to commonplace subjects. This I believe to exist in a correct understanding and application of the important principle of *rhythmus* in our language, first demonstrated by Sir Joshua Steele, and developed by later writers (chief amongst whom was Dr. Barber) into a practical working system.

An understanding of the subject as explained by these writers will show the student that, while rhythm is an ornament to oral language, it is also an essential, based upon a law which lies deep in the nature of the vocal organism, and which governs its correct and healthful action in utterance. It will also show him that the correct observance of a rhythmic movement does not imply that the voice shall strictly follow the mere mechanism of verse, although necessarily marking the latter sufficiently to preserve the effect arising from poetic numbers.

Moreover, he will learn that syllabic measure, or metrical progression in speech, is not confined to verse alone, but exists as well in all well constructed prose.

It may be said that, in a certain sense, there is prose in poetry and poetry in prose, and the true art of the reader will enable him to so deal with both as to render poetry independent of the mere tyranny of meter, without robbing it positively of measured forms, and to give to prose a proper degree of rhythmic latitude.

The end proposed, by a happy combination of the art of the reader and the poet, is not only to reach the understanding, but to appeal beyond to the soul through the fancy and the imagination.

The ear that is not educated to an appreciation of measured sounds in their relations to the utterance of the language of poetic fervor or exaltation, will never enable the reader to attain to this consummate power.

If, then, in the course of study by which we educate our youth to an effective exercise of their vocal powers, the principles of meter and rhythm be ignored, not only must the organs of voice suffer in consequence, but the emotional and imaginative nature will be deprived of one of its most effective means of expression in language.

Desiring to give place in this volume to Dr. Barber's valuable essay on rhythmus, and some scored examples to illustrate the principles of measure in speech, I offer the following outline, containing briefly the substance of his explanation of the subject, which will be necessary to the reader to apprehend the value and application of the essay and examples in question.

All oral language, whether consisting of prose or poetry, if correctly delivered, is divided into metrical cadences or measures, each of which, as in music, ought to occupy the same length of time in the utterance.

A cadence, or measure in speech, consists of a heavy or accented portion of sound, followed by one or more light or unaccented portions.

This succession of heavy and light, or of accented and unaccented sounds, is dependent upon a law belonging to the primary organ of voice, by which that organ is inevitably subjected to the alternate action and reaction of pulsation and remission, in sympathy with the lungs and heart.

A measure or cadence, then, may be said to have two elementary portions,— a heavy and a light. Steele designated these portions of the cadence by the term *poise*,— heavy poise and light poise, or *thesis* and *arsis*. By heavy poise was meant that property of a syllable which has acquired for it the term *accented*, and by light poise, that which, as contradistinguished from the other, has been called *unaccented*. The terms accented and unaccented, for the sake of simplifying the treatment of the subject, will be substituted, therefore, for the term *poise;* and for the same reason the word measure will be used in preference to cadence.*

The accented portion of a measure is marked to the eye thus △, and the unaccented thus ∴.

The word temper exhibits a perfect measure.
△ ∴

---

* This is not only to simplify terms by using but one term for the same thing, but to avoid the use of *cadence* in more than one sense, as this term will be employed hereafter exclusively to designate the melodic close of a sentence.

The Principles of Rhythmus. 251

The difference between a perfect *measure* and a perfect *metrical foot*, consists in the following:

A metrical foot is composed of one syllable, or any number of syllables, not exceeding five, *occupying the duration of a measure*.

Thus the word temper exhibits a perfect metrical foot, the accented portion of the measure being on the first syllable, and the unaccented on the second.

In the word temperance, we have a metrical foot of three syllables, occupying the same measure of time as the preceding, the unaccented portion of the measure being divided into two short syllables. The light or unaccented portion of the measure may be similarly broken up or articulated into three and even four syllables in rapid utterance; as, spir-it-u-al, spir-it-u-al-ly, beau-ti-ful-ly.

In such cases the metrical foot is different in form, but the measure remains the same.

Two heavy or accented sounds can never be uttered in immediate succession, like the heavy and the light sounds,—for the same reason that the hand, having closed by a contraction of the muscles, can not be closed again until it has been intermediately opened. Thus the word *baker* may be uttered with one effort of the voice, the first syllable being produced by the pulsative, and the second by the remiss, action of the larynx, alternating with each other as accented and unaccented sounds.

But the words *bake*, *bake*, can not be uttered in immediate succession. Each word being on the pulsative, there will be a perceptible hiatus or pause between them, for if the light portion of a measure does not follow the pulsative effort of the larynx, the remission must take place in pause or silence.

In this case the time of such remission will measure the same as that which would be occupied in the utterance of the light part of the measure. Thus:

"My hopes, fears, joys, pains, all centre in you,"

will occupy exactly the same time in the utterance as

"My hopes and fears and joys and pains all centre in you."

Heavy and light sounds in immediate succession constitute the base of such words as

fan-cy, pict-ure, tem-per, etc.;

light and heavy sounds, such words as

ab-hor, de-test, a-void, etc.

Monosyllables constituting nouns and verbs, not merely auxiliary, are almost always affected to the heavy or accented function of the voice, and particles to the light or unaccented,—thus:

Man, boy, beast, bid, break, hill; of, to, he, it, from.

Certain syllables are affected, either to the accented or unaccented portion of the measure, ac-

The Principles of Rhythmus.

cording to the syllables with which they are associated, or according to their relative importance in the sentence,— thus:

   let, let; will, will; can, can.

This is the case of all auxiliaries, expletives, and monosyllables of intermediate importance:

  Let him go where'er he will, man shall still be man.

A bar (|) is a technical invention used to separate the successive measures of speech to the eye, and is here employed as in music, the time of all the bars being equal.

An imperfect metrical foot is one in which either the accented or the unaccented portion of the measure is wanting. In such cases the time of the bar is completed by a corresponding rest or pause, marked thus ⌇, as in the line following:

 'Twas at the | roy-al | feast | ⌇ for | Per-sia | won. ⌇ |

Here "feast" forms an imperfect foot representing only the accented portion of the measure; and "for," an imperfect measure in which this order is reversed.

A single syllable may constitute an entire measure if it be extended in time, in which case the pulsative and remiss action takes place on its first and latter part, the *first part* being perceptibly heavier, and the latter part lighter. Syllables such as

    hail, star, joy,

admit of a pulsation and remission as palpably as though they consisted of two syllables.

Such syllables may be pronounced so as to constitute a part or a full measure, at the option of the speaker. In the latter case, the syllable comprises an emphatic foot,—thus:

Hail, | ho - ly | Light! ⁊ |

A measure may be in common or triple time, according to the character of the foot.

A metrical foot of two syllables constitutes a measure of common time; as,

Nat-ure's | change-ful | form. |

A measure of triple time is composed of three syllables:

The | mur-mur-ing | stream-let winds |
Clear thro' the | vale.

When either of these feet predominate in verse it is said to be in *common* or *triple time*.

These are considered the most perfect feet. Next comes the emphatic foot or measure of a single syllable, already described.

The third form is the foot of four syllables, constituting the accelerated measure, the syllables of which are uttered with more than ordinary quickness, or, more technically, with very short quantity; for since every bar occupies the same space, it must be evident that the pronunciation must be accelerated according to the number of syllables.

The following are examples of this kind of metrical foot:

Cit-i-zens of | Lon-don. |

To | mo-men-ta-ry | con-scious-ness a- | woke.

He had a | fever | when he was in | Spain.

The foot of five syllables is called a base foot, and is only employed in the measures of familiar prose; and even there it exists rather as a license of carelessness in the speaker, as in the following:

If the | soul | ❤ be happily dis- | posed ❤ | every thing be-comes | ca-pa-ble of af- | ford-ing en-ter- | tain-ment. |

Such a measure necessitates extreme acceleration or rapidity in its utterance, and would, therefore, in a more dignified reading, be broken up into two measures,—thus:

| Capable | ❤ of af | fording. |

We never find in the verse of Shakespeare or Milton a measure of more than four syllables.

From the preceding it will be seen that the quantities perpetually vary in speech, as in music,— that is, that while each entire bar in a succession measures the same in time, the quotional parts of these bars will constantly vary as to time.

In a succession of measures, beside the slight pauses arising from the rests of the imperfect measure, the time of a whole bar, or of several bars, may pass in silence when the longer pauses of discourse require such continued suspension of the voice. Such pauses separate language into clausular divisions.

The "*rests*" of imperfect measures, together with the measures of complete silence, permit a constant supply of breath to the speaker without any interference with the natural flow of continued utterance.

The time or rate of utterance may be either rapid or slow, but in all cases it is susceptible of measured progressions in accordance with the principles I have endeavored to explain.

The rhythmus of speech consists in an arrangement of measures or metrical feet in clauses more or less distinguishable by the ear, and of more or less obvious proportion in their periods and responses.

If a discourse or paragraph were composed or delivered without such clausular divisions and responses, though it were ever so perfect in its metre, it would have no *rhythmus*.

Verse is composed of a regular succession of metrical feet or similarly constructed measures, so divided by pauses into proportioned parts or clauses, as to present, at certain intervals, sensible responses to the ear.

Prose is composed of all sorts of measures, arranged without attention to obvious rule, and divided into clausular divisions that have no obvious proportion, and present no responses to the ear at any determined intervals.

The broad distinction, then, between prose and verse consists in the more regular sequence of accent, quantity, and pause in the latter than in the former.

The Principles of Rhythmus. 257

But in their respective attempts at rhythmic excellence, they seem to approach each other in a compromise which adds to the regularity of one and diminishes that of the other. Thus the best poetic rhythmus is that which admits occasional deviations from the current of similar metrical successions, so ordered that they may not continue long enough to destroy the general character of regularity, whilst the most skillfully arranged prose is constantly showing the beginning of a regular metrical arrangement, which loses itself in a new series of measures before the ear has time to become impressed with any determinate order.

The beauty of poetry, then, may be said to consist in such a nice adjustment of the several kinds of measures and the various rests or pauses, as will produce an agreeable rhythmus without interfering with the regular mechanism of the verse.

The following lines will afford instances of agreeable rhythmus in use:

Arms and the | man, I | sing | ♩ ♩ | who ♩ | forced by | fate. |

Hail, | holy | Light! ♩ | offspring of | heaven | first | born. |

Rocks, ♩ | caves, ♩ | lakes, ♩ | fens, ♩ | bogs, ♩ | dens, and | shades of | death. |

♩ A | u-ni-verse of | death | ♩ which | God by | curse | ♩ Cre | ated | evil, | ♩ for | evil | only | good ♩ |

From a mistaken idea as to the nature of quantity in our language, but little attention has, as yet, been paid, in the study of reading, to the rhythm of prose; yet numberless beautiful passages from the writings of our best authors attest their appreciation of the effects of this symmetrical arrangement of time, accent, and pause. The following passage from Dickens, whose writings abound in similar instances, will furnish an example of the charm of rhythmic prose:

Dear, | gentle, | patient, | noble | Nell | ᵕ was | dead. | ᵕ ᵕ |
ᵕ Her | little | bird, | ᵕ a | poor ᵕ | slight ᵕ | thing, | ᵕ the | pressure of a | finger would have | crushed, ᵕ | ᵕ was | stirring | nimbly | ᵕ in its | cage, | ᵕ and the | strong | heart | ᵕ of its | child- mistress | ᵕ was | still | ᵕ and | motionless | ᵕ for | ever. |

Language, ever obedient to those subtle laws by which the mind is directed in its tendencies, and made, as it were, involuntarily to choose certain modes of giving expression to its emotions, becomes naturally rhythmical in proportion to the dignity and elevation of the thoughts which seek utterance.

The ancients, with whom speech was an esthetic art, laid much stress upon the beauty and dignity of rhythm in language, and they considered that there could be no grace or excellence of style without a well ordered arrangement of accentual force, quantity, and pause. Quintilian wrote copiously on the subject; so did Dionysius of Halicarnassus. The latter speaks of rhythmus as "supporting or sustaining the voice;" which it does by preserving it from that careless and imperfect utterance in which the words stumble and run against each other, as it were, in such a manner as to arrest the even step of language, and thwart the expectation of both the ear and the mind.

An important fact to be pointed out in reading according to the division of language by musical time, as here explained, is that, in order to produce harmonious succession, *the voice must always move perceptibly from the accented or heavy to the light or unaccented syllable, and never from the light to the heavy.* Such a progress is essential to the facility, force, and harmony of delivery in natural, continued utterance. If, therefore, a line begin, as many of our lines do, both in poetry and prose, with a light or unaccented sound, the voice must sound lightly the first syllable, and then the progress through the line or passage is from heavy to light. The imperfect bar would be marked by a rest; the same rule applies to the musical bar. Such a passage would begin with an imperfect foot, as in the following:

Ye | airy | sprites who | oft as | fancy | calls.

The physical cause of this alternation of accented and unaccented sounds in language may be demonstrated not only by anatomy, but by the united senses of vision and touch in examining the action of the living throat in the act of energetic speaking.

It is this principle, and not the mere arrangement of long and short syllables, which constitutes the natural basis of rhythmus in our language; but it must be remembered that the perfection of that rhythmus must depend upon the nice adaptation of quantities to fill out properly the physical alternation, and preserve a due proportion in the measures and clauses.

If the enunciated sounds of continued speech, together with its rests and pauses, are subjected to musical time, as here explained, the respiration will never become disturbed even by the most energetic speaking; but in proportion as speech is not accurately divided by syllabic measures, will the respiration become laborious, and the physical powers be so far ineffectually applied.

The division of language, moreover, by musical time, is not only essential to easy, correct, and forcibly continued utterance, but the law of relation is carried still farther, for it will be found that the grammatical sense of the language always corresponds with the natural division.of its parts into accentual measures.

Chapter II.

Essay on Rhythmus. By Dr. Barber, 1823.

THE general neglect of the science of rhythmus has been peculiarly hostile to the improvement of our national elocution.

It is a question whether the principles upon which the rhythmus of our language depends have been even ascertained by grammarians and professed instructors. I think they have not. Indeed, with the exception of the works of Joshua Steele, the Rev. Mr. Odell, and Professor Thelwell, I know of no others who throw light upon the nature and character of a "cadence," or an English metrical foot.

I have been greatly indebted to an unpublished lecture by the last-named gentleman for important information in this preliminary essay. With the exception of what I have learned from these sources, I have met with nothing on the subject of the delivery of our language which has not appeared to me more or less defective in theory.

An ignorance of certain physical facts has led many writers on rhythmus to ascribe to mere election and voluntary taste what has its origin in the indispensable attributes of organic action.

It was this ignorance which prevented Mr. Roe [a contemporary writer] from perceiving the necessity of the mensuration of pauses; and which led him to deny that the crotchet and quaver rests constitute a part of the elocutionary as well as of the musical bar. He has, accordingly, amused the eye with cadences of a length which no human organs can utter, to say nothing of the confusion and deformity which his theory is calculated, in other respects, to introduce into the pronunciation of English verse. It is only by a consideration of the *necessary* pulsation in the *first* place, and of the equally necessary *alternate* remission in the second, of the primary organ of voice, that we can ascertain what constitutes a cadence, or one simple measure, and where such simple measure *begins*.

But the true nature of a cadence being once understood, we can not fail to apprehend the metrical proportion of our language; nor can we fail to perceive *how it happens* that persons who speak with harmony and facility, speak in *metrical* cadences. If our conception of a metrical foot be accurate, we shall be able to detect, moreover, the fallacy into which those have fallen who have hitherto confounded *poise* (or heavy and light) with *quantity;* or, in other words, the arbitrary adjustment of long and short syllables, in Latin scanning, with the inevitable recurrence of *thesis* and *arsis*. No person can read Latin intelligibly if he reads as he has been taught to *scan;* but, by means of a scoring which accurately marks the periodical recurrence of *thesis* and *arsis,* or of heavy and light syllables, as dependent on the action and reaction of the organ of voice, not only may every individual read as he scans, but, as the scoring will be found invariably to ascertain the grammatical sense, a deviation in actual delivery from the rule ascertained by that scoring will be found, in the precise degree of such deviation, to involve the trifold sacrifice of the sense, the harmony, and the undisturbed tenor of the respiration. If we bear in mind the precise meaning of heavy and light poise (or accented and unaccented sounds) *as distinguished from all other attributes of speech*, we shall find no difficulty in detecting the difference between the commencement of a line, or of a passage, and the commencement of a foot; we shall perceive that the speaker or the poet, equally with the musician, may *commence* with an initial or imperfect bar; and we shall be successful in our attempts to divide into their primitive metrical parts such passages as are so commenced.

Nothing is at present more fully ascertained than the mathematical proportion of the bars of music,— the general agreement of integral bars (in a given time or passage) amidst the boundless varieties of parts and fractions of which those integers are composed. But let us suppose that one of the fine passages from Handel or from Haydn were presented to us, with every part of its notation complete except the division into bars, and that we were to proceed (taking *numbers*, instead of *proportions*, as the basis of our metrical divisions) to write it into score, and were, unfortunately, to begin from an improper note,—what would, in that case, become of the proportion of the bars, as far as related to their impression upon the eye? And yet, how easy would it be to amuse a person ignorant of the science of sounds, with plausible declamation upon the want of time and measure in the music of Handel and Haydn!

These observations strictly apply to those persons who have denied a measure to English speech, and who have refined, with great apparent profundity, on the rhythmus and structure of our language. No wonder it is, that, under such circumstances, the six proportioned but varied cadences that constitute (in its simplest form) an English heroic line, should ·have been reduced, by false theory, into five disproportioned and incongruous feet; that the measure of harmonious prose should have been peremptorily denied, and that even the magnificent, the infinitely diversified, but mathematically perfect, measure of the immortal Milton (who never deviates into a discord or neglects a quantity but when he has some emotion to represent which would be marred by the incongruity of harmonic smoothness) should have been theorized into chaotic disorder and dissonance by secluded critics who have never learned to scan his verse with their *ears*, nor to utter it with their *oral organs*.

But the misfortune as regards the practical ends of delivery is, that false theory has led to bad habits of utterance. It is as *practicable* (however opposed to nature and instinct) to present inverted cadences or measures to the ear as to the eye; that is, measures in which the voice proceeds from light to heavy, instead of in the natural order from heavy to light. This error constitutes an impropriety of utterance which offends more frequently than any other the ear of taste and sensibility, in the harsh and labored elocution of artificial speakers. Its effects are perceptible to all hearers. The detection of its cause lies deep in the first principles of the science of speech.

The *indication* of a division or mode of progress from heavy to light, from the *accented* to the *unaccented* syllables, instead of the reverse of this, is in the natural organic action of the speaker. Its result is force and harmony. This *instinctive* progress from heavy to light, as distinguishable from that of from light to heavy, it is most essential to comprehend and *feel*. The metrical principle, manifested by the *first* of these movements, applies, not only to human speech, but to the vocal efforts, however limited and imperfect, of all the tribes of voice.*

I am aware that it is extremely difficult to render the subject fully comprehensible without the aid of patient and repeated oral demonstration, or to put persons in possession of a practical rule of scoring by which those axioms may be habitually applied — first in the reading lesson, and afterwards in spontaneous delivery. By means of such a scoring, however, they are susceptible both of easy comprehension and application; and, by

---

* With the exception of the duck, which has no alternation, but measures its cadences by heavy poise *alone*, and the Guinea hen, which marks its note from *light* to *heavy*.

an attention to them, it will be found that the rhythmus of our language is one of rigid measure, and that its utterance, conformably to such measure, is compatible with a forcible and harmonious delivery; that, above all, such a delivery will never be found to necessitate any disturbance to respiration.

The truth of the foregoing remarks may be easily demonstrated. The author could safely engage to take any single period, smoothly and harmoniously uttered in spontaneous speech, to repeat it in the tones of the speaker, to beat time to it with complete regularity as he repeated it, and then to write it out into score, with all the divisions of its respective cadences; and to demonstrate the quantities of every foot and the measure of every pause by which those cadences were occupied.

Might he be permitted to add that an adherence, in spontaneous delivery and in reading, to the scoring which would in such case be instituted, is the only secret by which he has been enabled to read and speak with emphasis many hours every day, without injury to lungs highly susceptible, and a constitution by no means vigorous.

He ventures, moreover, to maintain that where there is no measure there can be neither smoothness nor harmony; for harmony in speech is the combined effect of measure, melody, and euphony. But where there is neither smoothness nor harmony there is like to be perpetual hesitation and frequent impediment. Common as these blemishes are, there remain, however, a sufficient number of good speakers of English to demonstrate that cluttering and hesitation are rather the results of *bad habits* of delivery, than of necessities in the language.

Let it be once admitted that our language is a language susceptible of musical admeasurement (and the examples by which these elements are illustrated are practical exhibitions of such admeasurement), and the student may always be directed to read as he scans and scores.

The learner, while the system is yet new to him, will necessarily be more deliberate and formal than when a due comprehension of the metrical principle is attained, and the habits of delivery incident to it are fully formed. He will have to ascend, in due gradation, from the mere abstract to the rhetorical rhythmus; that is to say, from that skeleton rhythmus which recognizes only the mere inherent qualities of the elements and syllables arranged, to *that vital and more authentic rhythmus which results from the mingled considerations of sentiment, pause, and emphasis, and which assigns to each of these its just proportions of measured quantity.* But the latter rhythmus, differing from the former only in its perfection and expressive beauty, is based on the same simple and original principle of measure, founded on the alternate, voluntary action and re-action of the glottis; and the pupil is not only to *read* his Milton and his Shakespeare as he would *scan* them, but is to *speak* as he would *scan*, whether addressing an assembly or unbending in easy pleasantry at the tea-table. Conversational rhythmus is, indeed, very different in effect from the rhythmus of oratory; but it is rhythmus still, and rhythmus dependent upon the *metrical* proportions of cadences and feet. Its proportions are more difficult of detection than those of the more stately kind; the proportions of all prose, more difficult than those of verse; and the proportions of blank verse more difficult, because more diversified, than those of our heroic couplet. But the grace of *all* utterance must nevertheless depend upon proportion. Therefore, the student, the orator, or the man of the world, who would improve — the first, the impressiveness of his instruction; the second, the energy of his declamation; and the third, the grace and harmony of his conversation, — will do wisely in cultivating his metrical perception as applicable to *all* spoken language. But he who would surmount an impediment of speech, natural or acquired, or emancipate himself from other troublesome and deforming defects of utterance, should cultivate that perception as his only redeeming principle; he should, *especially*, aim at a practical precision and harmony of cadence, which might insure their full effects to the noblest effusions of poetry and eloquence.

It is important to remark that the rhythmus of our language should first be studied through the medium of verse; because it is there that it appears in its simplest and most perfect state; and because the fixed and determinate arrangement of the syllables and cadences enable the teacher to lay down rules which assist in educating the ear; while in prose composition, it is the ear and the perception *alone* that can guide the reader in ascertaining the cadence; it being the indispensable characteristic of prose, not only that it should be perpetually varying in the length of the clauses and the recurrence of emphasis, but that it should proceed through all the practical *varieties* of cadence. In the midst of that variety, however, if smooth and flowing, it will be found susceptible of an accurate notation, and will preserve, subject to such notation, its metrical proportions.

So obvious and indisputable are the propriety and advantages of commencing the study of elocution through the medium of verse, that the author does not believe it possible to acquire the art of reading prose with expressive harmony through the medium of prose *alone;* while, on the contrary, he has never, in a single instance, known an individual attain facility in reading our best poets, without being able to read prose, at the same time, with emphasis and harmony.

Chapter III.

Selections Scored for Illustration.

By closely following the examples scored according to the previous explanations, the reader may satisfy himself how far his method of reading aloud may be in accord with the principles of rhythm, as illustrated in the application of accent, quantity, and pause to the extracts here given. The musical ear, of course, very quickly catches the rhythmic flow; where the ear is sluggish from lack of cultivation, it can soon be taught to recognize the ease with which language may be measured, and the beauty of such a measurement.

In the first attempts to follow the scorings, the effect will be necessarily mechanical, but successive repetitions will accustom the reader to pronounce the words "trippingly on the tongue,"— the voice passing smoothly from accent to accent without making the "beat" of the measure offensively apparent to the ear.

The following points should be remembered in reading the scored extracts:

Every bar, as in music, is to occupy the same time. This time is to be consumed in the pronunciation of the syllables contained in the bars, or the syllables and pauses, or the pauses alone, where the whole bar is devoted to rest.

The mark △ shows that a syllable is heavy or accented; the mark . ·. shows that a syllable is light or unaccented; the mark ⁌ indicates that a rest or pause is to be made.

A long syllable can be extended through the whole time of a bar, and may be made heavy or accented in its opening, and light at its termination; a short one can not fill a bar.

When the mark ⁌ is omitted after a *short* heavy syllable, standing alone in a bar, a pause is to be made as if it were present.

Lastly, the progress of the voice is to be distinct from the accented to the unaccented syllable, or from heavy to light, and not from light to heavy.

It will be observed that some of the exercises have the heavy (△) and light (. ·.) marks omitted. Where these marks are wanting, the position of the syllables in their relation to the bars will be sufficient indication to the reader.

The use of the exercises will convince most persons that they are deficient in rhythm in reading both prose and poetry, particularly the latter.

They mark the metre, but do not introduce either pause or time, consequently the beat becomes painful to the cultivated ear. By an exact observation and application of the laws of rhythm, reading ceases to be laborious, and the sense will be rendered perfectly clear, as far as it is dependent on the capital point of the distribution of measure.

The Hermit.

At the | close of the | day, | when the | hamlet is | still, |
And | mortals | the | sweets of for | getfulness | prove, |
When | nought but the | torrent | is | heard on the | hill, |
And | nought but the | nightingale's | song | in the | grove: |
It was | thus, | by the | cave of the | mountain a | far, |
While his | harp rung sym | phonious, | a | hermit be- | gan; |
No | more with him | self, | or with | nature at | war, |
He | thought as a | sage | tho' he | felt as a | man. |

Ah, | why | all a | bandon'd to | darkness and | woe, |
Why, | lone Philo | mela, | that | languishing | fall? |
For | spring shall re | turn, | and a | lover be | stow, |
And | sorrow | no | longer thy | bosom en | thrall, |
But if | pity in | spire thee, | re | new the sad | lay; |
Mourn, | sweetest com | plainer, | man | calls thee to | mourn; |
Oh, | soothe him | whose | pleasures, | like | thine | pass a | way; |
Full | quickly they | pass: | but they | never re | turn. |

Selections for Illustration.

Now | gliding re | mote, | ♥ on the | verge of the | sky, |
♥ The | moon half ex | tinguished, | ♥ her | crescent dis- | plays; |
♥ But | lately I | marked | ♥ when ma | jestic on | high; |
♥ She | shone, | ♥ and the | planets were | lost in the | blaze. |
Roll | on, thou fair | orb, | ♥ and with | gladness pur | sue |
♥ The | path | ♥ that con | ducts thee to | splendor a- | gain; |
♥ But | man's faded | glory | ♥ what | change shall re- | new? |
Ah, | fool! | ♥ to ex | ult in a | glory so | vain! | |

♥ 'Tis | night, | ♥ and the | landscape is | lovely no | more; |
♥ I | mourn, | ♥ but ye | woodlands I | mourn not for | you; |
♥ For | morn is ap | proaching, | ♥ your | charms to re- | store, |
♥ Per | fum'd with fresh | fragrance, | ♥ and |.glittering with | dew. |
♥ Nor | yet | ♥ for the | ravage of | winter I | mourn; |
Kind | nature | ♥ the | embryo | blossom will | save; |
♥ But | when shall | spring | visit the | mouldering | urn? |
Oh, | when shall it | dawn | ♥ on the | night of the | grave! |
 | | |

It was | thus, | by the | glare of false | science be- |
tray'd, |

That | leads to be | wilder; | and | dazzles to | blind: |
My | thoughts wont to | roam, | from | shade | onward
to | shade, | |

De | struction be | fore me, | and | sorrow be | hind, |
"Oh, | pity! | great | Father of | light," | then I | cried, | |
"Thy | creature, | who | fain would not | wander from |
thee; |

Lo! | humble in | dust, | I re | linquish my | pride: |
From | doubt and from | darkness, | thou | only canst |
free." | | |

And | darkness and | doubt | are now | flying a | way, |
No | longer I | roam in de | jection for | lorn, | |
So | breaks on the | traveler, | | faint and a | stray, |
The | bright and the | balmy ef | fulgence of | morn. |
|

See | truth, love and | mercy | in | triumph de | scending, |
And | Nature | all | glowing in | Eden's first | bloom ! |
On the | cold cheek of | death, | smiles and | roses are |
blending, |

And | beauty im | mortal | a | wakes from the | tomb. |
| |
—*Beattie.*

APOSTROPHE TO LIGHT.

Hail | holy | Light, | | offspring of | Heav'n | first | born, |
  | Or of the E | ternal | | co-e | ternal | beam, | |
May I ex | press | thee | un | blam'd? | | | Since | God |
   is | light, |
   And | never | but in | unap | proached | light |
Dwelt from e | ternity, | | dwelt | then in | thee, |
  | Bright | effluence | of | bright | essence | incre | ate. |
     | |
   Or | hears't thou | rather, | | pure e | thereal | stream. |
       |
   Whose | fountain | who shall | tell? | | Be | fore the | sun, |
   Be | fore the | Heav'ns | thou | wert, | | and at the | voice |
   Of | God | | as with a | mantle, | didst in | vest |
   The | rising | world of | waters | | dark | and | deep |
  | Won from | the | void | and | formless | infinite. |
    | |

Thee I re | visit | now | with | bolder | wing, |
   Es | cap'd the | Stygian | pool | | though | long de- | tain'd |
   In | that ob | scure so | journ | | while | in my | flight |

♪ Through | utter | ♪ and through | middle | darkness | borne, |
♪ With | other | notes | than to the Or | phean | lyre |
♪ I | sung of | chaos | ♪ and e | ternal | night, | | |
Taught by the | heavenly | Muse | ♪ to | venture | down |
♪ The | dark de | scent | | ♪ and | up to | re-as | cend |
♪ Though | hard | ♪ and | rare ; | | thee I re | visit | safe |
♪ And | feel thy | sov'reign | vital | lamp : | | ♪ but | thou |
♪ Re | visit'st | not | these | eyes, | ♪ that | roll in | vain |
♪ To | find thy | piercing | ray, | | ♪ and | find | no | dawn ; | |
♪ So | thick a | drop se | rene | ♪ hath | quench'd their | orbs | |
♪ Or | dim suf | fusion | veil'd | | | Yet not the | more |
Cease I to | wander | | where the | muses | haunt, |
Clear | spring | ♪ or | shady | grove, | ♪ or | sunny | hill, |
| Smit with the | love of | sacred | song ; | | ♪ but | chief |
Thee | Sion, | ♪ and the | flow'ry | brooks be | neath |
♪ That | wash | thy | hallow'd | feet, | ♪ and | warbling | flow, |
| Nightly | ♪ I | visit : | | ♪ nor | some | times | ♪ for | get |

Selections for Illustration. 277

Those | other | two | equal'd with | me in | fate, |
| So were | I | equal'd with | them in re | nown |
| Blind | Thamyris, | ⸿ and | blind Mæ | onides, |
⸿ And Ty | resias | ⸿ and | Phineus, | | prophets | old: |
|
Then | feed on | thoughts, | ⸿ that | voluntary | move |
⸿ Har | monious | numbers; | ⸿ as the | wakeful | bird |
Sings | darkling | ⸿ and in | shadiest | covert | hid |
| Tunes her noc | turnal | note. | | | Thus with the | year |
Seasons | ⸿ re | turn, | ⸿ but | not to | me | ⸿ re | turns |
Day | ⸿ or the | sweet ap | proach of | ev'n | ⸿ and | morn; |
|
⸿ Or | sight of | vernal | bloom, | ⸿ or | summer's | rose,
| |
⸿ Or | flocks, | ⸿ or | herds, | | ⸿ or | human | face di- | vine; | |
⸿ But | cloud | ⸿ in | stead, | ⸿ and | ever | during | dark |
⸿ Sur | rounds me, | ⸿ from the | cheerful | ways of | men |
Cut | off, | and for the | book of | knowledge | fair |
⸿ Pre | sented | ⸿ with a | uni | versal | blank |
⸿ Of | Nature's | works | | ⸿ to | me | ⸿ ex | pung'd and | raz'd | |
⸿ And | Wisdom, | ⸿ at | one | entrance, | | quite shut | out. | | |

So much the | rather | thou, | ♥ ce | lestial | Light |
Shine | inward, | | ♥ and the | mind | ♥ through | all her | powers |
♥ Ir | radiate, | | there | plant | eyes, | | all | mist from | thence |
| Purge and dis | perse, | | that I may | see | ♥ and | tell |
♥ Of | things in | visible | ♥ to | mortal | sight. | | |
—*Milton.*

ST. PAUL'S DEFENSE BEFORE KING AGRIPPA.

THEN A | grippa | said unto | Paul, | | Thou art per- | mitted to | speak for thy | self. | | | Then | Paul | stretched forth the | hand, | ♥ and | answered | ♥ for him | self. | | |
♥ I | think myself | happy, | | King A | grippa, | ♥ be- | cause I shall | answer for my | self | this | day | ♥ be | fore | thee, | touching | all the | things | ♥ where | of | ♥ I am ac- | cused | ♥ of the | Jews: | | wherefore | ♥ I be | seech thee | ♥ to | hear me | patiently. |
| | ♥ My | manner of | life | ♥ from my | youth, | | which was at the | first | ♥ a | mong mine | own | nation | ♥ at Je | rusalem, | know | all the | Jews; | | ♥ which | knew me | ♥ from the be | ginning, | if they would | testify; | ♥ that | after the | most | straitest | sect | ♥ of our re | ligion | ♥ I | lived a | Pharisee. | |
| ♥ And | now | ♥ I | stand | ♥ and am | judged | ♥ for the | hope of the | promise | made of | God | ♥ unto our | fathers: | | ♥ unto | which | promise | ♥ our | twelve | tribes, | instantly | serving | God | day and | night, | hope to | come.
| | | ♥ For | which | hope's | sake, | King A | grippa, | I am ac | cused | ♥ of the | Jews. | | | Why | should it be | thought | ♥ a | thing in | credible | ♥ with | you, | ♥ that | God | ♥ should | raise the | dead? | | | I | verily |

thought with my | self, | ❡ that I | ought to | do | many things | contrary | ❡ to the | name of | Jesus of | Nazareth. |
 | | ❡ Which | thing | ❡ I | also | did | ❡ in Je | rusalem: | ❡ and | many of the | saints | ❡ did I | shut up in | prison, | | having re | ceived au | thority | ❡ from the | chief | priests; | | ❡ and | when they were | put to | death, | ❡ I | gave | my | voice | ❡ a | gainst them. | | | ❡ And I | punished them | oft | ❡ in | every | synagogue, | ❡ and com | pelled them | ❡ to blas | pheme; | | ❡ and | being ex | ceedingly | mad a | gainst them, | ❡ I | persecuted them | even unto | strange | cities. | | | Whereupon as I | went to Da- | mascus, | | ❡ with au | thority, | ❡ and com | mission | ❡ from the | chief | priests, | ❡ at | mid | day, | O | king, | ❡ I | saw in the | way | ❡ a | light from | heaven, | ❡ a | bove the | brightness | ❡ of the | sun, | | shining | round a | bout | me, | ❡ and | them which | journeyed | with me. | | | ❡ And | when we were | all | fallen to the | earth, | ❡ I | heard a | voice | speaking unto me, | ❡ and | saying | ❡ in the | Hebrew | tongue, | | Saul, | | Saul, | why | persecutest thou | me? | | ❡ It is | hard | for thee | ❡ to | kick a | gainst the | pricks. | | | ❡ And I | said, | Who | art thou, | Lord? | | | ❡ And he | said, | ❡ I am | Jesus, | | whom thou | persecutest. | | | ❡ But | rise | ❡ and | stand upon thy | feet; | | ❡ for | I have ap | peared unto thee | ❡ for | this | purpose, | ❡ to | make thee a | minister | ❡ and a | witness | both of | these | things | which thou hast | seen, | ❡ and of | those | things | ❡ in the | which | ❡ I will ap | pear unto thee; | | ❡ de | livering thee | ❡ from the | people, | ❡ and from the | Gentiles, | ❡ unto | whom | now I | send thee; | ❡ to | open their | eyes, | ❡ and to | turn them | ❡ from | darkness | ❡ to | light, | ❡ and from the | power of | Satan | ❡ unto | God; | | ❡ that | they may re | ceive | ❡ for | giveness of | sins, | ❡ and in | heritance | ❡ a | mong | them which are | sanctified, | ❡ by | faith | ❡ that is in | nte. | | | Whereup- | on, | O | king A | grippa, | | I was | not diso | bedient | ❡ unto the | heavenly | vision: | | ❡ but | showed | first | ❡ unto | them of Da | mascus, | | ❡ and at Je | rusalem, | ❡ and through | out | all the | coasts of Ju | dea, | ❡ and | then | ❡

to the | Gentiles, | | that they should re | pent | ᛜ and | turn to | God, | ᛜ and | do | works | meet for re | pentance. | | | ᛜ For | these | causes | ᛜ the | Jews | caught me in the | temple, | | ᛜ and | went a | bout | ᛜ to | kill me. | | | Having | therefore | ᛜ ob | tained | help of | God, | ᛜ I con | tinue | ᛜ unto | this | day, | witnessing | both to | small and | great, | | saying | none | other | things | ᛜ than | those | ᛜ which the | prophets | ᛜ and | Moses | ᛜ did | say, | ᛜ should | come. | | | ᛜ That | Christ | ᛜ should | suffer, | ᛜ and that | he should be the | first | ᛜ that should | rise from the | dead, | ᛜ and should | shew | light | ᛜ unto the | people, | and | ᛜ to the | Gentiles. | | | ᛜ And as he | thus | spake for himself, | | Festus | said with a | loud | voice, | | Paul, | thou art be | side thyself; | | much | learning | ᛜ doth | make thee | mad. | | | But he | said, | ᛜ I am | not | mad, | ᛜ most | noble | Festus, | ᛜ but | speak forth the | words of | truth | ᛜ and | soberness. | | | ᛜ For the | king | knoweth of | these | things, | ᛜ be | fore | whom | also | ᛜ I | speak | freely: | | ᛜ for | I am per | suaded | ᛜ that | none of | these | things | ᛜ are | hidden from | him; | | ᛜ for | this | thing | ᛜ was | not | done in a | corner. | | | King A | grippa, | ᛜ be- | lievest thou the | prophets? | | | ᛜ I | know | ᛜ that thou be | lievest. | | | Then | ᛜ A | grippa | said unto | Paul, | Al | most | thou per | suadest | me | ᛜ to be a | Christian. | | ᛜ And | Paul | said, | ᛜ I | would to | God, | ᛜ that | not only | thou, | ᛜ but | also | all that | hear me | this | day, | ᛜ were | both | al | most, | ᛜ and | alto | gether | such as | I am, | ex | cept | these | bonds. | | | —*Acts* xxxvi., 1–29.

THE OCEAN.

Roll | on, | ᛜ thou | deep | ᛜ and | dark | blue | ocean, | |
roll! | | |
ᛜ Ten | thousand | fleets | | sweep over | thee, | ᛜ in | vain, | | |

Selections for Illustration.

Man | marks the | earth | with | ruin | | his control |

Stops with the | shore; | | upon the | watery | plain |

The | wrecks are | all | thy | deed; | | nor doth remain |

A | shadow of | man's | ravage, | | save his | own, | |

When for a | moment, | | like a | drop of | rain, |

He | sinks | into | thy | depths | with | bubbling | groan, |

With | out a | grave, | | un | knell'd, | un | coffin'd, | and un | known. | | |

The armaments, | which | thunderstrike | the | walls |

Of | rock-built | cities, | | bidding | nations | quake, |

And | monarchs | | tremble | in their | capitals, |

| The | oak le | viathans, | whose | huge | ribs | make |

Their | clay cre | ator | the vain | title | take, |

Of | lord of | thee, | and | arbiter of | war! |

These are thy | toys, | | and as the | snowy | flake, |

They | melt into thy | yeast of | waves, | which | mar |

A | like the Ar | mada's | pride, | or | spoils of | Trafalgar. | | |

Thy | shores are | empires, | | chang'd in | all | save | thee, |

A Plea for Spoken Language.

| ♩ As | syria, | | Greece, | | Rome, | | Carthage, |
| what are | they? |
♩ Thy | waters | wasted them | | while they were | free, |
| ♩ And | many a | tyrant | since: | | ♩ their | shores |
♩ o | bey |
♩ The | stranger, | slave, | ♩ or | savage; | ♩ their de | cay |
♩ Has | dried up | realms | ♩ to | deserts, | | not | so |
thou, | |
Un | changeable, | | save to thy | wild | waves | play: |
|
Time | writes | no | wrinkle | ♩ on | thine | azure | brow; |
| Such as cre | ation's | dawn | ♩ be | held, | | thou |
rollest | now. | | |
Thou | glorious | mirror, | where the Al | mighty's | form |
Glasses it | self in | tempests; | ♩ in | all | time, |
Calm | ♩ or con | vuls'd, | | ♩ in | breeze, | ♩ or | gale, |
♩ or | storm, |
| Icing the | pole, | or in the | torrid | clime |
Dark | heaving; | | boundless, | | endless, | | ♩ and
sub | lime. | |
♩ The | image of E | ternity! | | ♩ the | throne |
♩ Of the In | visible; | | even from | out thy | slime |
♩ The | monsters of the | deep | ♩ are | made: | | each |
zone |
♩ O | beys thee; | | thou | goest | forth, | dread, | fathom-
less, | ♩ a | lone. | | | —*Byron.*

Without God in the World.

The exclusion of a Supreme Being, and of a superintending providence, tends directly to the destruction of moral taste. It robs the universe of all finished and consummate excellence, even in idea. The admiration of perfect wisdom and goodness for which we are formed, and which kindles such unspeakable rapture in the soul, finding in the regions of scepticism nothing to which it corresponds, droops and languishes. In a world which presents a fair spectacle of order and beauty, of a vast family, nourished and supported by an Almighty Parent; in a world, which leads the devout mind, step by step, to the contemplation of the first fair and the first good, the sceptic is encompassed with nothing but obscurity, meanness, and disorder.

When we reflect on the manner in which the idea of Deity is formed, we must be convinced, that such an idea, intimately present to the mind, must have a most powerful effect in refining the moral taste. Composed of the richest elements, it embraces, in the character of a beneficent Parent, and Almighty Ruler, whatever is venerable in wisdom, whatever is awful in authority, whatever is touching in goodness.

Human excellence is blended with many imperfections, and seen under many limitations. It is beheld only in detached and separate portions, nor ever appears in any one character, whole and entire. So that, when, in imitation of the stoics, we wish to form out of these fragments, the notion of a perfectly wise and good man, we know it is a mere fiction of the mind, without any real being in whom it is embodied

A Plea for Spoken Language.

and | realized. | | | In the | be | lief of a | Deity, | these con | ceptions | are re | duced to re | ality: | | the | scattered | rays | of an i | deal | excellence | are con- | centrated, | | and be | cometh | real | attributes | of | that | Being, | with | whom | we | stand in the | nearest re | lation, | who | sits su | preme | at the | head of the | universe, | is | armed with | infinite | power, | and per- | vades | all | nature | with his | presence. | | |

The | efficacy of | these | sentiments | in pro | ducing | and aug | menting | a | virtuous | taste, | will in | deed | be pro | portioned | to the | vividness | with | which they are | formed, | and the | frequency | with | which they re | cur; | | yet | some | benefit | will not | fail to re | sult from them, | | even in their | lowest de | gree. | | |

The i | dea | of the Su | preme | Being | has | this pe | culiar | property; | | that | as it ad | mits of | no | sub- stitute, | so, | from the | first | moment it is im | pressed, | it is | capable | of con | tinual growth | and en- | largement. | | | God | him | self | is im | mutable: | | but | our con | ception | of his | character | is con | tin- ually | re | ceiving | fresh ac | cessions; | | is con | tin- ually | growing | more ex | tended and re | fulgent, | by | having trans | ferred upon it | new per | ceptions, | of | beauty, | and | goodness; | | by at | tracting to it | self, | as a | centre, | what | ever | bears the | impress of | dignity, | order, | or | happiness. | | | It | borrows | splendour, | from | all that is | fair, | sub | ordinates | to it | self | all that is | great, | and | sits en | throned, | on the | riches of the | universe. | | | —*Rev. Robert Hall.*

Chapter IV.

Hill's Essay.

As all things relating to the proper expression of the sentiments and passions of mankind claim a kindred relationship, the dramatic art in its highest and noblest sense is closely allied to, and, in a certain sense, inseparable from, the art oratorical. I have, therefore, thought it would be well to introduce, with slight alterations, as an addenda to the ideas presented in this volume concerning a study of the expressive attributes of spoken language, Aaron Hill's quaint essay on the nature of the human passions and their expression in voice and action.

Its contents can not fail to throw light on the psychological features of the study of elocution, containing, as they do, the analysis (and the enforcement of such analysis or the essential basis of all studies in expression) of those mental phenomena known as passions, which have their outward manifestation in vocal and physical signs,—signs by which the soul speaks, as it were, through the medium of the senses.

Hill's advice to the delineator of the passions can not fail, therefore, to furnish valuable food for reflection to the orator, reader, or speaker, of whatever class, as well as to the actor, since each must obtain from it a certain insight into the spring of his emotional nature, and a stimulus to its manifestation in outward expression,—a matter of primary necessity to every student of expressive language.

I think no more just and vivid enforcement of the necessity of "suiting the action to the word, and the word to the action," can be found outside of Shakespeare's memorable injunction "not to o'erstep the modesty of nature,"—advice which, for three hundred years, has been looked upon as the living model for all who seek, through the medium of voice and action,

"To wake the soul by tender strokes of art,
To raise the genius and to mend the heart."

AN ESSAY ON THE DRAMATIC PASSIONS, IN WHICH THEY ARE PROPERLY DEFINED AND DESCRIBED; WITH APPLICATIONS OF THE RULES PECULIAR TO EACH, AND SELECTED PASSAGES FOR PRACTICE. BY AARON HILL.*

"Weak of themselves are what we beauties call,
It is the manner which gives strength to all."—*Churchill.*

The first dramatic principle is the following:

To act a passion well, the actor must never attempt its imitation till his fancy has conceived so

---

* Aaron Hill was contemporary with Garrick. This essay was published 1779.

strong an image, or idea of it, as to move the same impressive springs within his mind which form that passion when it is undesigned and natural.

This is absolutely necessary, and the only general rule. The practice of it shall be laid down clearly; and it will be found extremely easy and delightful, both in study and execution. And the truth of its foundation that it is wholly built on nature is evident, beyond dispute, upon examining its effects in this deduction from their causes.

First, The imagination must conceive a strong idea of the passion.

Secondly, But that idea can not strongly be conceived without impressing its own form upon the muscles of the face.

Thirdly, Nor can the look be muscularly stamped, without communicating, instantly, the same impressions to the muscles of the body.

Fourthly, The muscles of the body (braced or slack, as the idea was an active or passive one), must, in their natural, and not-to-be-avoided consequence, by impelling or retarding the flow of the animal spirits, transmit their own conceived sensation to the sound of the voice and disposition of the gesture.

And this is a short abstract of the art, in its most comprehensive and reduced idea. But there must follow applications of the general rule, by particular references, for practical use.

And, first, it should be noted that there are only ten dramatic passions; that is, passions which can be distinguished by their outward marks in action; all others being relative to, and but varied degrees of the foregoing.

These are the dramatic passions: Joy, Grief, Fear, Anger, Pity, Scorn, Hatred, Jealousy, Wonder, Love.

And now, for application of the rule to each of these in its particular distinction, in which an actor will be fully prepared for the expression of either, or all, of the above passions.

APPLICATION I.—OF JOY.

Definition.—Joy is Pride possessed of Triumph.

It is a warm and conscious expansion of the heart, indulging a sense of present pleasure, and comparing it with past affliction. It can not, therefore, be expressed without vivacity in look, air, and accent. But it will be proper, for distinguishing the modes of representing this and every other passion, to consider their effect on speeches, wherein that particular passion governs, which is about to be attempted by the speaker.

And let it be the first and chief care to discover where the author has intended any change of passions. For unless the passion is first known, how is it possible it should be painted?

Joy, for instance, is the passion in the following transport of Torrismond:

"Oh, heaven! she pities me.
And pity, still, foreruns approaching love,

As lightning does the thunder. Tune your harps,
Ye angels! to that sound; and thou, my heart,
Make room—to entertain the flowing joy!"

When the actor has discovered that the passion in this place is joy, he must not, upon any account, attempt the utterance of one single word till he has first compelled his fancy to conceive an idea of joy, to suppose that he is, really, Torrismond,—that he is in love with Leonora, and has been blessed, beyond his hope, by her kind declaration in his favor.

But there is a shorter road to the same end, and it shall, in due place, be shewn him. When he believes himself possessed of such an idea of joy, that would not fail to warm a strong conception, let him not imagine the impression rightly hit till he has examined both his face and air in a looking-glass; for there only will he meet with a sincere and undeceivable test of his having strongly enough, or too slackly, adapted his fancy to the purpose before him.

If, for example, his brow appears bent or cloudy, his neck bowing and relaxed; if he sees his arm swing languid or hang motionless, and the joints of his hip, knee, and ankle not strong braced, by swelling out the sinews to their full extent;—all or any of these spiritless signs in the glass may convince him that he has too faintly conceived the impression; and, at once, to prove it to his own full satisfaction, let him, at that time, endeavor to speak out, with a voice as high raised as he pleases, he will find that, in that languid state of muscles, he can never bring it to sound joy; no, not though the sense of the words were all rapture; but in spite of the utmost possible strain upon his lungs, his tone will be too sullen or too mournful, and carry none of the music of sprightliness. But if, on the contrary, he has hit the conception exactly, he will have the pleasure, in that case, to observe that his forehead appears raised, his eye smiling and sparkling, his neck will be stretched and erect, without stiffness, as if it would add new height to his stature; his chest will be inflated, and all the joints of his body will be high-strung and braced boldly. And now, if he attempts to speak joy, all the spirit of the passion will ascend in his accents, and the very tone of his voice will seem to out-rapture the meaning.

As to the reason of all this, it is as clear as the consequence. For these are nature's own marks and impressions on the body, in cases where the passion is produced by involuntary emotions. And when natural impressions are imitated exactly by art, the effect of such art must seem natural.

But because difficulties would arise in the practice of so strong a conception, before fancy is become ductile enough to assume such impressions at will (as in the instance of joy, now before us), the actor, taking the shorter road above promised him, may help his defective idea in a moment by annexing at once the look to the idea, in the very instant while he is bracing his nerves into springiness; for so the image, the look, and the muscles, all concurring at once to the purpose, their effect will be the same as if each had succeeded another progressively.

To convince himself of the natural truth of these principles, he has nothing to do but, first, to speak the foregoing example of joy, with his look grave or idle, and his nerves eased or languid; and immediately afterwards repeat the same speech with a smile of delight in his eye, with his joints all high-braced, and his sinews extended — his own ear will become his acknowledged instructor.

APPLICATION II.—OF GRIEF.

Definition.—Grief is Disappointment void of Hope.

It is a mournful and unstruggling resignation of defense to apprehension of calamity; and, therefore, must require, to express it rightly, a sad look, careless air, and voice unraised and indolent.

For a speech, wherein this melancholy reverse of the foregoing passion is expressed to the wish of an actor, we may borrow a second time from the same Torrismond:

> "But, I have been in such a dismal place!
> Where joy ne'er enters, which the sun ne'er cheers,
> Bound in with darkness, overspread with damps,
> Where I have seen—if I could say, I saw—
> The good old king—majestic ev'n in bonds!
> And, 'midst his griefs, most venerably great!
> By a dim, winking lamp, that feebly broke
> The gloomy vapors, he lay stretch'd along,
> Upon th' unwholesome ground, his eyes cast low;
> And, ever and anon, a silent tear
> Stole down, and trickled from his aged cheek."

A speaker, who would distress his imagination into a complete assumption of the sorrow expressed in these lines, will first consider that grief, being a passion the most opposite in nature to joy, his look that was before enlivened, must now, in a moment, take a mournful and declined impression. His muscles must fall loose and be embraced into the habit of languor. And then, no sooner shall his nerves have formed themselves to this lax disposition for complying with the melancholy demand of the sentiments, than his voice also will associate its sound to the plaintive resignation of his gesture, and the result, both in air and accent, will be the most moving resemblance of a heartfelt and passionate sorrow. Whereas, let him endeavor, with all possible industry, so to sadden his voice, without a previous accommodation of his look and his sinews to the faintness of the image intended, his tone will be hard, austere, and unfeeling, and more and more remote from the true sound of distress, in exact proportion to the spring he had retained on his nerves, and the vigor that had overanimated his eye, or too ardently quickened his gesture.

APPLICATION III.—OF FEAR.

Definition.—Fear is Grief, discerning and avoiding Danger.

It is an apprehensive but unsinewed struggle betwixt caution and despair. It can not, therefore, be expressed but by a look alarmed and watchful, with a voice and air unanimated.

Take, for example of this passion, the following short speech from Clarence, in Shakespeare's Richard the Third:

> "Oh, I have passed a miserable night!
> So full of fearful dreams! of ugly sights!
> That, as I am a Christian, faithful man,
> I would not spend another such a night,
> Tho' 'twere to buy a world of happy days!
> So full of dismal terror was the time!"

Here an actor, who would impress his imagination with a natural idea of fear, will most effectually represent it by assuming the same languor in look and in muscles, that was just here described as peculiar to grief. For then, if he would strike out, in an instant, the distinction by which fear is diversified from sorrow, let him only, in place of that resigned, plaintive, passive distress that is proper to grief, add (without altering the relaxed state of his nerves) a starting, apprehensive, and listening alarm to his look, keeping his eyes widely stretched, but unfixed; his mouth still, open; his steps light and shifting,—yet, his joints unbraced, faint, nerveless. And then will his whole air express the true picture of fear, and his voice, too, sound it significantly.

But still, this caution let the actor take care to remember,—that he is not to begin to utter a single word till he has first reflected on and felt the idea, and then adapted his look, and his nerves to express it. But as soon as this pathetic sensation has strongly and fully imprinted his fancy, let him then, and not before, attempt to give the speech due utterance. So shall he always hit the right and touching sensibility of tone, and move his auditors impressingly; whereas, should he, with unfeeling volubility, hurry on from one overleaped distinction to another, without due adaptation of his look and muscles to the meaning proper to the passion, he will never speak to hearts, nor move himself nor any of his audience, beyond the simple and unanimating verbal sense, without the spirit of the writer.

Besides the reputation of a fine and pathetic speaker, and a feeler and inspirer of the passions, he will derive another benefit and grace from such a natural practice; for the time which it must necessarily take, so to conform his look and nerves to the successive changes of the passions, will *preserve his voice at every turn, by giving it due rests;* allowing *frequent* and *repeated opportunities for* a *recovery of its wasted strength, in easy and unnoted breathings.* And yet, all such beautiful and pensive pausing places will, at the same time, appear to an audience but the strong and natural attitudes of thinking, and the inward agitations of a heart that is, in truth, disturbed and shaken. Whereas, the glib, round, rolling emptiness of an unpausing insignificance in speaking (far from painting or resembling nature), represents no image at all to a discerning audience, but that of a player pouring out his words, without meaning, in a voice that neither touches, nor is touched by, nature.

Application IV.—Of Anger.

Definition.—Anger is Pride provoked beyond regard of Caution.

It is a fierce and unrestrained effusion of reproach and insult. It must, therefore, be expressed impatiently, by a fiery eye, a disturbed and threatening air, and a voice strong, swift, and often interrupted by high swells of choking indignation.

To explain this passion, two examples will be necessary; the first, not so much for containing the passion itself, as a great actor's rules for feeling and expressing it with nature's spirit and propriety. And I do this justice to Shakespeare with a double pleasure, as the instance carries with it a clear evidence how much the play-house, old tradition wrongs his memory; for they report him a performer of no power or compass, and but of low rate in his profession as to action.

The second speech shall be for an example of the passion, with an explanation of two different modes, whereby nature has distinguished its expression.

Shakespeare's comes first, and is, at once, a rule and example:

> "Now imitate the action of a tiger;
> Stiffen the sinews, summon up the blood;
> Lend fierce and dreadful aspect to the eye:
> Set the teeth close, and stretch the nostril wide,
> Hold hard the breath, and bend up every spirit
> To its full height."

It were impossible to draw a picture of anger

more naturally, or an instruction more complete and clear for expressing it.

First, The sinews being braced strong through all the joints of the body, the blood (as a consequence unavoidable) is summoned up, that is, impelled into violent motion.

Secondly, The look becomes adapted, and adds fierceness, to the passion by the fire that flashes from the eye.

Thirdly, The setting of the teeth and wide expansion of the nostrils, follow naturally, because inseparable from an enraged bent of the eyebrow.

And, fourthly, The breath being held hard, is interrupted or restrained by the tumultuous precipitation of the spirits, they must necessarily become inflamed themselves, and will communicate their ardor to the voice and motion. And thus, this passion of anger is bent up to its full height, as Shakespeare, with allusion to the spring upon the sinews, hath expressed it.

I explain this passage to demonstrate his great skill in acting; and in hopes the players' observation that this favorite genius of their own profession had ideas of the art (so plainly founded on the very principles sustained in this essay), will recommend it with more weight from the partiality of their affection.

But to return. It here deserves reflection by how very small a separation nature has disjoined the outlines of two passions, seemingly the least conformable to one another. Few would imagine that the lineaments of joy and anger should unite in any

Hill's Essay. 297

point of strong resemblance! And yet it is evident they only differ in a change of look. For, as to the intensely bracing up the nerves, that is the same, exactly, in both passions, and the sole distinction lies in this: — a smile upon the eye, in bodies strongly-braced, compels the voice to sound of joy, — while frowns, in the same eye (without the smallest alteration of muscles), immediately transform the gay sound to a dreadful one.

The second speech, which will be necessary to explain the natural difference above declared, relating to two modes of anger, may be taken from the Orphan, and it is Chamont who speaks:

"I say my sister's wrong'd;
Monimia — my sister; born as high,
And noble as Castalio. Do her justice,
Or, by the gods! I'll lay a scene of blood,
Shall make this dwelling horrible to nature;
I'll do it! * Hark you, my lord!
—— your son — Castalio —
Take him to your closet, and there, teach him manners."

Though the passion, throughout all this speech, is furious and intemperate anger, yet nature has divided it into two such different tones of utterance that, though it would be impropriety to a degree of folly to pronounce that part foregoing the star in the sixth line any other way than with a fierce, vindictive air, and voice high raised, insulting, and impatient, the remainder (from that star) must, on the contrary, be expressed by affectation of a low, constrained, and almost whispered composure, concealing a slow, smothered, inward rancor, by a muttered, ironical repression of the voice, strained through the teeth, in a pretended restraint of indignation. And when, from such reliefs, as it were, of passion, the rage breaks out again into shrill and exclamatory loudness, the representation becomes movingly varied and natural; and the voice seems to preserve a kind of musical modulation even in madness.

APPLICATION V.—OF PITY.

Definition.—Pity is active Grief for another's Affliction.

It is a social sadness of heart, propelled by an auxiliary disposition of the spirits giving tension to impressed and straining muscles. It can not, therefore, be expressed but by a look of sorrow, with a braced and animated gesture.

Take the following example, from Belmour, in Fatal Extravagance:

> "Oh! could I feel no misery but my own,
> How easy were it for this sword to free me
> From every anguish that embitters life!
> But, when the grave has given my sorrows rest,
> Where shall my miserable wife find comfort?
> Unfriended and alone, in want's bleak storm,
> Not all th' angelic virtues of her mind .
> Will shield her from th' unpitying world's derision.
> Can it be kind to leave her so exposed?"

If an actor should endeavor to touch the expressiveness of the passion conceived in this speech, without having previously adapted his look to the sensation peculiar to pity, he would never (though his voice were the finest and most musical in nature) be able to succeed in his purpose; for, his tone would be sometimes too earnest and sharp, and sometimes too languid and melancholy. But let him, first, strain his muscles into the tension above required for expression of joy, and if then he adds the look that is proper to grief, the result of this mixed co-operation of contraries (of a visage peculiar to sorrow, with a spring on the muscles adapted to joy) will immediately produce the gesture, the voice, and the feeling expression of pity. And the more strongly he braces his nerves in opposition to the distress that relaxes his look, the more beautifully will he touch the concern, till his utterance paints it, as one may say, to the ear. For, by effect of a struggle that will be formed in his mind between the grief that has softened his eye and the force that invigorates his muscles, there will arise a pathetic and trembling interruptedness of sensible sound that must affect a whole audience, with a participated concern in the passion.

APPLICATION VI.—OF SCORN.

Definition.—Scorn is negligent Anger.

That is, anger against objects, which excite no esteem. It is, therefore, unbraced into easiness. See an example in the following answer of Bajazet to Axalla's declaration, from Tamerlane:

"Bear back thy fulsome greeting to thy master;
Tell him, I'll none on't. . . . .

> *"Had he been a god,
> All his omnipotence could not restore
> The radiancy of majesty eclipsed.*
> For aught besides, it is not worth my care:
> The giver and his gifts are both despised!"

In this speech, the beginning and the end contain manifest scorn. But in the middle part, which is, therefore, distinguished between the stars, the passion rises into nervous and exclamatory violence. All the rest, to be rightly expressed in the acting, will require the seeming contrast of an unsinewy slackness of muscles to a look that flames with anger and insult.

There is, however, (and a skillful actor will always remember to note it,) a gayer and very different species of scorn, on less solemn occasions, where the lowness of figure, or of power, in some slight, insignificant subject, or the unalarming impertinence of some vain, but not dangerous, levity, only calls for contempt, unconnected with anger. And this lighter expression of scorn will be hit most effectually by preserving the same disposition of muscles that was required in the other, but accompanied by a look that is smiling and placid, instead of the frown that took place in the former.

APPLICATION VII.—OF HATRED.

Definition.—Hatred is restrained yet lasting Anger.

It is a close, abhorrent, hostile disposition of the heart, averted by ill-will, but guarded by precaution. To express it rightly, it demands a look of malice, with a gesture of restrained impatience.

Bajazet will give example in another speech, concerning Tamerlane:

> "The Tartar is my bane—I can not bear him,
> One heaven and earth can never hold us both.
> Still shall we hate, and, with defiance deadly,
> Keep rage alive—till one be lost, forever.
> As if two suns should meet in the meridian,
> And strive, in fiery combat, for the passage."

Unless an actor has accustomed his reflection to examine distinctions in passion, he will be surprised to be told in this place that there is no other difference but the turn of an eye in the expression of hatred and pity. Yet his experience will find it a palpable truth. For, first, pity and hatred, both of them require the same intense brace upon the joints and sinews; and then the characterizing distinction between them is this (I mean only what regards their expression, that is, the outward marks they impress on the body): pity, by a look of inclination, implies affection and desire to relieve; whereas, hatred, by averting the visage, and accompanying that look of abhorrence with gestures of malice and disapprobation, proclaims animosity and purpose of mischief. The nerves must be braced in both passions alike, because pity is earnest and hatred is earnest, and therefore, the muscles, to express either passion (however opposite they may seem to each other), must be springy, and bent into promptitude.

But the look must be different in each, because

pity is earnest for beneficence; and therefore, the eye (which is the show-glass of the soul) must be impressed with ideas of goodness, whereas hatred is earnest for mischief, and the eye must, in consequence of a malignant intent in the will, reflect an image of meditated evil.

APPLICATION VIII.—OF JEALOUSY.

Definition.—Jealousy is doubtful Anger struggling against Faith and Pity.

It is a painful softness in the heart, resisted by a vindictive disposition in the spirits. It can not, therefore, be expressed without a doubtful variation, both in look and air, divided and suspended betwixt wavering passions.

But there are two degrees of jealousy, and they require different modes for their expression. So that two examples will be necessary, and Othello will supply us with them both.

We shall see in this that follows that first stage of jealousy, which is alarmed, but doubtfully suspicious, and not yet confirmed into the violence of positive belief and its warm consequences:

"By heaven, he echoes me!
As if there were some monster in his thought
Too hideous to be shown!—Thou dost mean something—
I heard thee say even now, thou likedst not that,
When Cassio left my wife,—What didst not like?
And when I told thee he was of my counsel
In my whole course of wooing, thou criedst 'Indeed!'
And didst contract and purse thy brow together, ...
        If thou dost love me,
Show me thy thought."

For expressing, in a natural manner, these unfixed, apprehensive, reluctant first dawnings of jealousy, the brace upon the nerves must be but conformable to the unsettled idea. It must be half bent and half languid. The look, too, under the same inconclusive alarm, must act its part with the indolent muscles; that is, it must partake of two opposite passions,—anger, as disposed to catch flame, under sense of such injury; and pity, as unwilling to give way to distrust against an object so endeared by affection.

The other species, or rather degree of this passion, is where jealousy extracts confirmation from appearances, which concur towards a proof.

In this case, the nerves must assume the strong brace that is proper to anger; and the look must express a turbulent mixture of anguish from a struggle between fury and sorrow. See Othello again:

> "I think my wife be honest—and think she is not!
> I think that thou art just, and think thou art not!
> I'll have some proof. Her name that was as fresh
> As Dian's visage, is now begrimed and black
> As mine own face! If there be cords or knives,
> Poison or fire, or suffocating streams,
> I'll not endure it. Would I were satisfied!"

We see in this speech doubt inflamed into agony. It is still, indeed, distrust; but it is, at the same time, indignation and bitterness. And this is the utmost pitch whereto jealousy (as jealousy) can by nature extend itself. For the least step beyond it is anger, which, unless mixed with and restrained by some tempering conceit of uncertainty, is no longer the jealousy we are considering, but a distinct and new passion, the effect, it is true, of the former, yet itself quite of a different species. So that jealousy can be divided no farther than into the two foregoing distinctions.

APPLICATION IX.—OF WONDER.

Definition.—Wonder is inquisitive Fear.

It is an ebb of spirits rushing back upon the heart, but leaving an alarm upon the muscles that invigorates them towards defense and opposition. No actor can imitate this passion with its natural propriety and force without dividing its idea into the two following degrees of distinction:

The first degree is amazement — the second is astonishment. In amazement, the conception catching alarm from the image of something strangely or unnaturally terrible, the nerves, upon a start of apprehension, brace at once into an involuntary rigor of intenseness, under a defensive disposition of the will, that would resist and repel the object.

But, in astonishment, the recoil of the animal spirits, hurried back in too precipitate a motion, drives the blood upon the heart with such oppressive redundance, as retarding circulation, almost stagnates the vital progression; and, arresting the breath, eyes, gesture, and every power and faculty of the body, occasions such an interruption of their several uses as would bring on an actual cessation; but that the reason, struggling slowly to relieve the apprehension, gives a kind of hesitative articulation to the utterance, and a gradual motion and recovery to the look, the limbs, and the countenance.

In the following lines from Hamlet, we shall see an instance of the first degree of wonder, while it reaches only to amazement, and suspends, not stagnates, the free motion of the blood and spirits:

> "O day, and night!—but this is wondrous strange!

and, again:

> "Angels and ministers of grace defend us!
> Be thou a spirit of health—or goblin damn'd,
> Bring with thee airs from heaven or blasts from hell,
> Be thy intents wicked or charitable,
> Thou com'st in such a questionable shape
> That I will speak to thee!"

There is manifest, in the beginning of this speech, the starting spring upon the nerves that follows the first shock of apprehension.

In the middle is discerned, as plainly, the slow, struggling, reasoning recollection of the shaken understanding; and in the two concluding lines, the resolution of recovered firmness to examine and determine steadfastly.

But in examples where the passion rises to astonishment, as in this below, from Belmour, see an almost total deprivation, for the time, of all the powers of sense and motion, except only that exerted reason, laboring against oppressive congelation, barely seems to hold breath in by force, and make life sensible:

> "I feel my blood
> Cool and grow thick; as melted lead flows heavy,
> And hardens in its motion. A little longer,
> And I, who have heart already marble—
> Shall petrify throughout—and be—a statue."

It would be impossible, after an actor had conceived an idea correspondent to the picture in the words in this, not to impress every lineament of the passion upon his look, and every attitude of it upon his gesture; and then, the tone of his voice, concurring, can not fail to sound the slow, conflicting struggle of astonishment.

APPLICATION X.—OF LOVE.

Definition.—Love is Desire kept temperate by Reverence.

It is expanded softness in the heart, indulged attachment in the fancy, and an awe (from fear to be distasteful where we wish to please), upon the spirits. It can never, therefore, rightly be expressed without a look of apprehensive tenderness, that softens a high-braced and animated air and casts a modest cloud of diffidence over too quick a sense of transport. And thus we are come, at last, to a passion the true name whereof might be legion; for it includes all the other, in all their degrees and varieties. It has, therefore, been postponed, and kept to bring up the rear; though, from the weight and extent of its influence, it ought to have taken place in the front of the number.

There is, however, independent of its auxiliary

and occasional passions, a distinct air and gesture, look, and manner of speaking peculiar to love, in its serene and unruffled impressiveness. And because there are not many actors in whom nature has done all that appears necessary for expressing the gentleness and the softness, together with the freedom and the fire, which unite their contraries, of setting off the spirit of this passion, it is necessary to reflect a little on the reason why it is common to see love unfeelingly, affectedly, and even ridiculously acted.

The lazy cause is want of tenderness, or at least of application, to conceive the true idea. For this passion, more than any other, lends a tongue to every look, and sheds an eloquence on every motion. It can not bear, then, a cold, formal emptiness; a big, broad, mellow troll of smooth, unanimated wordiness. It asks for soul in thought, air, movement. It exacts such strict confederacy between the heart, the mien, the eye, and tongue, that it disdains to pardon a bold, voluble, and lecture-like (however musical and sounding) insignificancy. The idea, then, to be conceived by one who would express love elegantly is that of joy combined with fear. It is a conscious and triumphant swell of hope, intimidated by respectful apprehension of offending where we long to seem agreeable. It is the exhalation of a soft desire, which to the warmth inspired by wishes, joins the modesty of a submissive doubtfulness.

It is complaint made amiable by gracefulness, reproach endeared by tenderness, and rapture awed by reverence. Without a previous fixed idea of the passion, in this native light, the finest of all human voices would in vain attempt to touch it tenderly. And this might be immediately found evident to the attentive actor's ear, in making trial on some speech, like this of Edgar, in the Tragedy of Athelwold:

> "Why have those piercing eyes so ill distinguish'd
> The reverence of my ardor? License and Freedom
> Would, in your presence, be dissolv'd to awe,
> And flow in sighs to soften you. This hand!
> Oh! give it me—and I will swear upon it
> That my charm'd spirits never rose, till now,
> In such a tide of ecstasy!—that heaven
> Has left your sex in shade to light up you
> With every grace that swells desire in mortals,
> Or gives your guardian angel pride to view you!"

Here, if the nerves are braced with proper warmth to the high pitch of joy, and the inclining look divided gracefully betwixt a tender fear and a triumphant pleasure, every accent will confess the passion in a soft, impressive touchingness. Whereas, without such previous disposition for attaining the idea, the vague, undirected tone would sometimes sound too faint, sometimes too harsh; and always insincere, declamatory, and unstriking.

I have done with the application of the general principle to particular examples of the passions.

I proceed to a justification of the mechanism in the rules foregoing by demonstrating its foundation on clear, natural causes.

I will only interpose a short digression for discovering the reason why it is so rare to see an actor elegantly qualified to represent a love part. I said before, and shall produce the proof immediately, that love includes, occasionally, all other passions.

He, then, who is not master of a power to represent them all in the distinct propriety of each, must, of necessity (so far as his defect in any one of them extends), be found an incomplete and disapproved sustainer of a lover's character.

And that every other of the passions hitherto described occurs, occasionally, in that comprehensive one of love, see proofs in these plain instances:

AN EXAMPLE OF JOY IN LOVE.

Thou art a cold describer!—oh, the day!
The dear remember'd day! when, at the altar,
Where, in thanksgiving, I had bow'd to heaven,
Heaven seem'd descending on me—my rais'd eye
Met her flash'd charms amidst a gazing crowd,
Who, from the scaffolded cathedral's sides,
Pour'd their bold looks upon me. Greatness and languor
Flow'd in a soften'd radiance from her mien,
And kindled every shrine with new divinity!
Sweetness sat smiling on her humid eye-balls,
And light-wing'd fancy danc'd, and flam'd about her!

AN EXAMPLE OF GRIEF IN LOVE.

Oh! what a dreadful change in my poor heart
Has one weak moment made!—scorn'd, like the vile,
Dishonor'd, infamous; expell'd forever,
I must become a wand'rer round the world;

Meet cold and hunger, poverty and shame,
Anguish and insult—better all, than man!
The faithless murd'rer, man! What am I doom'd to!
Whom have I trusted!—oh! revenging heaven!
See my distress, and punish me with more.
I can not be too wretched. Begone, deceiver,
I would not curse thee—I will not wish thee pain;
But never, never, let me see thee more!

An Example of Fear in Love.

She's gone—and I am left, to walk the world,
Like a pale shade, that shuns the paths of men.
Light searches me too deep: my conscious soul
Starts inward—and escapes the eye of day.
Oh! bosom peace, now lost!—were there, in guilt,
No weight more painful, than this lour of brow,
Yet, shun it all,—you, who have hearts, like men—
That you may raise the front, and look, like virtue.

An Example of Anger in Love.

Patience!—curse patience—why dost thou talk of patience,
With the same breath, the same cold, tasteless calmness,
That spoke distraction to me? Hast thou not told me
That she confesses it? that this proud beauty,
This haughty, fierce, disdainful, marbly virtue,
That scorn'd my honest passion—this austere frowner,
Has been—perdition on the name! 'twould choke me.
Hast thou not fir'd me with the basest truth
That ever stung the heart of a fool lover?
And dost thou talk of patience!—give it to statesmen;
I spurn the servile lesson. Patience, saidst thou?
Rage and despair have broke upon my soul
And wash'd away all patience.

AN EXAMPLE OF PITY IN LOVE.

When the blood boils, and beauty fires the soul,
What will the tongue not swear? Discretion, then,
Does with a peacock's feather fan the sun.
Yet, in the midst of all my wild desires,
Thou wert the warmest wish my heart pursu'd.
My love to thee was permanent and strong.
Thy beauties were my waking theme, and night
Grew charming by soft dreams of thy perfection.
Still I regard thee with the same desires;
Gaze, with the same transporting pity, on thee,
As dying fathers bless a weeping child with.

AN EXAMPLE OF SCORN IN LOVE.

Yes! virtue!—Thou hast every well-known virtue
That thy whole sex is fam'd for:—kind, soft virtues!
Spleen, affectation, pride, ill-nature, noise,
Lightness in reason, insolence in will,
Giddy ambition's ever-varied whirl,
Wishes that change till ev'n distaste grows pleasing,
And tenderness, all tir'd, makes room for fury.
Virtues?—immortal gods!—Your best weigh'd virtues
Serve but to smile deceit from heart to heart,
Till, for your idol, dear variety!
Loathing an angel's form, you grasp a devil's!

AN EXAMPLE OF HATRED IN LOVE.

Bane of my peace, life, fame!—my sick'ning soul
Shrinks with indignant shame from her idea!
All that she once betray'd me to believe
Turns poison on my fancy. Each loath'd beauty
Serves but to feed the fire with which I hate her.
I know her to the heart; I see her, now,

Not thro' her smiles—I reach her thro' her falsehood,
View her all black with guilt, all base with infamy.
Light and elusive as the wand'ring fires
Which gleam, destructive, on the edge of night,
And tempt to waylaid fens the flatter'd traveler.
Oh! I could curse her all-bewitching charms,
That (shun'd and hated), still persist to hold me,
And hang their drowning grasp about my fancy.

AN EXAMPLE OF JEALOUSY IN LOVE.

But why, and whence, her tears? those looks? her flight?
That grief, so strangely stamp'd on every feature?
If it has been that Frenchman—what a thought!
How low, how horrid, a suspicion, that!
The dreadful flash at once gives light, and kills me.
An infidel! a slave!—A heart like mine
Reduced to suffer from so vile a rival!
But tell me, didst thou mark them at their parting?
Didst thou observe the language of their eyes?
Hide nothing from me!—Is my love betray'd?
Tell me my whole disgrace.—Nay, if thou tremblest,
I hear thy pity speak, tho' thou art silent.

AN EXAMPLE OF WONDER IN LOVE.

I stand immovable—like senseless marble!
Horror had frozen my suspended tongue,
And an astonish'd silence robb'd my will
Of power to tell her—that she shock'd my soul.
Spoke she to me? Sure I misunderstood her!
Could it be to me, she left!—what have I seen!
Orasmin! what a change is here! she's gone!
And I permitted it—I know not how.

AN EXAMPLE OF LOVE, UNMIXED AND SOLITARY.

    Oh, let them never love who never tri'd!
    They brought a paper to me to be sign'd;
    Thinking on him, I quite forgot my name,
    And writ, for Leonora, Torrismond.
    I went to bed, and, to myself, I thought
    That I would think on Torrismond no more.
    I clos'd my eyes, but could not shut out him.
    Tumbling, I tri'd each downy corner's aid
    To find if sleep was there; but sleep was not.
    Fev'rish for want of rest, I rose and walk'd,
    And by the moonshine to my window went;
    There, hopeful to exclude him from my thoughts,—
    But, looking out upon the neighb'ring plains,
    Soft sighs, unsummon'd, whisper'd to my soul,
    There fought my Torrismond.

I believe that it remains evident by this time that the lover's comprehends all serious dramatic characters that an actor can expect to shine by. Let us cease, then, to wonder that we can so seldom see it touched upon the stage.

And now we consider the natural foundation of that mechanism in the art described whereby the springs are moved to represent the passions outwardly.

It will have been observed that their specific differences are far from being so remote as the repugnance of the passions would appear to place them.

See this in all the ten examples: Joy is expressed by muscles intense and a smile in the eye; anger, by muscles intense and a frown in the eye;

pity, by muscles intense and a sadness in the eye; hatred, by muscles intense and aversion in the eye; wonder, by muscles intense and an awful alarm in the eye; love, by muscles intense and a respectful attachment in the eye; grief, by neither muscles nor eye intense, but both languid; fear, by muscles and look both languid, with an alarm in eye and motion.

Scorn, by muscles languid and neglected, with a smile in the eye to express the light, or a frown in the eye for the serious species.

Jealousy, by muscles intense and the look pensive; or the look intense and muscles languid, interchangeably. And if the natural causes of such near resemblance in the mechanism of opposite passions be inquired into, they will all be evidently deduced from the reflections following.

QUESTIONS AND ANSWERS.

Demonstrating the natural Causes of the Mechanism in the Rules foregoing.

QUESTION I. Why is joy expressed by muscles intense and a smile in the eye?

ANSWER. Joy is pride possessed of triumph. Pride and triumph give inflated ideas, and high raised and bold conceptions. But the muscles must be intense when they express elevation, because relaxed nerves are peculiar to depressed conception, and the eye must be smiling before it can paint satisfaction, because a frown would imply discontent; and to conceive joy with displeasure is a false, because an unnatural, impression.

Ques. II. Why is anger expressed with muscles intense and a frown in the eye?

Ans. Anger is pride provoked beyond regard of caution. Uncautious pride exults in menaces and arrogance. But neither arrogance nor menaces can consist with relaxation of the nerves, because slack muscles are a consequence of weak and faint, not boastful and avowed, ideas.

The eye, too, in this passion, is overclouded by a frown, because it catches sense of indignation from vindictive and distasteful images; and not to show that outward mark of the mind, agitation inwardly would be assuming a disguise to cover sensibility,—a prudence never natural in anger, because its great characteristic property is rash and open insult.

Ques. III. Why is pity expressed by muscles intense and a sadness in the eye?

Ans. Pity is active grief for another's afflictions. But we can never sincerely mourn distresses when we do not feel them touchingly. Whatever we so feel we look,—by natural inclination and necessity. No visage but a sad one, therefore, can consist with the distress of pity. But the muscles, to express this passion, must be braced; because, whatever we pity we intensely wish to give relief to; and since the will, when active, compels active fibers, it remains a natural consequence that this seeming contrariety between the gesture and the look is the true medium to express compassion; for, being nature's own effect, when she impresses marks of pity in her usual manner, art, assuming the same outward springs to work by, can not fail to represent her with exactness.

QUES. IV. Why is hatred expressed by muscles intense and aversion in the eye?

ANS. Hatred is restrained yet lasting anger. Anger inflames the will, and as the will, becoming active, actuates the muscles, they must necessarily be strained hard, and prompt to violent exertion when they would express this passion properly. But then as it is anger not thrown out, but patient, covered, and restrained, the eye withdraws itself from a distasteful object to imply aversion in restraint of fury; and herein consists the natural distinction that paints hatred on the outward lineaments.

QUES. V. Why is wonder expressed by muscles intense and an awful alarm in the eye?

ANS. Wonder is inquisitive fear. As it is inquisitive, it is steadfast, and demands firm muscles. But as it is fear it can not justly be expressed without the marks of apprehension and alarm. Were this alarm a too-disturbed one, full of motion and anxiety, it would paint fear instead of wonder, and would carry no consistence with braced muscles. It is, therefore, firmly nerved, because inquisitive with purpose of defense; and so this application of alarm, with resolution to examine steadfastly, must constitute a nervous, awful, and fixed attentiveness, and give the picture of the passion naturally.

QUES. VI. Why is love expressed by muscles intense and a respectful attachment in the eye?

Ans. Love is desire kept temperate by reverence. Desire must be attached, and, as in love, its object is a visible one, desire of objects visible must show itself most plainly in the eye. But then our fear to give distaste, attempering desire with reverence, creates respectful softness in the look and attitude. And this external softness, being strengthened by an inward brace upon the nerves (the natural consequence of hope and joy), enlivening reverence by effusion of a sparkling pleasure, there is transmitted to the eye, the ear, and heart of an attentive audience, the same impression which the actor's spirits are impelled by.

Ques. VII. Why is grief expressed by neither muscles nor look intense, but both languid?

Ans. Grief is disappointment void of hope; but muscles braced intense imply hope strongly, and a spirited vivacity in the eye is the effect of pleasure and elevation. These are naturally consistent with a passage that depresses, which grief manifestly does, because depression slackens all the nerves; nerves unbraced deject the look, and air, in necessary consequence, and, therefore, a relaxed mien and languid eye must form the truest picture of a natural sorrow.

Ques. VIII. Why is fear expressed by languid look and muscles, with alarm in eye and motion?

Ans. Fear is grief discerning and avoiding danger. As it is grief, it must depress the spirits and unbrace the muscles, whence the languid air becomes adapted and characteristic. But, as it is grief, not careless and resigned, but apprehensive, fugitive, and starting, it demands a lightness in the motion, with a watchful, though unanimated, sharpness in the eye, because the fancy has a conceived idea of threatening mischief; but the object, overcharging the imagination, has relaxed the unconcurring fibers into a debility, unable to obey the will, which, therefore, but evades, and not resists, the danger.

QUES. IX. Why is scorn expressed by languid muscles, with a smile upon the eye in the light species, or a frown to hit the serious?

ANS. Scorn is negligent anger. It insinuates, therefore, by a voluntary slackness or disarming of the nerves, a known or a concluded absence of all power in the insulted object, even to make defense seem necessary. And the unbraced muscles are assisted in this show of contemptuous disregard by an affected smile upon the eye, because slack nerves, if, at the same time, the look were also languid, would too much resemble sorrow, or even fear; whereas, the purpose is disdain and insult. And though, in more provoking, serious cases, where the scorn admits disturbance, it assumes some sense of anger; it must still retain the slack, unguarded languor on the nerves, lest it should seem to have conceived impressions of some estimable or important weightiness, where its design is utter disregard and negligence.

QUES. X. Why is jealousy expressed by muscles intense, and the look pensive,— or by the look intense, and the muscles languid interchangeably?

ANS. Jealousy is doubtful anger struggling against

faith and pity. It is a tenderness resisted by resentment of suspected injury; and thence, the nerves, braced strong, imply determination of revenge and punishment. While, at the same time, a soft, pensive hesitation in the eye confesses a reluctance at the heart to part with, or efface, a gentle and indulged idea.

Sometimes, again, it is rage at a concluded infidelity, and then the eye receives and flashes out the sparklings of inflamed ideas; while the muscles, counteracting the will's violence, from a repressive disposition of the heart, grow slack and loose their spring, and so disarm, or modify enraged imagination.

And from this unsettled wavering in the balance of the purpose, where the heart and judgment weigh each other, and both scales, by turns, preponderate, is deduced a glowing picture of this passion.

I have traveled now through ten pathetic stages, where an actor must not stop for rest, as in his other journies, but for labor; and such a labor will he truly find it (if he enters naturally into the demand of those strong passions), that neither mind nor body can be capable of choosing a more healthfully fatiguing exercise.

And this remark brings into my remembrance a great and general mistake among the players at rehearsal, where it is their common practice to mutter over their parts inwardly, and keep in their voices with a misimagined purpose of preserving them against their evening acting; whereas, the surest natural means of strengthening their delivery would be to warm, de-phlegm, and clarify the thorax and wind-pipe by exerting (the more frequently the better) their fullest power of utterance; thereby to open and remove all hesitation, roughness, or obstruction, and to tune their voices by effect of such continual exercise, into habitual mellowness and ease of compass and inflection, just from the same reason that an active body is more strong and healthy than a sedentary one.

www.ingramcontent.com/pod-product-compliance
Lightning Source LLC
Chambersburg PA
CBHW022019240426
43667CB00042B/942